Handicap!

Finding the Key Horse

David L. Christopher
and
Albert C. Beerbower

LIBERTY PUBLISHING COMPANY
Deerfield Beach, Florida

© Liberty Publishing Company, Inc., 1992

Published by:
Liberty Publishing Company, Inc.
440 South Federal Highway
Deerfield Beach, Florida 33441

ISBN 0-89709-201-5

Manufactured USA

To Bud

King of the Double

TABLE OF CONTENTS

PART ONE

PART TWO

PREFACE

Between us, Al Beerbower and I have experienced more than sixty years of handicapping thousands of thoroughbred races. Both of us have found success, each with our own personal formula. Although we have each tackled the Great Riddle in a totally different way, the lessons that we've learned and the conclusions that we've reached, independently, over the past several decades are much the same. That is, we both look to the trainers, ultimately, as a good way to separate the last few choices before we go to the betting window.

As racing fans, Al and I differ in two primary respects: 1) I use a personal computer to measure the talents of each horse, to see the pace, and to identify the contenders; Al doesn't. 2) Al would rather bet a selection to *win*; while I prefer the higher rewards (and risks) of exotic wagering. However, the key horses on which our money will ride are often found in the same manner. And, fortunately, these horses are usually the first to cross the finish line -- an important ingredient in this sport, to be sure!

It is our objective to help the reader identify one or two "key horses" on which to bet, either alone, or in the exotics. For the purposes of this book, a "key horse" may be defined as one that is expected, with a high degree of confidence, to be first or second in the race.

Many of the valuable lessons that we've learned can be found between the covers of this book. We hope these guidelines will be as profitable for you as they have been for us.

David L. Christopher

INTRODUCTION

Many would say that the "art" of handicapping has developed into a science over the past thirty years or so. Perhaps. Today's racing students have more information at their fingertips than at any time in history. Many go to the track armed with win/loss records, momentum studies, and bloodline charts that expose almost every aspect of every horse's existence. A few in this sport have even gone to the preposterous extreme of measuring a horse's trip in HUNDREDTHS of a second!

Still, the challenge remains no less formidable. Only one favorite out of every three wins the race. And less than 5% of today's racegoers constitute that select list of regular visitors to the cashier's window. It was true three decades ago, and it's true today -- the new age of information notwithstanding!

In recent years, handicapping has taken on many new forms. Yet, as always, "class" handicappers are placed at one end of the spectrum, and "speed" handicappers at the other end. An analogy to this can be found on Wall Street where there is a conflict between the "fundamentalist," who studies industry and company reports, and the "technical analyst" who charts stock prices. Here, as on Wall Street, it's wrong to say that one or the other is THE answer. Usually, the best results are attained when these and other conflicting methods are used as a complement to one another. Exactly *how* they should be applied is one of the questions that will be addressed here.

This book is divided into two parts: The first section examines one reliable method by which a list of three or four contenders is developed; a list from which the key horse is expected to emerge. The second section illustrates several powerful spot play situations that can help us narrow this list further and identify our key horse(s) on which to wager.

PART ONE

The Contenders

For most fans, the initial stage in the handicap process involves dividing the field into two categories: Contenders and Non-contenders. Success at the windows depends to a large extent on the precision of this step. Most experienced handicappers prefer to attack the problem in reverse by first eliminating every horse that has little or no chance to win the race. Thus, a list of remaining "live" candidates can be devised through a logical process of elimination (either by class, form, trainer/jockey analysis, or by whatever other means). At this point, most fans continue the handicapping process in the same manner, or a new method is applied to separate the last few contenders.

Reducing a field of eight, ten, or twelve horses down to three or four can be accomplished any number of ways. It will not be our mission here to criticize any rational approach, although many are of dubious value. Most likely, you've heard them all...

1. "This baby won a $20,000 claiming race handily and finished only fourth when he was raised to Clm $25,000. He'll beat that $16,000 claimer EASILY!"

2. "Sunday Silence defeated him in the Derby and again in the Preakness. Beat Easy Goer in the Belmont? No problem!"

3. "That horse was no closer than eight lengths at every call in its last two races. It's going off form. Win? No way!"

4.   "In the paddock that animal was more alert than any other horse around. With that shiny coat, the prancing, and the alert ears, she appears to be the likely choice!"

5.   "The odds dropped from 8:1 to 5:2 during the post parade! Bet against that barn? Not on your life!"

6.   "That beast has never run on the grass before and wasn't bred for distance. Throw her out!"

In his popular guide, *Ten Steps to Winning*, author Danny Holmes applies a unique approach by using different handicapping methods for different types of races. For example, he identifies the contenders in a claiming SPRINT by analyzing "pace." However, "class" is used as the primary selection process when a claiming ROUTE is handicapped. Whether or not you agree with this approach, the book contains many valuable ideas.

William L. Scott's most recent book, *Total Victory at the Track*, walks the reader through a step-by-step procedure that essentially ranks each horse by its running positions at the second call point, at the finish, and by the number of horses it has beaten in those contests, coupled with various adjustments.

One of the more interesting books published within the past few years is *Modern Pace Handicapping*, by Tom Brohamer. This textbook explores the subject of pace in terms of feet-per-second and applies some of the ideas of Howard Sartin. Brohamer's book is an extension of Huey Mahl's pioneering work, written almost twenty years ago. His now-outdated guide, *The Race is Pace*, described a horse's momentum at various points in the race in terms of miles-per-hour.

In addition to these, there have been many good books written by popular authors such as Andy Beyer, James Quinn, Steven Davidowitz, and William Quirin. They, too, can offer valuable suggestions on analyzing the contestants. Obviously, there are many ways of separating the wheat from the chaff, as they say.

One of the major problems racing fans encounter in this endeavor is TIME. There are very few good handicapping methods that can be accomplished without investing at least several minutes per race -- especially without the aid of a personal computer. And even with the world's best machine and software, it still requires a few minutes to enter or retrieve data. In an effort to cut time, newcomers to computer handicapping should beware of any software packages that accept only one pace line of data per horse. It's impossible for a single past race to accurately measure a horse's overall capability.

The Influence of Pace

Serious students of this game never underestimate the importance of pace. If two sharp, evenly-matched, pacesetters are entered in a contest with six other horses, most experienced handicappers would give serious consideration to any strong, off-the-pace runners in the field. By merely scratching one of the two early speed horses, those same experts would very likely draw up an entirely new list of contenders, or at least bet the race in a totally different manner!

On any typical day at the track, the outcome of many, if not all, of the races will be dictated by pace. Therefore, recognizing the capabilities of every horse in the contest becomes paramount. Frequently the question is not whether the horse will win, but whether it could have a temporary influence on the pace or be a beneficiary of it. Of course, once the pace is determined, many can then be dismissed immediately as non-contenders. It is this aspect of horse racing that makes the personal computer an incredibly potent and valuable tool.

The "Key" Horse

Experienced handicappers universally agree that it is much more difficult to identify one "key" horse from three or four contenders than it is to narrow the field down to those few. The reason for this is simple: *Usually more than one contender is capable of winning!* In most cases, the final results often depend on the pace and, sometimes, racing luck. Therefore, to be consistently successful at the cashier's window, it is necessary for the handicapper to single out at least one "key" horse for betting purposes. Simply stated, this horse is expected (with a *high* degree of confidence) to finish first or second in the race.

Every once in a while, of course, one horse will appear to be a "lock" -- a
horse that can best be described as "The Monster." So dominant is this horse
that it, alone, can almost dictate the pace and win from nearly any part of the
track. However, rarely will this key horse go unnoticed by the bettors. This
winner among winners will be discussed in greater detail later.

Part 2 of this book offers a series of trainer moves, or what we prefer to call
"key horse patterns," that have demonstrated a notable record of success.
When they occur, these situations often point to particularly powerful key
horse candidates. Sometimes one or more of these patterns can be used to
select a single, specific, long shot or overlay, disregarding all other factors.
Traditionally, this is referred to in race track parlance as a "spot play." Or,
better yet, these situations can help us further narrow down our list of
contenders to two or, preferably, one key horse.

As it is with the computer, this approach to handicapping should be used
with care and forethought. Many of these ideas are independent situations
subject to other competitive aspects of the race. For example, we have
observed that a horse with improving form (described later) has a superior
chance of winning. This would be true, of course, if it is placed among a
field of horses that it can beat. We are assuming, therefore, that the trainer
has worked this horse purposefully into condition and is competent (smart?)
enough not to place the horse over its head. For this reason, we prefer to
apply these key horse patterns to our list of contenders rather than to use
them as spot plays.

Study these key horse patterns. Learn to recognize them. Some will work
better than others at your track; or you may discover variations indigenous
to your location. After all, they do, for the most part, reflect the habits of the
trainers at your track or circuit.

Speed Handicapping

In almost every type of contest, speed handicapping can be used effectively to separate the contenders from the also-rans.

The First Edition of *Winning at the Track*, published in 1983, attempted to provide a fast, easy, and reliable speed handicapping method of identifying contenders for the average racing fan. In effect, three recent races for each horse were adjusted and used to identify the top selections. Unfortunately, if many of the contestants happened to be changing from other distances or coming from other tracks, the hand-calculated numbers and the comparisons would be somewhat less reliable. Also, if pace figures were included in the handicap, the entire process would become a time-consuming effort the night before.

Two years later, the Second Edition was produced which included a description of the *Winning at the Track* computer program. With this inexpensive software, each horse's early speed, late speed, and overall capability could be measured accurately. Also, every contest in each horse's past performance history would be adjusted to today's distance and track -- regardless of where they occurred -- and up to eight past races could be entered into the computer for each horse.

For the first time, every major distance and track in North America, dirt or turf, could be equated to one another! But, most importantly, ALL the horses could be compared on an "apples-equals-apples" basis *and* it would be possible to examine each horse's entire past history without relying on only *one* pace line as the data input. Finally, and best of all, with the new database module introduced in early 1992, each horse's data can now be saved to be retrieved at a later date, thus reducing hours of data entry time into minutes.

The genesis of the method shown here was devised about thirty years ago and was initially published as a simple "shortcut" for identifying contenders. The "shortcut" approach is still being used by thousands of fans who have yet to buy their first computer. But times are changing! Today, the *Winning at the Track* computer program is one of the most popular handicapping software packages on the market.

One thing is now certain -- any racegoers who continue to ignore the computer and its application to this sport will eventually find themselves at a competitive disadvantage at the betting windows. With pari-mutuel wagering, fans are not betting against the "house." They are competing against all the other people at the track, and it stands to reason that well-informed bettors have an advantage.

The example to follow illustrates how an ordinary race can be handicapped using a standard personal computer and the *Winning at the Track* program.

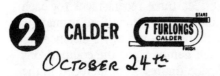

2 CALDER

OCTOBER 24th

7 FURLONGS. (1.23) CLAIMING. Purse $5,500. Fillies and mares, 3-year-olds and upward. Weight, 3-year-olds, 120 lbs. Older, 122 lbs. Non-winners of two races since September 19 allowed 2 lbs. A race since September 29 4 lbs. Two races since August 21 6 lbs. Claiming Price $5,500 for each $250 to $5,000 2 lbs.

LASIX—Jazzier, Another Smiso, Our Real Beauty, Sallie Blue, Belle's Tiny Tank, Stacie Blue Eyes.

Jazzier — B. m. 5, by An Eldorado—Jazzerciser, by Tarleton Oak — $5,000 — Br.—Sussex Racing Group (NY) — Tr.—Hyland Angel — 112
Own.—Hyland Angel
Lifetime 50 8 9 9 $74,635 — 1991 21 4 4 5 $14,674 — 1990 19 2 2 2 $12,361 — Turf 1 0 0 0

13Sep91- 4Tdn fst 6f	:23	:46^3	1:13	3↑ⒻClm 4000	5 3 5^{2½} 5^{6½} 4^{3½} 4^{2½}	Rivera H Jr	LBb 117	4.10	77-17 OverllChoice119^{nk}BrickCityMiss120^{2}NercticRlty116^{nk}	Evenly	6
6Sep91- 2TP fst 6f	:22^1	:45^4	1:13	3↑ⒻClm 4000	9 9 7^{7¾} 8^{8½} 8^8 6^{6¾}	Arguello F AJr^5	LBb 114	6.70	74-14 BoldMonik113^{1½}AggressivHony114^{2}CutiousDstny113^2	Evenly	12
25Aug91- 6Tdn fst 6f	:21^4	:45^4	1:13^1	3↑ⒻClm 5000	7 2 7^7 7^{11} 7^{6½} 4^{2½}	Rivera H Jr	LBb 119	4.30	77-22 OaterEater116^{nk}MightyKte115^{1½}DncinAnPrncin116½	Too late	7
9Aug91- 10Tdn sl 6f	:22^3	:46^3	1:13^1	3↑ⒻClm 4500	9 1 3^4 3^{2½} 4^{2½} 1^{nk}	Rivera H Jr	LBb 117	4.30	79-22 Jazzier117^{nk} Nearctic Reality116½ Pixie Quick119^1	Driving	9
26Jly91- 9Tdn fst 1	:48^1	1:13^3	1:40^4	3↑ⒻClm 4000	1 2 2^{2½} 2^4 2^5 3^{4¾}	Rivera H Jr	LBb 116	3.80	69-24 Lady Aristo119^{4½} Power Queen119^{nk} DH Jazzier116	Good try	6
26Jly91-Dead heat											
7Jly91- 7EIP fst 1	:47^3	1:14^1	1:42^1	ⒻClm 4000	3 4 6^{3¾} 6^{6¾} 7^{13} 6^{8¾}	Lopez R D	LBb 113	*2.30	53-35 Sundrop Sue112^5 Laurella106^{2½} Squaw Valley115^{hd}	No rally	11
29Jun91- 1Tdn fst 6f	:22^3	:46^3	1:12^3	3↑ⒻClm 4500	2 7 5^{4½} 5^{5½} 5^{3½} 2^{1½}	Rivera H Jr	LBb 119	5.80	81-17 Sweet Blue116^{1½} Jazzier119^{4½} Neals Sandy116½	Gaining	8
21Jun91- 2Tdn fst 6f	:22^2	:46^1	1:12^1	3↑ⒻClm 4500	8 1 6^3 5^{3½} 5^7 3^{3¾}	Rivera H Jr	LBb 116	6.30	80-14 Zoe Skates122^{1½} Silent June119^2 Jazzier116^{nk}	Too late	8
12Jun91- 9Tdn fst 6f	:22^2	:46^4	1:13^4	3↑ⒻClm 4000	8 1 5^{2¾} 3^{2½} 4^2 1^{nk}	Rivera H Jr	LBb 119	3.20	76-22 Jazzier119^{nk} Lady Aristo122^{1½} Racey Routte116½	Rallied	8
26May91- 4Tdn my 6f	:22^2	:47	1:14	3↑ⒻClm 4000	6 1 5^{7½} 6^{4¾} 4^1 1½	Navarro C J^5	LBb 111	2.40	75-21 Jazzier111½ Blitchton119^{nk} Tappa116^4	Driving	7

Speed Index: Last Race: -6.0 3-Race Avg.: -6.3 8-Race Avg.: -4.0 Overall Avg.: -5.1
LATEST WORKOUTS Sep 9 Tdn 4f fst :51^2 B

Edchabar — B. m. 5, by Nodouble—Bartered Goods, by Seattle Slew — $5,000 — Br.—Lin-Drake Farm (Fla) — Tr.—Moreno Jaime — 112
Own.—Rosa B & L
Lifetime 46 3 3 6 $42,579 — 1991 20 1 1 3 $9,222 — 1990 10 0 0 2 $3,320 — Turf 2 0 0 0 $285

17Oct91- 10Crc fst 1 1/16	:48^4	1:14^2	1:49^4	3↑ⒻClm 5500	8 4 3^{nk} 3^{1½} 10^{10} 10^{10½}	Varsi A M^{10}	Lb 109	14.50	62-22 Thorny Path113^{1¾} Bailador109½ Noble Shandey114^1	Gave way	12
4Oct91- 10Crc fst 1 70	:48^2	1:14^3	1:45^2	3↑ⒻClm 5500	4 4 4^{5½} 4^3 5^5 5^5	Varsi A M^{10}	Lb 107	7.20	81-12 Andr'sChrm116^{hd}HnrHnr109^{1½}SvnnhSnd116^{2½}	5 wide thruout	11
25Sep91- 10Crc fst 1 1/16	:48^4	1:14^4	1:48	3↑ⒻClm 5000	1 2 2^{hd} 1^1 2^{1½} 3^{1¾}	Alferez J O	Lb 112	5.60	80-16 FancyBluff110^{1½}SavannahSound120^{hd}Edchabr112^2	Weakened	11
19Sep91- 10Crc fst 1	:48^3	1:13^4	1:40^4	3↑ⒻClm 14000	5 7 8^{8¾} 8^{13} 8^{11} 8^{14}	Tatro J	Lb 112	24.00	75-18 Blue Jean Dream110^2 Bob'sOrbit118^{2}LittlePigeon111^1	Outrun	8
8Sep91- 6Crc sly 1 1/16	:48^4	1:13^4	1:48	3↑ⒻClm 11000	5 4 6^{8½} 8^{11} 7^7 7^8	Martinez R R^7	Lb 110	4.60	74-12 SweetPicclilli108^{hd}BlueJenDrem112^{2}LteBuddr110½	Gave way	9
29Aug91- 10Crc fst 1 70	:49	1:14^2	1:45^2	3↑ⒻClm 13000	6 4 5^4 6^{1¾} 5^{3½} 3^{1¾}	Cajamarca J M^7	L 109	39.10	84-11 Bob's Orbit116^{1¾} Chantely Blue106^{no} Edchabar109^{1½}	Rallied	8
29Aug91-Disqualified from purse money											
15Aug91- 2Crc fst 1	:47^4	1:14^1	1:41^3	3↑ⒻClm 8000	4 4 4^{7½} 5^{5½} 4^{4½} 4^{4¾}	Gaffalione S	Lb 116	4.50	80-08 HenriHenri106^{1½}JustMe109^{1}LockdOnTrgt112^{2½}	Showed little	5
4Aug91- 5Crc fst 1 1/16	:49	1:14^2	1:48	3↑ⒻClm 10000	7 4 3^2 3^{1½} 2^{3½} 2^2	Martinez R R^{10}	Lb 109	30.10	80-18 Another Smiso111^2 Edchabar108^2 Just Me108¾	2nd best	8
14Jly91- 11Crc fst 1	:48	1:13^3	1:40^2	3↑ⒻClm 11000	2 5 5^4 7^{6½} 5^6 7^{8½}	Bracho J A^7	Lb 108	29.90	82-12 Tarps Appeal116^{2½} Another Smiso116^{3½} Bald Cat116^1	Outrun	8
4Jly91- 4Crc fst 1 70	:47^2	1:13^3	1:45	3↑ⒻClm 14000	5 6 6^5 6^{6¾} 6^8 5^{5½}	Bracho J A^7	Lb 108	116.20	83-10 Starofanera116^{3½} Tarps Appeal116^{1}OverHeated116½	Mild gain	10

Speed Index: Last Race: (—) 3-Race Avg.: (—) 12-Race Avg.: (—) Overall Avg.: -8.0
LATEST WORKOUTS Oct 12 Crc 4f fst :49 B

Last Decree Ch. f. 3(Jan), by Nias—Rajab's Welcome, by Rajab
$5,500 Br.—Cassetta Mr-Mrs Al (Fla) Tr.—Hurtak Daniel C 114
Own.—Cassetta Al
Lifetime 34 2 2 4 $14,218 1991 21 1 1 4 $8,594 1990 13 1 1 0 $5,624

10Oct91- 2Crc gd 7f :224 :464 1:262 3+ⒻClm 5250 4 8 8¾ 87½ 55½ 3½ Toribio A R b 112 4.50 82-19 Ethel Dare118hd Be Proudest114½ Last Decree1122½ Rallied 9
2Oct91- 2Crc fst 7f :223 :462 1:27 3+ⒻClm 5250 2 10 1011 89¾ 54½ 21 Toribio A R b 112 10.40 79-10 HelloDink1111LstDecree112½NoOneTngod1201 Rallied inside 11
~~13Sep91- 2Crc fst 7f :231 :471 1:263 3+ⒻClm 6500 4 8 85½ 97½ 811 811½ Beitia A O b 113 11.70 70-12 FortunateOne1061Chelsea'sGold1132Usin-Ch1161 Never close 9~~
30Aug91-10Crc fst 7f :223 :462 1:262 3+ⒻClm 6250 7 8 87½ 73¾ 35 34 Beitia A O b 114 5.60 79-10 LockedOnTrget1141Andre'sChrm1123LstDcr1145 Lacked rally 9
17Aug91- 6Crc fst 7f :241 :48 1:27 3+ⒻClm 9000 4 1 51½ 55 57 55 Beitia A O b 116 3.80 75-16 MySisterMartina1161Usina-Ch116½FarNorthSong1133 Outrun 5
9Aug91-10Crc fst 7f :222 :46 1:264 ⒻClm 7500 12 1 912 78 3½ 11½ Beitia A O b 112 13.40 81-13 Last Decree1121½ Collaboration108no Jetazelle117hd Driving 12
1Aug91-11Crc sly 6f :221 :463 1:13 ⒻClm 7500 2 11 119½ 108½ 54 32½ Beitia A O b 112 71.30 82-16 GoodMornngSml1172½It'sYourOystr120noLstDcr1121 Fin. well 11
26Jly91- 4Crc fst 7f :23 :463 1:272 ⒻClm 7500 3 6 3½ 32 78 77 Sweeney K H b 112 53.50 71-16 FortuntOn113noSpcyPrl1135OnABroomstck107no Early factor 9
10Jly91- 6Crc fst 7f :223 :461 1:262 ⒻClm 7500 9 5 97 97½ 912 610½ Valles E S b 112 103.10 72-11 It's YourOyster1121DontAct1126FamilyDesire1171½ No threat 12
30Jun91- 5Crc sly 6f :223 :464 1:132 ⒻClm 7500 7 6 77 810 812 87 Valles E S b 112 21.20 76-12 ThisIsMyMystery112½It'sYourOystr1082TicStr117nk No threat 8

Speed Index: Last Race: +1.0 3–Race Avg.: –6.6 10–Race Avg.: –8.2 Overall Avg.: –8.2
LATEST WORKOUTS Sep 26 Crc 4f sly :512 B Sep 10 Crc 3f sly :36 H

Fortunate One Dk. b. or br. f. 3(Apr), by Fortunate Prospect—Peregrine Dancer, by Northern Hawk
$5,500 Br.—Burrows George (Fla) Tr.—Hale Robert A 109⁵
Own.—BobbieHale'sRacingStb&Kurlnd
Lifetime 25 5 0 4 $19,800 1991 18 3 0 4 $14,322 1990 7 2 0 0 $5,478

11Oct91- 8Crc fst 7f :223 :454 1:26 3+ⒻClm 7500 1 8 9¾ 914 67½ 34 Martinez R R7 111 3.60 81-14 MedievlPrincess1113MissStride1101FortuntOn1112 Late rally 9
13Sep91- 2Crc fst 7f :231 :471 1:263 3+ⒻClm 6500 9 1 11 1hd 1hd 11 Martinez R R7 106 8.60 82-12 Fortunate One1061 Chelsea's Gold1132 Usina-Ch1161 Driving 9
9Aug91-10Crc fst 7f :222 :46 1:264 ⒻClm 7500 4 11 1113 1115 73½ 62¾ Guerra A J5 112 5.70 78-13 Last Decree1121½ Collaboration108no Jetazelle117hd Mild bid 12
26Jly91- 4Crc fst 7f :23 :463 1:272 ⒻClm 7500 5 9 911 77 21 1no Guerra A J5 113 12.60 78-16 FortunteOne113noSpicyPerl1135OnABroomstick107no Just up 9
29Jun91- 2Crc fst 1 :48 1:14 1:424 ⒻClm 7500 2 3 44 511 811 76 Matutes L S7 109 13.00 73-14 SpielAppel1131Jetzelle118¾Helpmeifyoucn116hd Early factor 9
20Jun91- 4Crc sly 6½f :23 :462 1:193 ⒻⒷClm 7500 7 9 99½ 98¾ 79½ 44 Matutes L S7 110 6.10 83-14 She'll Solo117¾ Lace n'Things112½Silk'nScents1121 Good fin 9
13Jun91-10Crc fst 1⅛ :481 1:144 1:461 ⒻClm 7500 11 10 1112 76½ 58 49½ Matutes L S7 109 10.10 72-18 ⒹLorabecka1126½Jetazelle118½Goose'sGander1092½ No threat 12
13Jun91-Placed third through disqualification
7Jun91- 2Crc fst 7f :224 :463 1:28 ⒻClm 7500 5 6 98¾ 89½ 53 1nk Matutes L S7 107 14.30 75-20 FortntOn107nkHrrtlnCompny1121¾HrdlyProsprs107no Just up 9
22May91- 4Crc sly 1 :481 1:144 1:44 ⒻClm 7000 5 4 68¾ 65½ 76½ 86½ Rivera J A II 112 12.80 66-24 Otey112no Goose's Gander111hd Lorabecka1091¾ No rally 12
10May91- 4Crc fst 7f :223 :462 1:272 ⒻClm 7500 5 5 66½ 65¾ 56½ 33 Estevez R 112 9.00 75-16 OnABroomstick1171½Donn'sDsir1071¾FortuntOn1122¾ Gaining 9

Speed Index: Last Race: –5.0 3–Race Avg.: –6.6 7–Race Avg.: –6.1 Overall Avg.: –7.6
LATEST WORKOUTS Sep 12 Crc 3f fst :382 B

Be Proudest Dk. b. or br. f. 3(Jun), by Exclusive Era—Cosmic Time, by Jig Time
$5,250 Br.—Buck Nanay (Md) Tr.—Benson Alan 112
Own.—Scoon R
Lifetime 6 1 3 0 $6,510 1991 6 1 3 0 $6,510 1990 0 M 0 0

10Oct91- 2Crc gd 7f :224 :464 1:262 3+ⒻClm 5500 3 6 54 32½ 11½ 2hd Sweeney K H 114 19.70 83-19 EthelDare118hdBeProudest114½LstDecree1122½ Failed to last 9
31Jly91- 1Crc gd 7f :224 :464 1:281 3+ⒻMd 10000 4 8 72½ 63½ 31½ 1¾ Sweeney K H 117 *2.10 74-15 Be Proudest117¾ Chelsea's Gold1172 BlackRobe117nk Driving 12
19Jly91- 1Crc fst 6f :214 :462 1:14 3+ⒻMd 10000 2 7 63¾ 55½ 31½ 22 Gaffalione S 117 4.40 78-14 LoveCircle1172BeProudest1171½CocktilHour1122 Outfinished 12
7Jly91- 1Crc fst 6½f :224 :462 1:21 3+ⒻMd 10000 8 3 1hd 33 45 44 Lee M A 117 *.80 76-13 GodMrnngSml117½NghtyPtsr1172AmrcnSpd1101½ No late bid 10
27Jun91- 1Crc fst 6f :222 :462 1:133 3+ⒻMd 10000 1 4 44½ 45 33 22 Lee M A 115 11.70 80-14 Zydee'sLi'lLdy1152BeProudest115nkFineFortunt1151½ Gaining 12
19Jun91- 1Crc fst 6f :223 :464 1:133 3+ⒻMd 10000 5 9 95½ 1111 812 89½ Gold S10 105 24.40 72-14 MostKas1151LuckyLilHawk1081½SingleandCrazy1173 No rally 12

Speed Index: Last Race: +2.0 3–Race Avg.: –5.6 6–Race Avg.: –8.0 Overall Avg.: –8.0
LATEST WORKOUTS Oct 7 Crc 4f sly :484 B Oct 3 Crc 5f gd 1:031 B Sep 28 Crc 5f fst 1:034 B Sep 21 Crc 4f fst :51 B

Spirit of Finer Ch. f. 3(Feb), by World Appeal—Some One Finer, by Lord Rebeau
$5,250 Br.—Dawries E R (Fla) Tr.—Hurtak Daniel C 112
Own.—Larkin & Punches
Lifetime 10 2 0 3 $20,935 1991 6 0 0 2 $3,575 1990 4 2 0 1 $17,360

6Oct91- 2Crc fst 6f :22 :46 1:123 3+ⒻClm 5250 5 9 913 914 79½ 35 Ramos W S 113 8.90 92-12 Rowdy Dowdy1164½ Valid Polly105½ SpiritofFiner1131 Rallied 9
13Sep91- 8Crc fst 6½f :222 :453 1:182 3+ⒻClm 13000 5 7 710 713 612 514½ Ramos W S 112 12.30 78-12 MyfvortChrty1132SntLcn1128ChmpgnCnsl1161 Showed little 7
7Aug91- 5Crc fst 6½f :22 :454 1:194 ⒻClm 16000 7 1 710 79½ 69 610 Lee M A 116 3.30 76-16 Pshttothimt1121½DcptvBt112noHpfrMyLdy1131 Showed little 7
20Jly91- 7Crc fst 6½f :223 :454 1:183 3+ⒻAlw 10100 5 5 610 613 615 617½ Hernandez R 112 9.50 75-09 P.K.Cod120hdFullofstuff1124½AlotOfVison1114½ Showed little 6
~~28Jan91- 7GP fst 7f :223 :444 1:232 ⒻAlw 22000 2 5 56¾ 48½ 48 47½ Hernandez R 112 2.90 82-12 FntstcMornng1123ShnJult112nkFullofstuff1124 Checked early 5~~
6Jan91- 8Crc fst 6f :214 :452 1:114 ⒻAlw 15400 7 2 714 710 79 32¾ Hernandez R 112 5.10 88-09 PrisinFlight1122½Fullofstuff115nkSpiritofFinr1122 Closed fast 8
27Dec90- 9Crc fst 6½f :221 :453 1:183 ⒻAlw 14900 7 1 69½ 614 54 34 Hernandez R 113 24.40 89-12 Nny'sAppl1203FoolishlyWild1141SpiritofFinr1131 Closed well 7
22Sep90-10Crc fst 1⅛ :48 1:133 1:46 ⒻGardenia 6 5 76½ 814 818 826½ Hernandez R 112 12.60 58-16 Dordordor1121½Tppnze112¾ShogunShotgun1128 Showed little 8
24Aug90- 8Crc sly 6f :221 :463 1:141 ⒻAlw 13000 5 5 57 56½ 34 1hd Hernandez R 113 6.40 79-23 SprtofFnr113hdShogunShotgn113nkPrsnFlght1175½ Stiff drive 7
6May90- 3Crc fst 4½f :23 :482 :55 ⒻMd Sp Wt 8 4 67 45 11¾ Hernandez R 116 13.50 89-14 SpiritofFiner1161¾MisspntBucks116nkMjsticGm1161¼ Driving 10

Speed Index: Last Race: –6.0 3–Race Avg.: –8.0 9–Race Avg.: –4.8 Overall Avg.: –7.0
LATEST WORKOUTS Oct 2 Crc 5f fst 1:044 B Sep 27 Crc 4f fst :49 H Sep 9 Crc 5f sly 1:023 B Sep 2 Crc 4f fst :49 B

Another Smiso Ch. f. 4, by Naskra—Smile Softly, by Prince Tenderfoot
$5,500 Br.—Meadowhill (Ky) Tr.—Mello Ernest 116
Own.—Mello Sara & Mendenhall
Lifetime 30 4 5 3 $67,145 1991 15 3 2 1 $23,225 1990 15 1 3 2 $43,920 Turf 7 0 2 0 $11,010

11Sep91-10Crc fst 1⅛ :484 1:141 1:481 3+ⒻClm c-7500 8 6 51½ 44 56 55¾ Ramos W S Lb 122 *1.00 75-15 Zydee'sLi'lLdy113noHenriHnri1092FncyBluff1123 Lacked rally 8
29Aug91-10Crc fst 1⅛ :49 1:142 1:452 3+ⒻClm 12000 4 3 41½ 31 43½ 54 Hernandez R C5 Lb 115 *2.30 82-11 Bob's Orbit1161¾ Chantely Blue106no Edchabar1091½ Faltered 8
29Aug91-Awarded fourth purse money
18Aug91- 5Crc fst 1 :484 1:14 1:413 3+ⒻClm 12000 6 3 31 3½ 2hd 11 Guerra A J5 Lb 108 *2.60 85-13 Another Smiso1081 Tokyo Stutz1141 Love Cut114no Driving 7
4Aug91- 5Crc fst 1⅛ :49 1:142 1:48 3+ⒻClm 10000 4 2 21 1hd 13½ 12 Guerra A J5 Lb 111 3.10 82-18 Another Smiso1112 Edchabar1082 Just Me108¾ Driving 8
26Jly91- 7Crc fst 1⅛ :473 1:131 1:461 3+ⒻClm 12500 5 3 2½ 2hd 1hd 52 Rodriguez P A Lb 116 *1.50 80-16 CompromisdLdy1121Usin-Ch112hdJustM112no Led, weakened 9
14Jly91-11Crc fst 1 :48 1:133 1:402 3+ⒻClm 13000 7 3 2hd 1hd 2½ 22½ Lee M A Lb 116 2.50 88-12 Tarps Appeal1162½ Another Smiso1163½ BaldCat1161 Nice try 8
14Jun91- 6Crc fst 1⅛ :481 1:134 1:49 3+ⒻAlw 15800 3 2 1½ 12 2½ 45¾ Rodriguez P A Lb 117 2.90 71-19 ShrGold1081½Bldski'sFbl1103½PrstnMd1121½ Bore out stretch 8
24May91- 8Crc fst 1⅛ :483 1:141 1:461 3+ⒻAlw 14000 2 2 11 12 1½ 2¾ Lee M A Lb 119 *1.00 81-23 WhyBeNorml108¾AnotherSmiso1186½ClssicJd1082½ Held well 6
17May91- 5Crc fst 1⅛ :471 1:143 1:452 ⒻClm 10500 7 2 21½ 13 15 16½ Lee M A Lb 112 3.70 86-22 AnotherSmiso1126½SmeOldRin1146½BrifNot1141½ Ridden out 8
25Apr91- 8GP fm *1⅛ Ⓣ 1:442 ⒻAlw 23000 6 2 26 26 612 913½ Rodriguez P A Lb 112 9.30 76-13 AplcheeDwn112¾FlslyAccusd1134¾UrbnGirl1051¾ Early factor 10

Speed Index: Last Race: (—) 3–Race Avg.: (—) 12–Race Avg.: (—) Overall Avg.: –3.2

Realisticly True Ch. f. 4, by Tunerup—True Fire, by In Reality
$5,250 Br.—Schmidt Hilmer C (Fla) Tr.—Wolfson Milton W 1077
Lifetime 30 1 5 3 $12,733 | 1991 10 0 3 2 $4,833 | 1990 11 0 1 0 $1,710
Own.—Two Star Stable Inc

10Oct91-10Crc gd 7f :224 :463 1:27 3+ⒻClm 5250 3 9 9¾ 89 8½ 2½ Martinez R R7 b 108 6.20 77-19 AmtPrbh116²½RlstclyTr108noTrnr'sDghtr1111 Closed strongly 10
4Oct91-10Crc fst 1 70 :482 1:143 1:452 3+ⒻClm 5250 8 9 6¾ 33 43½ 44 Ramos W S b 114 3.90 82-12 Andre'sChrm116hdHnriHnri1091½SvnnhSound116²½ Weakened 11
20Sep91-10Crc fst 7f :224 :46 1:261 3+ⒻClm 5250 4 10 10¾ 914 77½ 33½ Matutes L S5 b 109 5.70 80-18 NoOneTngoed1141EthelDre113²½RelisticlyTrue1091 Late rally 11
6Sep91- 2Crc fst 7f :234 :474 1:27 3+ⒻClm 5250 6 2 52¾ 75½ 65¾ 21½ Matutes L S5 b 109 3.70 79-19 MissLughBid1141½RlisticlyTru109hdTrinr'sDughtr1161 Rallied 9
16Aug91- 2Crc fst 7f :232 :472 1:253 3+ⒻClm 5250 4 5 95½ 73½ 34½ 26½ Matutes L S5 b 109 18.40 80-14 SusiSouthworth113⁶½RlistclyTru109½Andr'sChrm116²½ Rallied 11
2Aug91- 2Crc fst 7f :222 :462 1:263 3+ⒻClm 5000 9 3 710 65½ 56½ 31 Matutes L S5 b 107 19.30 81-18 DandyDate1091Andre'sChrm116hdRelisticlyTrue107hd Gaining 10
26Jly91- 1Crc fst 6f :223 :461 1:13 3+ⒻClm 5000 3 8 95½ 914 611 46½ Alferez J O b 112 4.70 78-16 ToddBell1141½Andre'sChrm1125EmpressArcn112no Impr. pos. 9
17Jly91-10Crc fst 7f :221 :453 1:263 3+ⒻClm 5000 8 8 1010 1012 913 610½ Gonzalez M A b 112 17.10 71-16 SusieSouthworth1145SeaImage107hdEmaruba1071½ No factor 11
10Jly91- 1Crc fst 1 1/16 :492 1:153 1:49 3+ⒻClm 5000 6 5 31 31 813 811½ Alferez J O b 112 16.60 65-23 Sh'sSurShdy1121½Ctprs1161CompromsdLdy111hd Early factor 11
27Jun91-10Crc fst 6f :213 :453 1:133 3+ⒻClm 5000 10 10 1214 1116 78 65 Alferez J O b 112 24.50 77-14 Todd Bella1142 Ciel Bleu112hd Wendy's J. B.116½ No threat 12

Speed Index: Last Race: -4.0 3-Race Avg.: -2.6 8-Race Avg.: -5.3 Overall Avg.: -6.1

Trainer's Daughter Ch. f. 4, by Stutz Blackhawk—Too Nice, by Nice Catch
$5,500 Br.—October House Farm (Fla) Tr.—Mendez Jose A 10610
Lifetime 49 10 3 6 $75,589 | 1991 12 0 0 2 $2,024 | 1990 20 4 1 2 $25,590 | Turf 3 1 0 0 $7,210
Own.—Mendez Maria & Suchlick

18Oct91- 2Crc fst 6f :222 :462 1:13 3+ⒻClm 5500 5 5 41½ 43½ 55 44½ Felix J E 116 6.20 80-18 AmzngHppnng1123EmprssArcn113noTddBll1121½ Lacked rally 9
10Oct91-10Crc gd 7f :224 :463 1:27 3+ⒻClm 5500 5 4 12 11½ 21 32½ Matutes L S5 111 12.70 77-19 AmilPrbh116²½RlisticlyTru108noTrinr'sDughtr1111 Weakened 10
26Sep91-10Crc fst 6f :222 :462 1:132 3+ⒻClm 5500 2 10 63¾ 66 76½ 77 Toribio A R 116 11.10 76-16 Germana1182 Valid Polly1053½ Love Circle1081 Showed little 12
13Sep91- 2Crc fst 7f :231 :471 1:263 3+ⒻClm 6500 7 6 52¾ 62¾ 44 54 Toribio A R 116 10.50 78-12 Fortunate One1061 Chelsea's Gold1132Usina-Ch1161 Faltered 9
6Sep91- 2Crc fst 7f :234 :474 1:27 3+ⒻClm 5500 2 9 1hd 1hd 1hd 31½ Toribio A R 116 13.10 79-19 MissLughBd1141½RlstclyTru109hdTrnr'sDughtr1161 Weakened 9
22Aug91- 5Crc fst 6f :22 :454 1:122 3+ⒻClm 6500 4 4 32½ 45 55½ 811½ Vergara O 116 24.90 77-15 Rowdy Dowdy118no Lang Lang1166½ Lump ofJoy112nk Faded 8
12Jun91- 2Crc fst 6f :214 :46 1:131 3+ⒻClm 5250 11 2 67 58½ 98 106¾ Matutes L S7 107 13.90 77-13 BrazenRuckus1112½FancyBluff109¾Sunning114hd Early factor 12
31May91- 2Crc fst 7f :222 :462 1:273 ⒻClm 5000 4 9 43½ 43 55 64¾ Rydowski S R 112 5.10 72-32 Love Cut1121½ Intriguing Lil1121¾ Edie Mum1071½ Weakened 11
15May91- 2Crc fst 7f :22 :46 1:273 ⒻClm 6500 1 6 45½ 57 714 65½ Alferez J O 116 10.70 71-17 ExplosiveBank114¾GreyGator116²½Edchabr1121½ Early factor 11
5May91- 5Crc fst 1 1/16 :471 1:144 1:503 ⒻClm 8000 2 1 21½ 58 78¾ 610¾ Moore B G5 107 28.70 58-25 Same Old Rain116¾ Cutpurse1161½ Usina-Ch120¾ Used early 8

Speed Index: Last Race: -2.0 3-Race Avg.: -4.6 9-Race Avg.: -5.7 Overall Avg.: -6.9
LATEST WORKOUTS Oct 17 Crc 3f fst :381 B Oct 5 Crc 4f fst :49 H Sep 3 Crc 4f fst :51 B

Lukes Dancer Dk. b. or br. f. 4, by Minshaanshu Amad—Fair Loretta, by Judgable
$5,000 Br.—Sugar Hill Farm I (Fla) Tr.—Mercer F 1075
Lifetime 26 1 3 2 $5,780 | 1991 18 1 3 2 $5,362 | 1990 8 M 0 0 $418 | Turf 1 0 0 0
Own.—Luccarelli Alfred

15Sep91- 3Tdn fst 6f :231 :481 1:154 3+ⒻClm 4000 1 8 88 57½ 63½ 54 Medero F B 122 *1.70 62-26 ⒹWshty109nkBuck'sApple116hdToTheHvns1182 Broke slowly 8
8Sep91- 7Tdn fst 1 40 :471 1:144 1:46 3+ⒻClm 4000 9 9 816 70½ 67 56¾ Medero F B 118 17.80 56 — JoGetois1131LadyAlbon116hdWaltWinninWidow1175½ Gaining 12
29Aug91- 6Tdn fst 6f :223 :462 1:131 3+ⒻClm 4000 1 9 95½ 77 57¾ 25½ Medero F B 118 27.80 74-16 Classy Judi1095½LukesDancer118½SumSmartLady113½ Rallied 10
22Aug91-10Tdn fst 1 40 :481 1:143 1:454 3+ⒻClm 4000 9 2 21 23 68½ 68¾ Medero F B 118 19.20 55-28 JqueUzi1161SucyJn1101½WtlWinninWidow1153 Flattened out 11
10Aug91- 1Tdn fst 1 :493 1:162 1:443 3+ⒻMd 4000 6 3 11½ 15 15½ 15½ Medero F B 116 *2.00 55-37 LukesDncer1165½AmberAutumn117½NiceBuzz1159 Ridden out 7
3Aug91- 2Tdn fst 1 :484 1:164 1:45 3+ⒻMd 4000 2 7 712 69½ 69 513¾ Medero F B 116 3.50 39-32 Jaque Uzi1151½ Sins Hope1163 Katy Kerr1144¾ No factor 8
24Jly91- 1Tdn fst 1 :494 1:162 1:444 3+ⒻMd 4000 2 2 1hd 12 11 2hd Medero F B 118 31.80 54-36 PassingSpirits122hdLukesDncer118¾KtyKerr1146½ Just missed 8
14Jly91- 5Tdn fst 1 40 :492 1:161 1:463 3+ⒻMd 4000 7 4 31 56½ 511 510½ Medero F B 118 12.40 41-35 Jo Getois1131½ Passing Spirits1222 Katy Kerr1156¾ Evenly 10
4Jly91- 3Tdn fst 6f :224 :471 1:134 3+ⒻMd 3000 1 8 45½ 47½ 46½ 28¾ Medero F B 122 9.40 67-18 Little Silver Star1158¾ Lukes Dancer122½ Easybre1222 Rallied 10
27Jun91- 3Tdn fst 1 40 :473 1:132 1:421 3+ⒻMd 4000 3 7 611 511 59 613¾ Londono O A B 118 7.70e 68-18 Kandy Krash1181½ Thats aChopper1161½KatyKerr1149 Evenly 12

Speed Index: Last Race: -12.0 3-Race Avg.: -12.3 3-Race Avg.: -12.3 Overall Avg.: -18.3

Our Real Beauty Ch. f. 4, by Free Reality—Maltz's Lady, by Slady Castle
$5,500 Br.—Corsiglia Beatrice (NJ) Tr.—Imprescia Dominic Jr 1115
Lifetime 15 4 2 1 $56,280 | 1991 4 0 0 1 $770 | 1990 10 3 2 0 $44,290
Own.—Rocca Carol

10Oct91- 2Crc gd 7f :224 :464 1:262 3+ⒻClm 5250 8 1 2hd 2hd 77½ 75¾ Green B L 114 *2.10 77-19 Ethel Dare118hd Be Proudest114½ Last Decree112²½ Faltered 9
2Oct91- 4Crc fst 7f :23 :464 1:272 3+ⒻClm 5500 6 3 11½ 13 12½ 31 Green B L 116 5.10 77-18 EthelDare1131SweetPicclilli111hdOurRelBeuty1161 Weakened 10
26Sep91-10Crc fst 6f :222 :462 1:132 3+ⒻClm 5000 1 8 2hd 32½ 99¾ 1111½ Green B L 114 3.10 71-16 Germana1182 Valid Polly1053½ Love Circle1081 Faded 12
12Sep91- 2Crc fst 6f :221 :461 1:123 3+ⒻClm 5000 1 8 41½ 31 23½ 87½ Castillo H Jr L 112 *1.80 80-16 German1142NoOneTngoed1141½Belle'sTinyTnk1092½ Faltered 12
10Nov90- 8Med sly 6f :224 :464 1:113 3+ⒻⓈHandicap 7 2 62½ 87½ 813 832 Migliore R L 114 5.60 52-19 Natala1182 Crafty Tenderoni1165 Honest Uzi115¾ Outrun 8
28Oct90- 8Pha fst 6f :221 :453 1:111 ⒻⓇLadySlipper 2 3 21 3½ 41½ 55 Marquez C H Jr L 120 *1.50 83-13 Chrissy'sSecret1223ChangingProspects118noFuerza1222 Tired 8
11Oct90- 8Med fst 6f :214 :45 1:092 3+ⒻAlw 17000 2 1 21 21 12 12 Krone J A L 113 2.40 95-12 OurRealBeuty1132WildWrning1136MotherofEight1164 Driving 6
29Sep90- 8Med fst 6f :22 :45 1:11 3+ⒻⓈHandicap 5 3 11 12 2½ 54½ Smith M E L 112 5.50 83-16 Crafty Tenderoni110½Lena'sPrayer1191½HonestUzi116¾ Faded 8
7Sep90- 5Med fst 6f :221 :453 1:12 3+ⒻⓈAlw 21800 1 4 12 12½ 14 13 Smith M E L 114 *1.30 82-19 Our Real Beauty1143 SpecialVice1161½LauraWho1183 Driving 8
28Aug90- 5Pha gd 6½f :221 :444 1:16 3+ⒻAlw 12500 1 2 12 13 12 12½ Cordero A Jr L 113 *1.20 97-14 OrRlBt1132½ChngngPrspcts11412UpprClss114¾ Drifted, drvng 6

Speed Index: Last Race: -4.0 3-Race Avg.: -7.3 10-Race Avg.: -4.1 Overall Avg.: -4.1
LATEST WORKOUTS Sep 10 Crc 4f sly :501 B Aug 31 Crc 6f fst 1:16 B

Sallie Blue Dk. b. or br. m. 5, by Hall of Reason—Azure Main, by Big Burn
$5,500 Br.—Tamburo Mrs P A (Fla) Tr.—Posada Frank A 10610
Lifetime 99 1 3 10 $27,534 | 1991 30 1 0 1 $4,371 | 1990 31 M 3 5 $16,675 | Turf 2 0 0 1 $1,700
Own.—Llanes & Posada

6Oct91- 2Crc fst 6f :22 :46 1:123 3+ⒻClm 5500 4 5 76 711 98½ 89½ RasmussenSJ10 Lb 107 53.30 77-12 RowdyDowdy1164½ValidPolly105½SpiritofFiner1131 No factor 9
2Oct91- 4Crc fst 7f :23 :464 1:272 3+ⒻClm 5250 1 8 65 67½ 66¾ 66 Felix J E Lb 114 91.00 72-18 EthelDre1131SweetPicclilli111hdOurRlButy1161 Saved ground 10
26Sep91-10Crc fst 6f :222 :462 1:132 3+ⒻClm 5250 3 9 74½ 77½ 87¾ 87½ Alferez J O Lb 114 49.60 75-16 Germana1182 Valid Polly1053½ Love Circle1081 No threat 12
12Sep91- 2Crc fst 6f :221 :461 1:123 3+ⒻClm 5250 10 2 107½ 107½ 89½ 77 Acevedo D A L 114 70.90 80-16 Germn1142NoOneTngod1141½Bll'sTinyTnk1092½ Showed little 12
6Sep91- 2Crc fst 7f :234 :474 1:27 3+ⒻClm 5250 7 3 41¾ 43½ 77½ 76½ Acevedo D A L 114 22.00 73-19 MissLughBid1141½RlisticlyTru109hdTrnr'sDughtr1161 Stopped 9
28Aug91- 4Crc sly 6f :222 :462 1:133 3+ⒻClm 5500 2 10 118 98½ 75½ 64 Acevedo D A L 116 24.10 78-13 Todd Bella118nk Germana114¾ Tenn Is1142 Belated bid 11
24Aug91- 2Crc fst 6f :221 :462 1:132 3+ⒻClm 6000 8 1 76½ 65 54½ 33½ Acevedo D A L 112 67.90 79-15 Sajonia1162 No One Tangoed1081½SallieBlue112½ Closed well 8
7Aug91- 2Crc fst 6f :22 :46 1:131 3+ⒻClm 5250 7 10 107½ 1012 98 95½ Ramirez R T L 114 83.20 78-16 Lang Lang1141½ ValidPolly108¾ChrisGloryGirl1141½ No factor 12
26Jly91-10Crc fst 1⅛ :492 1:154 1:544 3+ⒻClm 30000 5 1 2hd — — — Kornmeyer L J L 112 47.50 — — Sonic Gray1121½ For Nando1121 Sweet Piccalilli1164½ Bolted 7
26Jly91-Originally scheduled on turf
17Jly91-10Crc fst 7f :221 :453 1:263 3+ⒻClm 5500 9 7 99½ 912 813 811¾ Blanford H A10 L 106 59.70 78-16 SusieSouthworth1145SeaImge107hdEmrub1071½ Showed little 11

Speed Index: Last Race: -11.0 3-Race Avg.: -10.0 9-Race Avg.: -8.5 Overall Avg.: -8.5

Below is the P/M Table from the *Winning at the Track* program. It displays the various capabilities of each horse.

```
Calder Race Crse  FL        October 24
2nd    Race                 7 f
```

PP	Horse	Notes	Odds	Ability Factor	Pure Speed	Early Speed	Late Speed	MF	P/M RATING
1	Jazzier	84/87	20:1	451	88	281	566	847	2516
2	Edchabar	78/73	20:1	455	94	254	591	845	2607
3	LastDecree	84/91	5:1	472	92	272	579	851	2577
4	FortunateOne	84/90	6:1	457	91	277	572	849	2552
5	BeProudest	85/92	10:1	463	92	288	579	867	2588
6	SpiritOfFiner	83/92	6:1	449	98	272	587	859	2637
7	AnotherSmiso	85/87	3:1	464	95	263	594	857	2631
8	RealistclyTrue	82/86	8:1	466	92	268	581	849	2578
9	TrainrsDaughtr	87/90	10:1	469	90	289	571	860	2554
10	LukesDancer	81/70	20:1	453	84	268	556	824	2450
11	OurRealBeauty	88/86	9:2	456	90	294	565	859	2538
12	SallieBlue	82/86	20:1	451	90	280	571	851	2543

The *Pace Analyst*, which is an additional module to *Winning at the Track*, shows "depth of talent" by ranking the best, the second-best, and third-best races for each horse. It displays these races in terms of Pole Speed (each horse's speed to the second call point) and Last Quarter (late speed) capabilities.

```
Race:  2   CRC      7 f
```

PP	Horse		Morn. Line	Pole Speed
11	OurRealBeauty	88/86	9:2	88
9	TrainrsDaughtr	87/90	10:1	84
6	SpiritOfFiner	83/92	6:1	83
5	BeProudest	85/92	10:1	83

PP	Horse		Morn. Line	Pole Speed
11	OurRealBeauty	88/86	9:2	86
1	Jazzier	84/87	20:1	84
5	BeProudest	85/92	10:1	83
9	TrainrsDaughtr	87/90	10:1	81

PP	Horse		Morn. Line	Pole Speed
11	OurRealBeauty	88/86	9:2	86
4	FortunateOne	84/90	6:1	84
5	BeProudest	85/92	10:1	83
7	AnotherSmiso	85/87	3:1	82

```
* PACE ANALYST *
Expected Pole Speed.... 88 - 0:46.2
Pure Speed Estimate.... 93 - 1:26.1
Required Last Quarter..119   L/S  576

CAPABLE AT THIS PACE:                    L/S
~~~~~~~~~~~~~~~~~~~~~~~ Best              ~~~
7-AnotherSmiso    85/87    81/130        594
2-Edchabar        78/73    78/132        591
6-SpiritOfFiner   83/92    83/129        587
8-RealistclyTrue  82/86    75/132        581
3-LastDecree      84/91    79/126        579
                          2nd
2-Edchabar        78/73    78/130        580
7-AnotherSmiso    85/87    79/128        579
3-LastDecree      84/91    79/127        579
6-SpiritOfFiner   83/92    78/129        578
                          3rd
2-Edchabar        78/73    75/131        578
6-SpiritOfFiner   83/92    76/130        577
7-AnotherSmiso    85/87    82/125        577
00-                        00/000       0000

       RACE FILE: 10-24-91.crc
       Pacesetters: # 11  #  5
```

Finally, the *Graphics* module allows the user to set the expected race criteria (pace and maximum lengths out at the second call point). The program then displays only those horses that qualify according to the standards set.

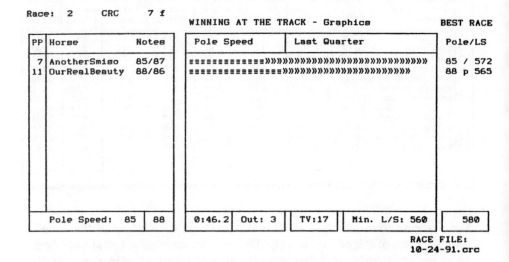

```
Race:  2      CRC      7 f
                               WINNING AT THE TRACK - Graphics              BEST RACE

 PP | Horse            Notes      Pole Speed       | Last Quarter              Pole/LS

  7 | AnotherSmiso     85/87   ===============»»»»»»»»»»»»»»»»»»»»»»»»»»»»»»   85 / 572
 11 | OurRealBeauty    88/86   ===============»»»»»»»»»»»»»»»»»»»»»»»»         88 p 565




         Pole Speed:  85    88    0:46.2  Out: 3    TV:17    Min. L/S: 560      580

                                                             RACE FILE:
                                                             10-24-91.crc
```

As the illustrations indicate, the four logical contenders in this race were ANOTHER SMISO, EDCHABAR, SPIRIT OF FINER, and OUR REAL BEAUTY. From this group, the following selections appeared to be the most promising:

1.   Another Smiso (A Naskra filly that seems to relish the idea of being in front in the first six panels of a contest. Today, Another Smiso is being offered at less than 50% of her claim value of 67 days earlier -- in a race she WON).

2.   Our Real Beauty (identified as one of three evenly-matched pacesetters and the horse to catch in the stretch); and

3.   Edchabar (a horse with plenty of late speed ability, being returned to action after 7 days).

Another Smiso, identified as the key horse in this race, and Edchabar were ideal lessons in "diametric handicapping." Both were route horses that had been competitive at higher levels, but were now being placed into a sprint -- normally a bad bet. However, the computer revealed that both had a good chance in this 7 furlong contest. Also, betting a horse that has just been claimed can be risky. Yet, Another Smiso's trainer was willing to take a family gamble (note the new owner) by waiting 30 days and then dropping her further down the ladder.

As it turned out, Another Smiso won by a comfortable 3-length margin, paying $11.80, $6.00, and $6.00; while Edchabar managed to catch Our Real Beauty in the stretch and paid $14.80 and $9.20. Our Real Beauty paid $9.00 for show. The perfecta was a respectable $178.00 and the trifecta paid $4,617.00 for each $2.00 ticket.

The Personal Computer

Regardless of the software being used, the computer is a tool. It's not a magic box; nor should it be used as such. The old saying holds true: "Garbage in, garbage out!" If the horse never produced the numbers and they were never entered into the computer in the first place, it would be wrong to blame the program for failing to identify the animal as a contender.

The following race is an example of what the computer *can't* do. Without handicapping the race, the huge payoff for this contest would not have been possible. Here is the way it appeared on November 29th:

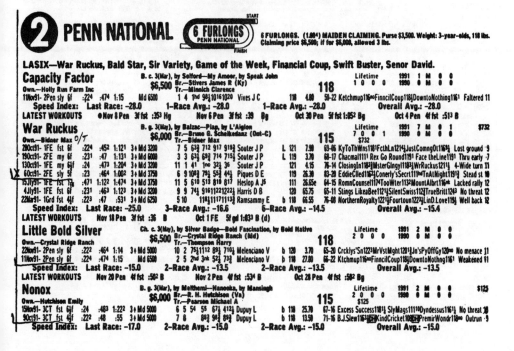

Lucky Mishap

Ch. c. 3(Feb), by Prince Bel Mar—Pachinka, by His B
$6,000
Own.—Gem Farms
Br.—George E. Meyers (Pa)
Tr.—Daninger Frank J Jr

											Lifetime	1991	3	M	0	0	$174
										115	3 0 0 0	1990	0	M	0	0	
											$174						

11Nov91- 3Pen sly 6f   :22² :47² 1:14⁴   3♦⒎Md 10000   2 3 3² 4⁴¹ 6⁷¹ 5¹³¹   Acksel J S   120   27.00   59-22 ChaceScore 120¹MyCptinDoc 120¹² ChinJumper 120²   Gave way 8
25Aug91- 3Pen fst 6f   :23¹ :47⁴ 1:14³   Md 10000   5 4 11¹ 53¹ 81⁶ 9²³   Baker C J   116   33.90   49-23 BareasSweet119¹FreestheSky115¹¹Bill'sWriter119¹¹   Stopped 9
18Feb91- 5Pen fst 6f   :22³ :46² 1:14   3♦⒎Md 10000   1 7 1ʰᵈ 65¹ 917 —   Salvaggio M V   118   14.70   — — Hay Bear118² Mr. Hogan118¹¹ Bill's Writer118³   Distanced 10

Speed Index: Last Race: -20.0   2-Race Avg.: -24.0   2-Race Avg.: -24.0   Overall Avg.: -24.0
LATEST WORKOUTS   Nov 1 Pen   3f fst :48² H   Oct 21 Pen   3f fst :38² B   Oct 4 Pen   4f fst :51¹ Bg

Bald Star

B. g. 3(Feb), by Cojak—Star Amber, by Barachois
$6,000
Own.—Lohman Richard E
Br.—Little Gordon E (Fla)
Tr.—Virts Joseph

											Lifetime	1991	7	M	0	3	$2,282
										115	7 0 0 3						
											$2,282						

16Nov91- 1Pha fst 6½f   :22⁴ :46⁴ 1:20   3♦ Md 7000   2 10 10¹⁴10⁹¹ 91⁴ 91³   Eldridge P K   L 117   7.90   65-14 Ashburn119³DottiesDelinqunt112³¹GnuinOnyx115¹   Off slowly 11
5Nov91- 4Pha fst 6½f   :22⁴ :46⁴ 1:13³   3♦ Md 7000   8 10 9¹⁵ 97 44 43³   Matz N⁵   L 112   11.70   72-17 Master Tillman112ʰᵈ ll Monello120³¹Rock'sPuff120³   Too late 12
19Oct91- 1Del fst 5f   :22 :46² :59¹   Md 5000   7 10 10¹⁵10¹⁶ 61⁵ 31⁸¹   Petersen J L   L 122   11.60   65-16 Pnnsylvnprnc116³HrdtoKnow116¹¹³BldStr122¹¹   Gained third 10
9Sep91- 6Del fst 6f   :22² :46 1:12²   Md 5000   7 12 12⁹¹12¹³10¹⁵ 81⁸¹   Hilburn K D   L 122   3.90   68-16 Hooryboy116ᵖᵒPnnsylvnprnc116¹⁰SvgMountn122²³   No threat 12
24Aug91- 1Tim fst 6f   :23² :47³ 1:19   3♦ Md 6500   2 4 6⁹ 7¹² 51⁰ 57   Douglas F G   117   *.50   76-10 Specific'sLestr122ⁿᵏMidnightGm112³ᵏJyBryrick117⁴¹   Outrun 10
26Jly91- 5Lrl fst 6f   :23 :47² 1:19¹   3♦ Md 6500   4 5 44 43 33¹ 35³   Wilson R   115   3.00   75-17 Place Line120³¹ Mardeka115²¹ Bald Star115³   Hung 14
21May91- 5Pim fst 6f   :23² :47¹ 1:14   3♦ Md 7500   9 7 89³ 81¹ 67¹ 34   Peterson T L⁵   105   8.50   71-21 Flat Note122ⁿᵒ Steptoe122⁴ Bald Star105³¹   Rallied 7

Speed Index: Last Race: -21.0   3-Race Avg.: -17.0   7-Race Avg.: -13.7   Overall Avg.: -13.7
LATEST WORKOUTS   Oct 10 Del   6f fst 1:17³ Bg   Oct 2 Del   5f fst 1:03 B

Sir Variety

Ch. g. 3(Apr), by Sir Raleigh—Grey Variety, by Grey Dawn II
$6,000
Own.—Szeyller Robert
Br.—Szeyller Mary R & R A (Pa)
Tr.—Iwersen David

											Lifetime	1991	5	M	0	0	$453
										115	5 0 0 0						
											$453						

11Nov91- 2Pen sly 6f   :22⁴ :47⁴ 1:15   Md 3500   10 9 10⁹³ 86¹ 76¹ 51¹   Hilburn K D   Lb 115   64.70   68-22 Ktchmup116ⁿᵒFinnclCoup118¹DowntoNothng116¹   No menace 11
30Oct91- 1Del fst 1½   :48 1:14⁴ 1:50³   3♦ Md 3500   1 13 12²⁵13²⁶13²⁹12³⁰³   Gunther S F   Lb 112   25.10   — — Stoney Hill118¹ Trachodon122³ Alfredo112¹   Outrun 13
20Oct91- 1Del fst 1   :48³ 1:15² 1:44   3♦ Md 4000   7 4 45¹ 58¹ 61² 62¹³   LizarzaburuPM   Lb 116   16.40   48-32 MightyBrev114¹¹BoldRuby122¹LostCrop117¹   Steadied far trn 12
20Oct91-Placed fifth through disqualification
25Sep91- 4Del sly 6f   :22³ :47¹ 1:14³   Md 3500   9 8 76 54 55 48   LizarzaburuPM   b 114   38.10   69-21 Noble Jason118³ Late Hitter114²³ Salopian105²¹   No menace 10
23Aug91- 8Del fst 6f   :22³ :46¹ 1:12²   Md 7500   6 9 81¹ 917 923 926   Gunther S F   b 118   28.90   59-17 CurrentTrnd122¹²DsrdGrk116ⁿᵏPnnsylvniprinc116¹   No factor 9

Speed Index: Last Race: -10.0   3-Race Avg.: -14.6   3-Race Avg.: -14.6   Overall Avg.: -18.0

Game of the Week

Ch. g. 3(Apr), by I Am the Game—Brave Peace, by Brave Emperor
$6,500
Own.—Krug Edward
Br.—James F Lewis & R R Rolapp (Md)
Tr.—Testerman Valora A

											Lifetime	1991	7	M	0	0	$200
										118	7 0 0 0						
											$200						

15Nov91- 3CT fst 6½f   :24 :48³ 1:22²   3♦ Md 5000   5 8 87 66 56¹ 61²¹   Lewis W R Jr   Lb 117   3.10   67-16 Excess Success118¹¹ Sly Mags111¹⁰Dyndessus118¹   Steadied 10
20Oct91- 6CT fst 6½f   :24² :48³ 1:22   3♦ Md 5000   5 5 64¹ 43¹ 35¹ 45¹   Lewis W R Jr   Lb 117   25.20   77-13 Widbll'sDight115¹GlHghFlyr117²¹JhnnyOnTm116²   No mishap 11
12Oct91- 6Del fst 1½   :47² 1:13³ 1:49⁴   Md 7500   3 3 36 48 71² 82⁵¹   Murphy C K   Lb 116   56.80   37-29 I'm Cocky Too116¹³Alfredo116²CorsicanPresident116ⁿᵒ   Tired 11
27Sep91- 5Pim fst 6f   :23¹ :47¹ 1:13²   3♦ Md 7500   2 9 10¹¹ 88 91¹ 91¹   Delgado G H   Lb 116   90.50   67-18 Lord Rop118³¹StormyTreasure118²FreddieHawkins116²   Wide 12
31Aug91- 5Tim fst 6f   :23³ :49 1:16²   3♦ Md 7000   9 2 3² 32¹ 51³ 829¹   McKnight R E   b 117   37.70   52-14 BitterDouble122⁷ThirdLanding117¹⒈FinlStep122⁷   Weakened 9
31Aug91-Placed seventh through disqualification
24Aug91- 1Tim fst 6f   :23² :47³ 1:19   3♦ Md 6500   1 3 45 69¹ 919 916   Ryan J S   b 117   15.10   67-10 Spcific'sLstr122ⁿᵏ MidnightGm112ⁿᵏ JyBryrick117⁴¹   Fell back 10
13Jly91- 9Pen fst 6f   :22² :46² 1:12²   Md 7000   8 7 85¹ 71² 712 913   Baker C J   b 116   4.50e   63-20 GophrGold118ⁿᵏKy'sMscMn118²SrInspctr118³¹   Raced poorly 11

Speed Index: Last Race: -17.0   3-Race Avg.: -14.0   6-Race Avg.: -19.5   Overall Avg.: -21.7

Financial Coup   RTE

Dk. b. or br. g. 3(Feb), by State Dinner—Sweet Innocence, by Wajima
$6,000
Own.—Pesaridan Stables
Br.—Racecourse Transportation Inc (Ont-C)
Tr.—Rowan Stephen C

											Lifetime	1991	10	M	1	1	$4,071
										115	10 0 1 1	1990	0	M	0	0	
											$4,071	Turf	1	0	0	0	

24Nov91- 2Pen sly 1½   :48² 1:15² 1:51   3♦ Md 5000   4 4 41¹ 42¹ 44¹ 44   Deibler C E III   Lb 119   *1.50   51-25 LndingScore122²¹SwiftHwk122ⁿᵒLovThtMgg119¹   No excuse 12
11Nov91- 2Pen sly 6f   :22⁴ :47⁴ 1:15   Md 3500   7 2 51¹ 44 1ʰᵈ 2ⁿᵏ   Deibler C E III   Lb 118   4.80   70-22 Ktchmup116ⁿᵒFinnclCoup118¹DowntoNothng116¹   No excuse 11
4Nov91- 9Pen fst 6f   :23¹ :48⁴ 1:16³   3♦ Md 5000   1 7 32¹ 41¹ 22¹ 3¹   Deibler C E III   Lb 120   2.20   61-27 RowingMedalist122ⁿᵏSirSatin123¹FinnclCoup120²   No excuse 10
21Oct91- 3Pen fst 170   :49¹ 1:14⁴ 1:46⁴   3♦ Md 5000   6 2 23 2³ 2³ 2³   Deibler C E III   Lb 118   2.80   71-19 Asmodeous122⁴FinnclCoup118²RowingMedalist122²   2nd best 7
14Oct91- 6Pen fst 6f   :22 :46 1:12⁴   Md 5000   6 7 66¹ 611 68¹ 411¹   Flores J L   Lb 118   9.10   63-21 Latin Label118⁵ GoldenPaces118ⁿᵏRegalMusic115¹   No menace 12
4Oct91- 10Pen fst 6f   :22³ :47 1:13²   3♦ Md 6500   1 9 63¹ 79³ 75¹ 510¹   Canon R A   Lb 119   *2.30   69-18 Long Stride118³ Bullea's Ally119ᵏ Swift Buster119¹   Outrun 10
16Sep91- 9Pen fst 6f   :22³ :46³ 1:14   Md 7500   3 3 32 3² 3ⁿᵏ 2ⁿᵏ   Canon R A   Lb 119   *1.20   75-14 Fredatius119ⁿᵏFinnclCoup119ⁿᵏSwiftBuster115²   No excuse 8
4Sep91- 1Pha fm 5f ① :23¹ :47¹ 1:01¹   3♦ Md 16000   11 1 74¹10⁹³10⁴³10⁸³   Canon R A   b 119   7.90   67-24 PrinceDekalb117²¹Epipsychidion107ⁿᵒNetecon117¹   No factor 11

Speed Index: Last Race: -8.0   3-Race Avg.: -10.0   5-Race Avg.: -11.2   Overall Avg.: -12.3

Swift Buster

Gr. g. 3(May), by Fuzzbuster—Self Feeder, by Pass Catcher
$6,000
Own.—Menke Fred R
Br.—Cummings Douglas M (Md)
Tr.—Castranze Charles A

											Lifetime	1991	8	M	1	2	$1,777
										115	8 0 1 2	1990	0	M	0	0	
											$1,777						

11Nov91- 2Pen sly 6f   :22⁴ :47⁴ 1:15   Md 6500   11 6 86¹ 76¹ 99¹ 83³   Acksel J S   Lb 118   3.70   66-22 Ktchmup116ⁿᵒFinnclCoup118¹DowntoNothing116¹   No factor 11
28Oct91- 6Del fst 1   :48 1:13² 1:42²   3♦ Md 6500   5 4 54 51¹ 3² 34   LaLande L   Lb 118   6.00   66-26 StealMyThunder116²³SwiftBuster118²LostCrop119¹⅓   Fin well 12
20Oct91- 1Del fst 1   :48³ 1:15² 1:44   Md 4000   6 5 57³10¹⁶ 816 72ⁿ   Moreno O   Lb 116   9.60   37-32 MightyBrv114¹BoldRuby122¹LostCrop117¹   Checked far turn 10
20Oct91-Placed sixth through disqualification
4Oct91- 10Pen fst 6f   :22³ :47 1:13²   3♦ Md 6500   7 4 97¹ 84 54¹ 39   Acksel J S   Lb 119   8.60   69-18 LongStride118³Bullea'sAlly119ᵏSwiftBuster119¹   Fin. willingly 10
16Sep91- 9Pen fst 6f   :22³ :46³ 1:14   Md 6500   1 8 44 52³ 2ʰᵈ 3ⁿᵏ   Acksel J S   Lb 119   7.30e   75-14 Fredtius119ⁿᵒFinnclCoup118ⁿᵏSwiftBustr115²   Saved ground 8
28Aug91- 1TAU fst 6f   :22³ :46¹ 1:14   3♦ Md 6500   2 10 76 69³ 57³ 53   Underwood S   Lb 113   32.70   70-16 PrinceofParadise118³Answered118³¹Mariachi117⁴¹   No factor 10
4Aug91- 3Lrl fst 1½   :48³ 1:14 1:54²   3♦ Md 8500   9 4 58 917 920 939¹   Luzzi M J   b 115   7.10   30-27 Mardeka119ⁿᵏ Mi Roy110⁷¹ Gunpowder Falls113ⁿᵏ   Outrun 10
21Jly91- 6Lrl fst 1½   :22⁴ :46 1:13   3♦ Md 8500   3 11 12¹¹12¹³11¹³ 76¹   Luzzi M J   Lb 115   10.10   69-18 Solo West115¹ No No Go 114¹³ML.AiryDestiny115ⁿᵒ   Outrun 12

Speed Index: Last Race: -12.0   3-Race Avg.: -12.0   5-Race Avg.: -12.6   Overall Avg.: -18.1
LATEST WORKOUTS   Nov 27 Pen   3f fst :37² B

Beau Bunctious

B. g. 3(Mar), by Spring Double—Barbara Bunctious, by Rambunctious
$6,500
Own.—Westland Dan D
Br.—Dan D. Westland (Md)
Tr.—Dilodovico Damon R

											Lifetime	1991	5	M	0	0	
										113⁵	5 0 0 0	1990	0	M	0	0	

15Nov91- 3Lrl fst 7f   :23³ :47² 1:26   3♦ Md 6500   11 9 87¹ 91²¹10¹¹12¹   Luzzi M J   b 120   11.70   52-21 Big A.120⁴ Standish120⁵ Bravo Caro120ⁿᵈ   No factor 11
28Aug91- 4Del fst 6f   :23² :46⁴ 1:14⁴   3♦ Md 25000   8 8 10¹²10¹²10¹⁰ 67³   Pino M G   b 114   16.30   78-13 Canterbury Kid108³¹Dr.Shot112ⁿᵒJustinsLaw114³   Belated bid 9
15Mar91- 10Pim sly 1½   :48² 1:13¹ 1:45¹   3♦ Md Sp Wt   1 8 88¹ 815 815 712   Peterson T L⁵   107   53.80   55-27 Roister107²¹ Lednak114³ Oh Marphe113¹⁵   Outrun 8
2Mar91- 4Lrl fst 6f   :22² :46¹ 1:12¹   Md Sp Wt   6 5 57¹ 51³ 51¹ 51¹²   Pino M G   120   12.70   67-20 FortySomething120⁴Aaron'sHalo120ⁿᵒRoister115¹⁴   No factor 7
18Feb91- 10Lrl fst 6½f   :22² :46¹ 1:18¹   Md Sp Wt   5 8 913 911 711 511   Pino M G   120   28.40   75-20 His Acallade120² Black Jim120³ Aaron's Halo120³   No factor 9

Speed Index: Last Race: -27.0   3-Race Avg.: -16.3   4-Race Avg.: -13.5   Overall Avg.: -14.4
LATEST WORKOUTS   Nov 8 Lrl   4f fst :50² Bg   Oct 4 Bow   3f fst :39   B

Based on the figures entered into the computer, the contenders in this race appeared to be WAR RUCKUS (the key horse selection), FINANCIAL COUP, BALD STAR, and BEAU BUNCTIOUS. This race was particularly interesting because the key horse was flashing on the board at 35 to 1! The track handicapper favored Financial Coup and Nonox, and the public agreed.

These are the *Winning at the Track* and *Pace Analyst* printouts as they appeared that day...

The *WATT* P/M Table:

```
Penn National      PA          November 29
2nd    Race                    6 f
```

PP	Horse	Notes	Odds	Ability Factor	Pure Speed	Early Speed	Late Speed	MF	P/M RATING
1	CapacityFactor	73/56	15:1	384	56	272	676	948	2579
2	WarRuckus	82/77	20:1	431	85	280	755	1035	3019
3	LittleBoldSlvr	81/71	20:1	428	72	277	718	995	2822
4	Nonox	72/68	15:1	422	71	263	722	985	2813
5	LuckyMishap	78/68	8:1	398	68	275	708	983	2758
6	BaldStar	79/69	8:1	418	79	261	744	1005	2929
7	SirVariety	80/74	8:1	429	74	258	729	987	2851
8	Game ot Week	76/68	15:1	417	78	267	738	1005	2909
9	FinancialCoup	81/65	2:1	436	76	277	730	1007	2885
10	SwiftBuster	84/72	5:1	430	81	275	740	1015	2945
11	BeauBunctious	78/66	8:1	434	89	256	762	1018	3048

This was the Display screen from the *Pace Analyst* module:

```
Race:  2     PEN     6 f
```

PP	Likely Pacesetters		Best Race			Second Best			P/M Rating
			Pole Speed	Last Qtr.	Late Speed	Pole Speed	Last Qtr.	Late Speed	
2	WarRuckus	82/77	77	186	755	82	181	746	3019
3	LittleBoldSlvr	81/71	74	176	718	81	170	718	2822

PP	Best-4 P/M Horses								
11	BeauBunctious	78/66	74	193	762	78	185	754	3048
2	WarRuckus	82/77	77	186	755	82	181	746	3019
10	SwiftBuster	84/72	68	186	740	84	176	735	2945
6	BaldStar	79/69	70	191	744	79	178	733	2929

PP	Selection - Display								
8	Game ot Week	76/68	73	185	738	76	180	733	2909
9	FinancialCoup	81/65	81	174	730	73	181	730	2885

RACE FILE: 11-29-91.pen

After reviewing the numbers, Beau Bunctious and War Ruckus were, by far, the two strongest in this race. Beau Bunctious appeared to be the "class" of this group, being the only horse that had run in non-claiming company. Also, it was dropping from higher levels of the better-quality Maryland circuit. However, the horse showed little inclination to perform on November 15 upon returning from his summer layoff.

Of the two expected pacesetters (War Ruckus and Little Bold Silver), War Ruckus is a much stronger horse by a wide margin. Therefore, War Ruckus became the horse to beat and the key in this race.

Now, which of the other horses could accompany him to the wire?

CAPACITY FACTOR? A good trainer and a small bullet workout, but it's doubtful that the horse has the ability.

LITTLE BOLD SILVER? No. He'll fold after the early pace.

NONOX or LUCKY MISHAP? No. It's unlikely that either one will be able to compete with this group.

BALD STAR? A good possibility.

SIR VARIETY? The horse was able to close on Financial Coup on November 11. Maybe.

GAME OF THE WEEK? This horse couldn't come close in a $4,000 claimer at Delaware Park. Why now? But wait! This is the son of the speedy I Am The Game, King Leatherbury's best-ever chance for a Triple Crown! In three straight races, I Am The Game chased Spend A Buck around the track ... including the 1985 Kentucky Derby! Game Of The Week has started seven times and has not earned enough money to pay for the van's gasoline! Could there be something here?

FINANCIAL COUP? Trainer Rowan is bringing the horse back into what appears to be a higher class after showing a little early speed in a route only five days earlier. Horses returning to a sprint from a route are normally a bad bet. However, maybe this will be an exception to the rule.

SWIFT BUSTER? This was another horse that closed on Financial Coup in the slop on November 11th. It can't be ignored.

BEAU BUNCTIOUS? The big question remains: Is this horse ready? Probably not. But if so, he'll be there.

We now have FIVE horses that could be with War Ruckus at the wire -- not including the unknown entity, Game Of The Week.

When the *WATT* race file is entered into the *Graphics* module, the field in this race appears as indicated below. The Pole Speed and Last Quarter capabilities are each illustrated with color bars extending from left to right on the screen.

The *Graphics* module:

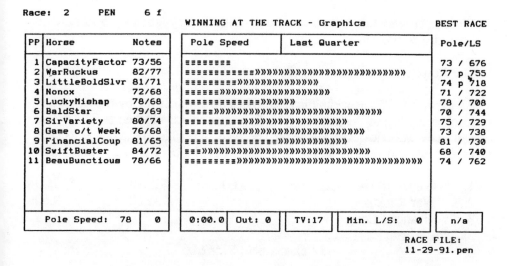

```
Race:   2      PEN      6 f
                            WINNING AT THE TRACK - Graphics              BEST RACE

PP│Horse          Notes      │Pole Speed    │Last Quarter   │     Pole/LS
 1│CapacityFactor 73/56      │                              │     73 / 676
 2│WarRuckus      82/77      │                              │     77 p 755
 3│LittleBoldSlvr 81/71      │                              │     74 p 718
 4│Nonox          72/68      │                              │     71 / 722
 5│LuckyMishap    78/68      │                              │     78 / 708
 6│BaldStar       79/69      │                              │     70 / 744
 7│SirVariety     80/74      │                              │     75 / 729
 8│Game o/t Week  76/68      │                              │     73 / 738
 9│FinancialCoup  81/65      │                              │     81 / 730
10│SwiftBuster    84/72      │                              │     68 / 740
11│BeauBunctious  78/66      │                              │     74 / 762

   Pole Speed:  78    0  │ 0:00.0│ Out: 0 │ TV:17 │ Min. L/S:  0 │  n/a
```

RACE FILE:
11-29-91.pen

If we enter our assumptions into the module, three horses appear on the screen. The assumptions were: An expected Pole Speed of 79 (a pace of 48 1/5 seconds) and a maximum of 6 Lengths Out at the half.

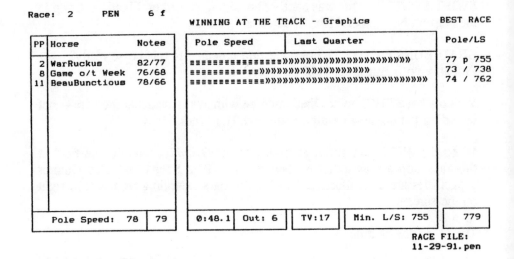

Race: 2   PEN   6 f

WINNING AT THE TRACK - Graphics

BEST RACE

PP	Horse	Notes
2	WarRuckus	82/77
8	Game o/t Week	76/68
11	BeauBunctious	78/66

Pole Speed	Last Quarter

Pole/LS
77 p 755
73 / 738
74 / 762

Pole Speed:	78	79

0:48.1	Out: 6	TV:17	Min. L/S: 755

779

RACE FILE:
11-29-91.pen

Would you play this race? If so, how? With the key horse at 35 to 1, it's a hard race to pass!

The Results:

As expected, War Ruckus disposed of Little Bold Silver by the time they reached the top of the stretch. The first quarter was clocked at 22 4/5; the half in 47 3/5. However, Game Of The Week was able to catch War Ruckus at the wire and won by a nose in a time of 1:14 1/5. Bald Star was fourth.

1.	Game Of The Week	$55.00	$22.80	$13.00
2.	War Ruckus		35.60	9.60
3.	Financial Coup			3.20

$2 exacta paid $1662.00

Game Of The Week had to run the best race of his life to win. Had it not been for remembering his daddy, I Am The Game, and seeing the *Graphics* printout, this horse could have gone completely unnoticed. It did not stand out as a major threat to War Ruckus.

Many seasoned handicappers will simply pass Maiden Special Weight and Maiden Claiming races knowing that a few of the contestants may have not yet demonstrated their talents. For those who are willing to assume risk in pursuit of a greater reward, here are four rules of advice for maiden races:

1.   Become familiar with the leading sires and broodmares of horses in or shipping into your local circuit(s).

2.   Learn which trainers are competent in races of this type.

3.   Avoid playing Maiden races in which there are more than TWO or THREE first-time starters.

4.   Consider passing a Maiden race when you do not have a solid key horse on which to wager.

There is another fact of life that racing fans must face when they use the computer for handicapping -- regardless of the type of race. If the horse is not ready to run today or if it encounters an especially bad trip, the machine cannot warn you against buying the tickets. After all, there is an element of chance to this sport.

We've found the computer to be the best way to separate the contenders in most races. It can accurately measure the capabilities of each horse and the expected pace of the race. It is, indeed, a remarkable handicapping tool, but it must be used intelligently. By applying the key horse patterns outlined later in this book to your list of contenders, you stand a good chance of being among the regulars who return to the cashier's window!

PART TWO

PART TWO

The Man Behind the Horse

"A trainer is a guy who'll work eighteen hours a day to avoid working eight for someone else." *Anonymous*

Whatever their motivation, trainers (men and women alike) really do devote long, tedious hours to their chosen calling. They work extremely long hours, stretching from crack-of-dawn workouts to late-night doctoring. And, there are seven of those days in every week. There are no weekends at the beach or Disney World with the family. Vacations, if any, are a catch-it-when--you-can affair. Question any trainer along the backside and you will be told: if you're not ready to spend the long hours and the endless weeks in the barns, you will never succeed in the profession.

Together with the gruelling hours comes a heavy burden of responsibility. It is always the trainer who is ultimately responsible for the well-being, the very life, of each horse in his charge. His stable of thoroughbreds may be worth many thousands of dollars -- or many millions of dollars.

While he may never bet a single dollar on the outcome of a race, and there are some who don't, the trainer is still a gambler every day of his working life.

He may be tricked into claiming a horse for a price above its true value. Or, he may lose a quality horse through that same claiming process. In the worst case scenario, his top runner, valued at a million dollars, breaks from the gate, runs a few furlongs, falls, breaks a leg, and is immediately destroyed. All in less than ten minutes. It does happen.

Much less spectacular, but also costly, is the horse which comes down with colic the night before a race it can win. Then, too, there is the race cancelled by the Racing Secretary after the trainer has his runner conditioned and ready to contend, right down to the wire.

Tracks are distributing millions of dollars in purse money to those trainers shrewd enough to enter their thoroughbreds in races in which they have a far-above-average chance of finishing first.

Every trainer knows -- or should know -- the schedule of upcoming races, including the dates, distances, allowances, claiming prices and much, much more. The successful trainers are those who will constantly condition and maneuver their horses into races where they will be strong contenders for top purse money. Much wealth is, indeed, available to the trainer capable of fully understanding and applying the fundamentals of his profession.

Unlike many professions of similar responsiblities and rewards, there is no formalized education, no college degree offered to the would-be trainer of race horses. Some schools are nibbling at the edges, offering courses in race track management. The University of Arizona is a pioneer in this field. Even so, these are all frontside programs. Little is available for the backside, where the trainer starts and, with much hard work and a generous dollop of luck, prospers.

The hard-knock education of the typical trainer is best summarized by an unknown philosopher: "Good judgment is acquired through experience. Experience is the result of bad judgment."

Numerous trainers come to the track by way of a farming or ranching background. A few are born into backside families. Many spent their childhood working with, riding, and caring for horses. Once in their teens, those choosing to leave the farm often gravitate to the circus, rodeo riding or the thoroughbred race track. Backstretch brats are already in their natural milieu.

Once into the backside of racing, the incipient jockey/trainer will work as a groom or exercise rider, or both. A trainer who probably followed the same path will often identify and assist a few above-average prospects. He may instruct and otherwise help an exercise rider obtain an apprentice jockey's license. A rider grown too heavy for competitive racing may be retained - formally or informally - as an assistant trainer, another form of apprenticeship. Those less-qualified will gradually drift away from the track. A few will continue walking, bathing, feeding, and otherwise caring for the stabled horses.

The neophyte trainer may start with a small stable of his own horses. Or he may start with a few animals owned by others willing to trust him with their stock. The majority start with a mixed stable of both horses owned and horses trained for other interests. All three modes of operation have their advocates and critics.

Most individuals make their training debut with horses in the cheapest claiming races. The more successful trainers work their way up the claiming ladder and on into allowance and stakes races. Following the course set by men like Lazaro Barrera, Woody Stephens and Charlie Whittingham, a few trainers progress all the way from cheap claimers to graded stakes racing, exclusively. The *creme de la creme* of the thoroughbred racing world.

Owner/trainer relationships play an extremely important role in the ultimate success of nearly every trainer. Successful doctors, lawyers or entertainers are often slow to recognize that the trainers of their horses know far more about conditioning and racing thoroughbreds than they ever will. As one popular, successful trainer explains:

"Quite often it's a matter of bringing the owner down to reality. Not every horse in his stable is a Triple Crown candidate. Very few horses are. I'll not run a horse beyond its ability, no matter the owner's opinion. I've seen too many good horses ruined by frequent overmatching. If they belong in cheap claimers, that's where I'll run them. Sure, I have a few claimed away from us, but I manage to claim a few good ones as replacements. I'm always upgrading the stable and, like every trainer on the grounds, I'm forever searching for that *bona fide* Triple Crown runner."

Even as he explains, the trainer is checking the feed tubs outside the stalls of his horses.

"I explain my philisophy to every owner, right up front. If they are unhappy, they are free to move their stock at any time. No hard feelings."

A review of this trainer's record explains the low turnover in his stable of thoroughbreds. He goes on to explain his reason for not owning any of the horses he handles.

"Every time you race one of your own horses against one you train for other owners, you're aggravating a sore spot. Conflict of interest. There's really no conflict, but I prefer to avoid the whole problem. I dropped my own horses many years ago."

A rival trainer takes an opposing view.

"Many of us condition our own stock along with that of our separate owners. I suppose we forever harbor a dream of actually owning that proverbial Triple Crown winner. No matter. The public is always protected. The horses are coupled as an entry whenever we run our own horses against those of our owners."

This rival trainer sports his own impressive record.

That long day mentioned earlier actually commences in the darkness before dawn. More than one trainer will be found rousting out his hired help.

First, there is a quick inspection along the rows of stalls. Each horse will have its bandages removed, its legs checked. The same for the mud packs previously applied to draw the heat from strained or tired legs.

Finely trained thoroughbreds are temperamental animals, not the docile pets that girl jockeys sing to in the films. One need only recall Crimson Satan, a stakes winner who frequently broke from the post parade to attack spectators along the rail. This bad actor was usually pushed backward into the starting gate -- from the front. Only half-jokingly the starting crew demanded combat pay.

The diet of these unpredictable animals must be checked daily. No overeating. No undereating. Any marked variation from the horse's norm is a cause for alarm, for further investigation.

The temperature of each horse must be recorded -- double checked if there is a hint of colic or a more serious virus along the backside. A hurried call for a veteranarian may be indicated.

Once the trainer is satisfied with his morning inspection, he will set the daily regimen for each horse. Those in recent races may be walked, bathed and rested. Others will be sent out for jogging or brief galloping, primarily a loosening exercise looking toward more vigorous workouts. Finally, there are the horses scheduled for the more serious, timed workouts, prepatory to upcoming races.

Exercise riders are combing through the barns, anxious to obtain mounts and riding fees. Several of the better jockeys are on hand to work the horses they will be riding in future races.

It may still be dark when the trainer leads his stock to the Gap. The Gap is the break in the backstretch rail where the horses enter for the morning workouts. Each horse is identified and passed through by the Gap Man, a track employee.

A few trainers of the cheaper claiming horses admit they prefer to reach the Gap in the dark.

"We're not trying to fool anyone, especially not the track officials or the public. We just don't want our rival trainers to know which of our runners are working good, which are having problems."

Our informant has a long record of success with a crowded stable of cheaper claimers. He asked that we not use his name.

"At our level, it's feint, punch and clinch. If we can sneak twelve-five quality into a race for sixty-two-fifties, we've outsnookered our rivals. If we can claim a twenty-five thousand dollar animal for fifteen, we might clear a few bucks. It's a two-way street, to be sure. We've claimed our own share of vet's list candidates for inflated prices."

Once the workouts are completed, the times recorded and reported by the track clockers, the trainer returns to his stables. He makes any necessary last-minute assignments and heads for the front office; the office of the Racing Secretary.

Here in the front office is the good news/bad news of the trainer's daily existence. There are always those races that do not fill. Others are ready and inserted as replacements. Bad news: The track has cancelled a race he was counting on; a race his entrant figured to win. Good news: An alternate allowance race at one mile has been scheduled and filled; ideal for the horse he is prepping for a sprint win. More good news: The maiden race for high-priced claimers has filled. His good allowance maiden will be a powerful contender.

As he continues to check through the condition book, the trainer is listening to the scuttlebutt whirling about him. Trainers, jockey's agents and track employees swap truths, half-truths and ripe rumors. Shrewdly, he separates the dross from the nuggets. The horse he feared most in Friday's third race is down with bucked shins; a doubtful starter. He will have the services of the perfect jockey for his front-runner on Saturday. His twenty thousand dollar claimer will definitely be outclassed in another race on Friday.

Returning to the backside, the trainer must now adjust his conditioning program for several horses in his stable. Some are still on the mainline for a potential win. Some are temporarily sidetracked and a few are completely derailed. The work and revised planning never end.

Every afternoon when he has horses racing, the trainer will spend much of his time in the saddling ring, the paddock. He may or may not lead his horses in from the receiving barn. He will definitely be in the paddock to check each horse's equipment, issue last minute instructions to each jockey and - when necessary - reassure a fretful owner.

The trainer will be especially careful to properly instruct a jockey riding one of his horses for the first time. Each animal has its own peculiarities which can affect the running of the race. Some horses run best when contending for the lead. Others stubbornly loaf down the backstretch, running only in the later stages of a race. Some horses sulk when whipped, others respond best to a hand ride. A close rapport between trainer and jockey will maximize the horse's efforts. Conversely, each is quick to blame a losing race on the shortcomings of the other.

Probably the greatest "condition freak" ever to frequent the winners circle is Bill Hartack. A top reinsman in every category, Hartack was involved in a love-hate relationship with half the trainers in America.

One of the many anecdotes told of Hartack has him warming up a horse for a major stakes race. As he nears the starting gate he jumps down from his mount and walks over to the track veterinarian who is watching the entrants from the back of his own horse.

Hartack squints up at the vet.

"Look, doc, I've ridden my share of the halt and the lame ..."

He points accusingly back toward his riderless animal.

"But, training wheels?"

The veterinarian gets the message and the horse is scratched from the race.

Once the last race is run, the crowd heads for home. Maybe an evening with the wife and kids in front of the TV. Perhaps a quiet dinner or a night of dancing. Not so with the successful trainer.

He may have a winner or one or two horses picked at random for the compulsory drug testing. If so, he may wait to lead his tested animals back to his barns. Possibly, he'll make one last check of the feed tubs, bandages, hot walkers and other matters he deems important. He will finally leave the stable for his personal quarters.

His evening may still be interrupted by an urgent call. A fractious filly has kicked at a groom, lost a shoe and injured her leg: a bleeder is having coughing fits. So, now it's midnight and the trainer is conferring with his veterinarian. The ailing horse has been examined, treatment prescribed and the adjusted regimen posted with the stable hands. At last, at the end of a long, long day he may enjoy a few hours sleep. All too soon, it's time to start the routine all over again. There surely must be times when the trainer covets that eight-hour job working for someone else.

Still, the monetary rewards available to the capable trainer are good. Aware
of his motivation and total involvement, we continue to watch the trainer --
not just his horse -- in the final stages of our handicapping.

Ready to Run?

The Hot Horse

When a horse is hot, it's hot! This tired, old cliche is just as true today as it was when first uttered by a Persian post rider some 3,000 years ago. That "hot" horse is still winning more races than any other animal competing on the modern track.

The hot (or sometimes called "live") horse is one adequately conditioned and ready to run a powerful race. The savvy trainer knows when his horse is ready. He also knows when and where to enter the animal for a potentially profitable run. Once we learn to recognize this trainer's tactics, we will cash a goodly number of winning tickets; many at very good prices.

As with human athletes preparing for the Olympic Games, or any other competition, the horse must be worked into condition for a winning performance. The javelin thrower must throw his javelins. The swimmer must swim, the diver dive, and the sprinter sprint. Most thoroughbreds, especially the claimers and cheaper allowance horses, must be raced into winning condition.

The trainer may enter his charge in several races; maybe only a few. He may race the horse several different distances over different surfaces with an assortment of jockeys. The speeds posted may vary from a track record to slow, very slow. These are all the trainer's legitimate concerns. Not ours. The trainer alone -- and possibly a few close backstretchers -- know when the animal is ready for that winning run.

The trainer will tell us, too, if we learn to read the trail he is leaving behind. If he isn't a mite too greedy or a tad too ambitious, we have an excellent chance for a win. To protect ourselves from the trainer's cupidity we have to insist upon the following criteria:

(1)   The horse must be racing within 9 days or less of its previous race. Ten days or more is a no-no. The date of each horse's last race is the all-important, controlling factor. Double check those dates.

(2)   The horse must be entered in the same -- or lower -- class as in its last race. A move up in class is a no-no.

Our criteria are readily explainable.

FIRST: We must be sure the trainer is going for the brass ring today, rather than waiting around for what might be a softer spot later. We could pick up a few more winners by extending our time limit to 10, 11, or 12 days. We would also be picking up too many losers by following the vacillating trainer.

SECOND: The horse must not be overmatched simply for the sake of higher odds, or to stroke the ego of the owner. Some trainers will deliberately overmatch a live horse, only to drop it back to its proper class for a winning race. Sometimes they get higher odds, sometimes not. Sometimes they win the race, sometimes not. This maneuver can be seen in examples elsewhere in this book. For now, we want the horse racing right back in its proper class. In essence, we want winners, not also-rans at higher prices. The following examples will illustrate the validity of our "hot horse" approach.

Finally, a word of caution here. This 9-day pattern is more valid at some tracks than others. Also, it works best when used in conjunction with other key horse patterns.

EXAMPLE: ONO GUMMO

This 9-year-old veteran has won 19 races and more than $340,000 campaigning on the Southern California circuit. Trainer Philip Hronec must fancy the tireless runner. He claimed the old-timer for a second time on December 15 -- out of our winning race.

Ono Gummo * B. h. 9, by Gummo—Dancing Alone, by Whodunit
PINCAY L JR $12,500 Br.—Thurman S M (Cal)
Own.—Carey & Ridgwd RcngStInc Tr.—Hronec Philip 115
Lifetime 81 19 15 19 $340,015 | 1991 3 0 1 1 $6,350 | 1990 18 4 6 1 $54,475 | Turf 6 0 0 3 $11,810

Feb91- 3SA	fst	6½f	:22	:45	1:162		Clm 16000	6	2	21	2hd	32	33	Desormeaux K J	LB	115	*1.90	85-20	McClymondsHgh114¾JkInLmLd1152½OnGmm115hd	Weakened	8
Jan91- 9SA	fst	1 1/16	:462	1:104	1:423		Clm 16000	12	6	45	45½	35½	45½	Pincay L Jr	LB	117	*2.90	85 13	GhttoBstr1152½PppyYokm1152¾Porchtto-Ar112hd	Wide early	12
Jan91- 1SA	fst	7f	:224	:452	1:232		Clm 12500	12	1	54¼	44	42	2hd	Garcia J A	LB	117	*2.70	86-14	NoStory115hdOnoGmm1172½DHPlymnmrtm115	4-wide stretch	12
Dec90- 1Hol	fst	1	:452	1:102	1:36	3↑	Clm c-12500	2	5	44½	32½	3nk	11½	Garcia J A	LB	115	4.30	84-11	OnoGummo1151½GryWritr114¾RoylCmronn113¾	Pinched start	8
Dec90- 5Hol	fst	1	:453	1:101	1:351	3↑	Clm 18000	8	3	32	42	63½	63½	Santos J A	LB	113	4.80	84-12	Histrion115nk Go Go Art1151 Charlatan1161	No excuse	11
Nov90- 5Hol	fst	7f	:214	:442	1:23	3↑	Clm 16000	9	6	85½	86¼	85¼	42	Santos J A	LB	117	6.30	88-09	Gö Dogs Go117¾ Moon Madness1171PapaStan112nk	Wide trip	11
Oct90- 9SA	fst	1 1/16	:461	1:104	1:432	3↑	Clm 16000	7	6	53½	52¼	52	21¾	Nakatani C S	LB	116	12.80	84-14	HonstJohn1161¾OnoGummo116noRoylCmronin1161¼	Good try	12
Oct90- 9SA	fst	1⅛	:461	1:102	1:483	3↑	Clm c-12500	4	3	2hd	2hd	42¼	710¼	Solis A	LB	116	5.50	83 07	DublinO'Bron1164½HonestJohn111¾TretToblyft1211¾	Stopped	12
Sep90- 5Dmr	fst	7f	:22	:442	1:221	3↑	Clm 25000	6	6	65	55½	89½	89¾	Solis A	LB	115	7.40	80-08	CsrEdurdo1152HghMs1152½HndsomKrt117hd	4-wide into lane	11
Aug90- 9Dmr	fst	1	:452	1:093	1:351	3↑	Clm 20000	5	3	34½	35½	35½	36	Solis A	LB	116	3.30	84-12	EsprtD'AmourII1092½MnfstDstny1203½OnoGmmo1162½	Evenly	10

Speed Index: Last Race: –2.0 3–Race Avg.: –3.6 6–Race Avg.: –4.5 Overall Avg.: –3.7
LATEST WORKOUTS Feb 16 SA 4f fst :504 H Jan 18 SA 4f fst :49 H Jan 11 SA 5f fst 1:042 H

31 Jan- Entered for $16,000 (a no-no) the horse ran back on 5 days rest and was beaten off by five lengths.

15 Dec- Running back on 7 days rest, the horse was dropped down in class ($18,000 to $12,500) and won, paying a nice $10.60.

20 Oct- Running back on 10 days rest (a no-no), Ono Gummo was entered for a higher claiming price (anotlicr no-no) and ran second.

While we did not know of it in advance, the claim by trainer Hronec confirmed our own faith in Ono Gummo. He then turned us off his newly re-claimed horse when he moved the animal up in class for its next race on January 31.

EXAMPLE: SYLVIA'S BABY

This 7-year-old gelding could be beginning in his "best-ever" year. His January win gets him off to a good start.

Sylvia's Baby * B. g. 7, by Smugglin George—Dominate Time, by Dominant Star
SANTOS J A $12,500 Br.—Boblitt Mr–Mrs D W (Wash)
Own.—Wachtel E Tr.—Stein Roger 115
Lifetime 59 8 12 9 $74,525 | 1991 3 1 0 0 $9,925 | 1990 11 1 0 1 $13,290 | Turf 2 0 0 0

20Feb91- 3SA	sly	1⅛	:473	1:121	1:503		Clm 16000	2	2	21	21	46	410½	Santos J A	LB	115	*1.40	65-20	Ri'sGrnBb115hdGibson'sChoic115¾ThrTimsOldr11510	Faltered	6
26Jan91- 9SA	fst	1⅛	:47	1:113	1:494		Clm 10000	9	3	21½	21	12	14	Santos J A	LB	115	4.70	81-13	Sylvi'sBby1154AbsolutRoux1144½Benidict'sPrintz115½	Driving	9
17Jan91- 1SA	fst	1 1/16	:464	1:111	1:442		Clm 10000	10	7	55	54½	54	44½	Santos J A	LB	115	4.50	76-18	Grey Writer117¾ Dyrai1142 Sammy's Birthday11513	Wide trip	11
23Dec90- 6BM	yl	1	①:483	1:141	1:403	3↑	Clm 22500	1	7	712	78	711	65½	Patterson A	LB	115	16.40	60-26	Haven Drive1171 Flint114nk Far Out Bet1174	Outrun	7
15Dec90- 2BM	gd	1	:454	1:101	1:363	3↑	Clm c-16000	1	5	59	511	512	58½	Mills J W	LB	110	2.90	79-12	StlshMjst117hdCncrdChr1172½MdnghtRckr1194	Showed little	6
30Nov90-10BM	fst	1	:461	1:101	1:343	3↑	Clm 20000	5	6	86½	75¼	55½	45	Mills J W	LB	117	7.30	93-12	SnstvProgrm1172GoStdyLd1192½MontnStrm112½	Evenly late	8
16Nov90- 7BM	fst	1	:464	1:103	1:353	3↑	Alw 19000	7	7	76	76½	44	43½	Mills J W	LB	117	15.80	89-13	Basingstoke117hd Soltau1103 Harry V.117½	Wide trip	8
3Nov90- 1BM	fst	1	:463	1:103	1:351	3↑	Clm 20000	7	5	65½	42	31	31¾	Belvoir V T5	LB	112	11.60	93-09	LDuckSlwp119nkWyykinRx1171½Sylvi'sBby112hd	Bumped late	7
13Oct90-10BM	fm	*1⅛	①:491	1:133	1:502	3↑	Clm 25000	3	7	75¾	74½	58½	64	Belvoir V T5	LB	112	19.30	74-23	Mr. Inovator1171 SirWilloughby1172Caballo-En117hd	No rally	10
5Oct90- 8BM	fst	6f	:222	:451	1:093	3↑	Alw 19000	6	9	99½	68½	55½	45¼	Warren R J Jr	LB	117	16.60	87-15	IccpdOnIc1172StormyRyStompr1122½BobbRobb117¾	No rally	9

Speed Index: Last Race: –14.0 3–Race Avg.: –8.6 7–Race Avg.: –3.7 Overall Avg.: –3.3
LATEST WORKOUTS Feb 22 SA 5f fst 1:03 H Feb 16 SA 5f fst 1:011 H Feb 10 SA 5f fst 1:033 H Jan 13 SA 4f fst :48 H

26 Jan-   With 9 days rest, Sylvia's Baby ran in the same $10,000 class
           and won, paying $11.40.

23 Dec-   Following his claim on 15 Dec, the new trainer, Roger Stein,
           entered his animal for $22,500 (a no-no) and watched it run
           sixth.

13 Oct-   Rested for 8 days, the horse was entered for $25,000 (a no-no)
           and ran out of the money.

Horses entered for a higher claiming price soon after being claimed are to
be avoided in most instances. For thirty days after a claim, the trainer
making the claim is required to run his newly-acquired animal for a price
above that of the claiming price. In the majority of these races, the new
trainer is simply ridding the horse of the temporary restriction on its claiming
price. The rule is a sound one, designed to prevent trainers from constantly
claiming horses and then immediately dropping them in class just to win a
quick purse.

EXAMPLE: JANITOR-Br

This 7-year-old gelding is a regular campaigner on the Santa Anita/Holly-
wood Park Axis. When he was shipped North to "steal" a purse at Golden
Gate Fields, he was overmatched and defeated. This situation will be
discussed in greater detail later.

22 Feb-   Running back in the same class after 8 days rest, Janitor was a
           winner. As a mild favorite, the horse paid $7.40.

14 Apr-   Janitor ran with 8 days rest for a $16,000 claiming price. As
expected, the jump in claiming price resulted in a six-length
defeat.

EXAMPLE: FIRST CLAUDIA-MX

With no success at Hollywood Park, this 4-year-old filly was sent barnstorm-
ing on the Northern California County Fair Circuit. At summer's end,
trainer Jim Argante settled his charge in for the autumn meet at Bay
Meadows.

12 Oct-   Running in her regular Md12500 class, First Claudia won,
paying a generous $19.80. The winner was running back on 8
days rest.

To further insure his victory, trainer Argante turned his filly over to Vern
Belvoir, a hot apprentice jockey riding on the Norcal circuit. When they
have a live horse ready to run, many trainers will turn to a hot apprentice.
Whether it's for the five pound weight allowance or a more aggresive ride,
it's immaterial. The trainer has tipped his hand just a wee bit more. We're
always grateful for the added confirmation.

Weight is an extremely important factor to a whole clutch of handicappers.
These weightniks carefully check and double check each jockey's daily
weight and his mount's overweights. They debate the merits of "live"
weight and "dead" weight. They argue the slowing effect of a few extra
pounds in the horse's saddlebags. Many of us wonder just what effect three
or four extra pounds can have on the back of a galloping half-ton thoroughbred. No matter. Many trainers will opt for the weight allowance
when they are sending a live horse to the post.

Mention weight to a racegoer and you are almost sure to hear the apocryphal story which probably originated in the stables of that Persian post rider. The current version being bruited about Golden Gate Fields features Jerry Hollendorfer, a leading trainer and his favorite rider, Ron Hansen.

Just back from a vacation, Ron runs into the trainer in the barn area. Hollendorfer greets the newly-returned jockey.

"Hey, Ron, how was the vacation?"

"Not so good. I fell in the bathtub and broke my collar bone."

"Tough."

"The Internal Revenue Service attached all my property."

"Pity."

"Then, last week, I buried my mother."

"Sorry."

The trainer finally gives Hansen a searching look.

"What do you weigh, now, Ron?"

"One hundred and seventeen pounds. Why?"

"My God, boy! You're two pounds over!"

EXAMPLE: MONSIER FRIJOLES

Trainer Howard Brewen keeps his steady 3-year-old racing in Northern California, including the County Fair circuit.

```
Monsier Frijoles                    B. g 3(Apr), by Bolger—Termon, by Beau Buck (Fra)
                                    Br.—Murphy Mrs W J (Cal)              1990  12  2  2  3      $18,900
  FRAZIER R L               117     Tr.—Brewen Howard        $10,000      1989   4  M  2  0       $4,400
  Own.— Murphy Mrs W J              Lifetime  16  2  4  3    $23,300
25Oct90-7BM   6f :222 :45 1:101ft  23 LB119  751 761 971 881  Frazier R L 2  12500 80-13 We'reJustBluff,NoDndy,B.J'sLw 12
 6Oct90-7BM   6f :222 :454 1:122ft   8 LB122  451 431 411 1hd Frazier R L 6  12500 78-19 MonsrFrjols,WhskyNt,WldLookot 9
 6Oct90- Finished wide
27Sep90-7BM   6f :222 :45 1:11 ft   61 LB120  53 321 32 411   MrtnzOA,Jr 9 [5] 10500 83-16 IrishBulldog,WillDuplict,Sliproo 11
25Aug90-9BM   6f :222 :451 1:104ft 9-5 LB117  331 32 32 21    Frazier R L 2   8000 85-15 NturBoy,MonsrFrjols,AskMToWn 8
 9Aug90-10Bmf 6f :222 :451 1:111ft  41 LB117  631 411 421 33  Hubbard N J 7   8000 81-16 GodTBKng,KnschPlsr,MnsrFrjls 10
27Jly90-10SR  6f :222 :443 1:111ft  16 L 116   651 571 44 21  Hubbard N J 4   8000 83-18 TimbrPoint,MonsrFrjols,NturBoy 8
10Jly90-9Sol  6f :22  :444 1:103ft  17 L 115   421 541 681 7121 Frazier R L 2 12500 75-14 Kyl'sEndvor,ClnlRmb,ScrpTwnty 9
22Jun90-11Stk 5f :214 :443 :563ft    4   120   311 3nk 221 381 Boag D R 6    16000 91-03 MolBrry,CoolAndSdt,MonsrFrjols 7
22Jun90- Wide
 9Jun90-7GG   6f :214 :442 1:10 ft  10   117   1hd 1hd 21 33  Frazier R L 2  12500 85-11 KlondikCl,AllRsons,MonsirFrijols 9
 9Jun90- Bumped at 1/8
28May90-7GG   6f :214 :451 1:112gd  21   117   2hd 2hd 31 441 Frazier R L 1  16000 77-15 DncngCrozr,GlxyGlory,StrttnJvP 9
  Speed Index: Last Race: -7.0      3-Race Avg.: -3.6    10-Race Avg.: -4.2    Overall Avg.: -4.2
  Oct 19 BM 4f ft :481 H        Sep 22 BM 4f ft :492 H    Sep 15 BM 5f ft :591 H    Sep 8 BM 4f ft :49 H
```

The gelding was trying with 11 days rest (9 Jun) and again (9 Aug) with 12 days rest. The horse ran third in both races. Finally, with 9 days rest, the animal finished in front on 6 Oct. A winning ticket paid $18.00.

Monsier Frijoles' past performances sharply underscore our insistence upon a return within *9 days or less*.

The horse's running lines also illustrate a "class trap" which sometimes misleads the uninitiated.

The animal appears to have risen in class for its winning race on 6 Oct. Not so. Entered in a race for $12,500 claimers on 27 Sept, Monsier Frijoles' trainer dropped his claiming price to $10,500 to receive a two pound weight allowance. Actually, the horse was running against the same class of stock in both races.

We have already discussed the importance some trainers attach to an increase or decrease in the mandatory weight carried by their charges. Recognizing this penchant, most tracks card numerous claiming races wherein the trainer may reduce the weight assigned the entry by reducing the claiming price. A line in the race conditions will read as follows:

> Claiming price $12,000; if for $10,500 allowed 2 lbs.
> Claiming price $25,000; if for $22,500 allowed 2 lbs.
> Claiming price $32,000; if for $30,000 allowed 2 lbs.

Frequently, what appears to be a slight jump in claiming price is, in reality, a reflection of the trainer's decision to waive the weight allowance.

EXAMPLE: CARI ON KATIE

Trainer John Stoker started his two-year-old at the Solano County Fair in Northern California. Following two races at Boise, he settled his horse in for a Fall campaign at Bay Meadows.

```
Cari On Katie                           Ch. f. 2(Apr), by Cari County—Katherine Swynford, by Night Invader
 CASTANON A L                           Br.—Gilliam-Fontaine-Bacus (Idaho)         1990  7  1  1  1          $6,903
                                116     Tr.—Stoker John                  $12,500
Own.—NewHorizonsPrtnrship&Bcus          Lifetime    7  1  1  1   $6,903
26Oct90-1BM   1  :463 1:123 1:403ft  21 LB114   43½ 32½ 32  33      Condie N R3 Ⓕ 10500 65-22 Nn'sProgrm,QueenSwep,CriOnKti8
  26Oct90—Wide trip
11Oct91-2BM   6f :224  :464 1:131ft  12 LB117   6½ 1hd 13  12½     CstnnAL12 ⒻM12500 74-17 CriOnKt,CntrOfGrvty,BrttnyFrst 12
30Oct90-2BM   6f :23   :47 1:132ft   25 B 117   9½ 63½ 55  47      CstnonAL1 ⒻM12500 66-20 Missy'sWish,PreferWin,Loxlyl c  10
30Aug90-3BM   6f :221  :471 1:131ft  31 B 117   7¾ 73  65½ 65½     GuerrroA5 ⒻM12500 68-19 StarClss,Unconventionl,Activity 12
  30Aug90—Steadied start
12Aug90-10Boi 7f :222  :454 1:262ft  25 B 117   811 87½102010 17½  OcaA7⑤Idaho Cnt Ft 67-12 ShdyDl,InfntryScrmblr,QutBlurr 10
1Aug90-3Boi   7f :232  :481 1:292ft  3½ B 122   75  42  36  25     Hoak J W6 ⑤Fut Trl 65-23 DoinNinety,CriOnKtie,MeritCrft  10
12Jly90-3Sol  5½f :222 :452 1:06½ft  20   117   75½ 68½ 410 58½    CortezAC1 ⒻM16000 73-10 IlliniSquw,PreferWine,LepyrRun 10
  12Jly90—Lugged out
 Speed Index: Last Race: -9.0    3-Race Avg.: -12.0   6-Race Avg.: -13.0      Overall Avg.: -13.0
Nov 6 BM 4fft :493 H      Oct 25 BM 3f ft :361 H     Oct 20 BM 4f ft :50 H      Oct 2 BM 3f ft :38 H
```

Stoker knew he had a potential winner when he entered his filly in a maiden race for $12,500 on 11 Oct. Coming off 8 days rest, Cari on Katie romped in, paying $26.00.

EXAMPLE: RACY GRACY

This oft-claimed filly is a regular contender in the cheaper claiming races at Hollywood Park and Santa Anita.

```
Racy Gracy                              Dk. b. or br. f. 4, by J Burns—Star Darling, by Diplomatic
 BERRIO O A                             Br.—Cree A E (Cal)                   1990 13 3  0  6          $32,775
                                1135    Tr.—Magana Pepe          $10,000     1989  7  1  2  0          $8,640
Own.—Ellis Susan                        Lifetime   20  4  2  6   $41,415
25Oct90-9SA   1  :47 1:113 1:37 ft   6 LB116   107½ 96  54½ 49     Meza R Q4 Ⓕ 12500 74-16 Frnchised,Linguistic,l,FrenchSuc 10
  25Oct90—Broke slowly
4Oct90-1SA    6f :213  :444 1:102ft  4½ LB118   3½ 31  21½ 1nk     FlorsDR9 Ⓕ⑤c10000 84-11 RcyGrcy,NturlRd,It'sAnothrTurn 12
24Aug90-1Dmr  7f :221  :45 1:233ft  *8-5 LR115  74½ 43½ 1½  12     Flores D R1 Ⓕ 10000 83-15 Racy Gracy, Best NewsYet,Akalli 9
16Aug90-1Dmr  6½f :22  :451 1:17 ft  40 LB115   72½ 32  32½ 31     Flores D R6 Ⓕ 10000 82-10 SuForLibl,Wink'sWitch,RcyGrcy 10
5Jly90-1Hol   6f :214  :453 1:12 ft  6 L 116    55  54½ 33  33      PdrozMA3 Ⓕc10000 77-16 BestNewsYel,ChrmStp,RcyGrcy 12
14Jun90-3Hol  7f :213  :441 1:23½ft  5½  116    63½ 32  31  32½    PdrozMA4 Ⓕ⑤ 12500 87-07 J.D.'sLove,ToBeImprssiv,RcyGrcy 8
19May90-1Hol  7f :221  :451 1:23 ft  4½  116    41½ 1hd 12½ 11½    Lopez A D10 Ⓕ 10000 90-10 RacyGracy,LiftTicket,Helg'sDoll 10
  19May90—Wide backstretch
27Apr90-1Hol  6f :221  :452 1:11½ft  12  116    62½ 41½ 42½ 3½     MezaRQ10 Ⓕ⑤ 10000 83-11 Natural Red, Valhalla,RacyGracy 12
  27Apr90—Wide throughout
23Mar90-1SA   6f :221  :46 1:122ft  11  116    1½ 2hd 32  75½      PedrozMA2 Ⓕ 10000 69-20 SidewlkMeting,MyFirst,ElgntPrl 12
8Mar90-1SA    6f :221  :452 1:11½ft  9½  1115   41½ 52½ 54½ 710½   MorlsCE J Ⓕ⑤ 10000 69-16 SueForLibel,OkPortl,Tsh'sStorm 12
 Speed Index: Last Race: -5.0    3-Race Avg.: -5.0   9-Race Avg.: -6.6      Overall Avg.: -7.0
Oct 15 Hol 4f ft :50 H      Sep 26 SA 5f ft :591 H     Sep 18 SA 4f ft :491 H
```

This 4-year-old was made the 8 to 5 favorite on 24 Aug at Del Mar. Racy Gracy had been rested for 8 days and then won by two lengths.

The betting public is quick to spot many of the more obvious horses meeting our requirements. We occasionally find ourselves betting on the favorite.

Fine. Other bettors have joined us in identifying the winner. In the Racy Gracy race, the claim entered by trainer Pepe Magana serves to emphasize the reliability of our pattern.

Del Mar, like Saratoga in the East, is a short-run, vacation track. Both tracks offer purses competitive with those of neighboring major tracks. See our reference to "Allowance Purse Index" in a later section.

This combination of a short season and rich purses prompts a coterie of trainers to deliberately prepare a select few of their horses for racing at these relatively rich "resort" tracks each year. Many of these runners will appear two or more times. Past performance dates are doubly crucial at Del Mar and Saratoga.

EXAMPLE: SERGEANT JAY TEE

Within little more than ninety days this young gelding has run the gamut of California racing. In July and August, the horse was running in County Fair meets in Northern California. In late October, Sergeant Jay Tee was already a serious contender in claiming races at Santa Anita - the State's richest, most prestigious track. In the months ahead, the horse may climb still further up the class ladder.

13 Sep-   With only 7 days rest, Sergeant Jay Tee romped in easily at Fairplex, paying a nice $11.00. Hallelujah? No. No bet for two reasons:

(1) The horse was switching from a track in Northern California to a track in Southern California. We will sometimes bet on

a horse switching between neighboring tracks of equal class - Bay Meadows/Golden Gate Fields, or Santa Anita/ Hollywood Park - but these tracks are too far apart. Too far apart in both geography and class.

(2) The horse was racing for the first time after winning its maiden race. We never bet on a horse in this situation. We wait for the trainer to establish the proper claiming price for his maiden winner.

20 Sep-   After another 7 days rest, trainer Ted West ran his horse way over its head for a claiming price of $22,500. The outclassed animal was badly beaten by nearly 20 lengths.

27 Sep-   Finally, the trainer is ready. So is his horse. Rested still another 7 days, Sergeant Jay Tee was dropped into a $10,000 claimer where he won, paying $12.00.

The limited number of racing days at Fairplex, the former Los Angeles County Fair track in Pomona, leads to a rich mix of "right back" horses. Good pickings for the local players. The same can be said for the summer races on the Northern California County Fair circuit. Racing at most of these tracks is limited to no more than 14 days; sometimes less.

Trainers will be trainers from coast to coast and at all points between. They rely on the same ploys, regardless of the track. The criteria established in this section apply equally well at any track across the country.

Those who live in Northern California are in a position to make occasional visits to the legal race books of Lake Tahoe and Reno. Here, live horses running at tracks from New York to California can be found. The bettor's day can be a long one, with the first races starting shortly after 9 A.M. and concluding sometime after 6:30 P.M. The recent addition of night racing can stretch the racing day to more than twelve hours. However, as much as we love the sport, this is not a life for most of us! The true "professional" handicappers will privately admit that three or four playable races a day is all that's needed to make a nice living.

EXAMPLE: KINKLETS

This New Yorker actually ran second four times before winning her maiden race.

Kinklets Gr. f. 3(Apr), by Drone—Julia Jane, by Mr Prospector
Br.—Shehan William R (NJ) 1990 12 1 5 0 $29,380
Own.—Schoninger B 1097 Tr.—Hertler John O $35,000 1989 2 M 0 0 $900
Lifetime 14 1 5 0 $30,280 Turf 1 0 0 0
29Aug90-4Bel 6½f :23 :464 1:181gd 4½ 1097 75 64½ 59 58¾ Carbajal L 6 Ⓕ 50000 78-14 GntlCurvs,MonMssmo,TrzvntTrsr 8
8Aug90 6Sar 6f :214 :45 1:103gd 36 1097 78 75½ 53 2¾ Carbajal L 10 Ⓕ 47500 90-07 Shenndoh,Kinklets,WinningStyl 10
21Jly90-3Bel 7f :231 :47 1:253ft 17 1077 63½ 53½ 31 33¾ Carbajal L 3 Ⓕ 45000 72-15 OrientlFith,‡ATimeThtWs,Kinklts 6
21Jly90—Placed second through disqualification
1Jly90-2Bel 1 1/16 :471 1:121 1:451m 24 116 53¾ 31 31½ 43¾ Rojas R I 4 Ⓕ 25000 72-18 TopTomto,ThnkDoubl,MyBlSttz 11
14Jun90-9Bel 1 1/16 Ⓣ:46 1:10 1:413fm 57 109 84½ 913 1125 1134½ RojasRI 12 ⒻAw29000 58-09 Chandelier,MissOtis,DancinBaba 12
22Apr90-2Aqu 6f :23 :473 1:132ft 2¾ 115 1½ 1hd 1½ 1nk Smith ME 1 ⒻM35000 73-19 Kinklets, Mineral Bath, Miss Otis 9
17Apr90-5Aqu 6f :222 :462 1:12 ft 3½ 115 1hd 32 31 22¾ VelsquezJ 1 ⒻM35000 77-17 SaratogStyle,Kinklets,MinerlBth 12
16Mar90-2Aqu 7f :23 :463 1:261ft 4 121 1hd 2½ 31½ 22½ VelsquezJ 1 ⒻM35000 68-20 JazzBallet,Kinklets,Certification 14
Speed Index: Last Race: -10.0 1-Race Avg.: -10.0 1-Race Avg.: -10.0 Overall Avg.: -11.6
Aug 19 Sar tr.t 4f ft :54 B Aug 3 Sar tr.t 4f ft :523 B Jly 18 Bel 4f ft :472 H

Trainer John Hertier really telegraphed his punch when he raced Kinklets in her regular M35000 class on only 5 days rest. Even with heavy public backing the filly managed a winning run worth $7.50.

EXAMPLE: DAUGHTER OF WOLF

The scene shifts to the Middle West. Arlington Park. Cesare's fleet Chicago runner wins her share of allowance races.

Daughter Of Wolf B. f. 3(Feb), by Wolf Power—Leade Me Holme, by Noholme II
SANTOS J A Br.—Baskin, Small, Port &Poncher (Ky) 1990 13 3 1 2 $43,785
112 Tr.—Cesare William Turf 4 1 0 1 $13,865
Own.—Baskin & Port Trust Lifetime 13 3 1 2 $43,785
1Oct90-7AP 1 :451 1:104 1:38 ft 11 L 115 65½ 69½ 619 620 RmosWS2 ⒻAw19000 61-28 Nurse Dopey, Jewel Ball,SunLuck 7
16Sep90-8AP 1⅛ :462 1:111 1:502ft 41 L 113 1012 1018 1124 1127¾ RazoEJr4 ⒻArl Oaks 63-17 Ovrturnd,TrinRobbry,MrcdsMiss 12
3Sep90-9AP 1 1/16 Ⓣ:483 1:124 1:431fm 5½ L 116 45½ 45½ 46½ 54¾ Ramos W S7 ⒻHcp0 86-83 SecretAdvice,Elegnce,ButifullyBr 8
3Sep90—Wide turn
12Aug90-9AP 1 :464 1:132 1:402sy 2 L 112 21½ 2hd 13 14½ Day P3 ⒻAw24225 69-31 DghtrofWolf,BrbryCrse,IglNymph 3
1Aug90-9AP a1 1/16 Ⓣ:484 1:142 1:462fm 4½ L 115 105¾ 83½ 31½ 11½ RmosWS1 ⒻAw17500 – – DughtrofWolf,Splic,IndinFshion 11
23Jly90-7AP a1 1/16 Ⓣ:482 1:133 1:463gd 6 L 108 1hd 2hd 3nk 55¾ Day P1 ⒻAw17500 – – SecretiveLdy,BlletTroupe,Leering 7
23Jly90—Steadied str
7Jly90-10AP 1 Ⓣ:472 1:13 1:372fm 7¾ L 115 53 63¾ 36 37½ RmosWS5 ⒻAw19000 82-11 Elgnc,CocktlsnSpn,DghtrofWolf 12
22Jun90-8AP 7f :22 :443 1:243sy *6-5 115 47 411 411 310 Day P4 ⒻAw18000 77-15 Pongee,ForevrFun,DughtrofWolf 8
4Jun90-3AP 6f :221 :462 1:104ft 2¾ 108 32½ 32½ 47½ 49 Day P6 ⒻAw18000 86-11 Lit'l Rose, Liquid Fill, I LikeThat 8
4Jun90—Wide early
26May90-7AP 7f :231 :47 1:26 sy 2¾ 115 3½ 21½ 21 2¾ RomrRP5 ⒻAw18000 79-15 LdySrtog,DughterofWolf,Elegnce 5
26May90—Wide turn
Speed Index: Last Race: -11.0 2-Race Avg.: -9.0 2-Race Avg.: -9.0 Overall Avg.: -9.2
●Oct 25 Hol 5f ft :593 H Oct 15 Hol 5f ft 1:003 H Sep 26 AP Ⓣ 5f fm 1:024 H (d)

1 Aug- After running fifth on 23 Jul, Daughter of Wolf comes back to win and pay $11.50.

EXAMPLE: SILK SKIRTS

For most racing fans, Canterbury Downs is nothing more than a symbol - Cby - in *The Daily Racing Form's* list of Thoroughbred Race Tracks in North America. Actually, it's a quality operation in a location far from the mainstream of U.S. racing. But we've also seen convincing evidence of the profitability of our treatment of live horses there. Silk Skirts' past performance lines offer an outstanding object lesson in the application of our restrictions.

13 Jun-	Coming back in 12 days, Anderson dropped his mare in class. The horse won, paying $15.00. However, we would have never considered her had we insisted on our "9-day rule." Read on.
24 Jun-	Eleven days later the horse is raced in a higher class and finishes eighth in a field of twelve.
13 Jul-	Silk Skirts ran back in the same class after 20 days rest. She continued to finish out of the money.
25 Jul-	Rested for 12 days, the mare was dropped back in class but could manage only a fourth place finish.
4 Aug-	Ten days later the trainer entered Silk Skirts in the same class and saw her beaten by 12 lengths.
16 Aug-	Rested for 12 days, the horse is dropped back in class and manages a second place finish.

30 Aug-   Two weeks later we find the mare raised in claiming price from
           $12,500 to $18,000. As expected, the runner finishes a beaten
           fourth.

7 Sep-   Finally. *Der Tag*. The day. Silk Skirts is running back in *8
           days* and is entered for her proper claiming price. The 5-year-
           old finishes first and pays $6.50.

As it was pointed out earlier, trainers across the map are following the same
patterns as they prepare each horse for its winning race. Whenever you can
visit a racebook with nationwide service, you can multiply your opportunities
to ferret out winning runners. They are entered every day at every track.

People returning from our gambling Meccas - Las Vegas, Atlantic City,
Nassau, Reno - like to boast of their winnings. Whether it's slot machines,
blackjack or craps, they have glowing tales to tell of their prowess at the
tables or machines. Never a word do we hear about any losses incurred in
intervening visits. Do we really believe they never lose? Of course not. We
all suffer losses along with our winnings. Sometimes when least expected.

EXAMPLE: SAUCY SAM

The sudden switch to a top jockey - Chris McCarron - is another key horse
pattern that is discussed in detail later.

30 Jun-   With 8 days rest the 5-year-old gelding dropped in class and
           won a hefty $29.80 mutuel.

4 Aug- Again dropping in class, Saucy Sam came back in 7 days and missed a $21.00 payoff by a neck. A fifty–fifty split will never hurt the pocketbook.

EXAMPLE: SHADY LACE

Trainer Cametta's five-year-old mare is a regular runner in cheap claiming races at Bay Meadows and Golden Gate Fields.

Shady Lace Dk. b. or br. m. 5, by Maheras—Pappa's Image, by Silent Pappa
CASTANON A L $8,000 Br.—Shady Valley Ranch (Wash) **116**
Own.—Camotta O R Tr.—Camotta Otis R
Lifetime 34 3 9 4 $29,980 — 1991 3 0 2 0 $3,400 — 1990 27 2 7 4 $24,215

9Feb91- 1GG	fst	6f	:222	:454	1:103	ⒻClm 10000	7	2	31	63½	79	77½	Castanon A L	LBb	116	7.70	77-10	DstnyUnknown118hdSombdySd118¾MgcDy1161½	Steadied 1/4	7
18Jan91- 7BM	fst	6f	:222	:454	1:111	ⒻClm 8000	5	2	2½	1hd	11	22	Gonzalez R M	LBb	118	3.30	70-20	MagicDay1162ShadyLace118hdPrevilingWinds116nk	Game 2nd	10
4Jan91- 6BM	fst	6f	:221	:45	1:102	ⒻClm 8000	7	3	34	33	31	21	Castanon A L	LBb	118	2.60	83-17	MaybeMaybenot1161ShadyLace1182PlceSet1171	Game finish	8
28Dec90- 6BM	fst	6f	:223	:453	1:102	3↑ⒻClm 8000	1	1	3nk	32	34	34	Castanon A L	LBb	118	3.80	84-17	SomebodySid1153½HerComsShdy116½ShdyLc1181	Evenly late	7
14Dec90- 1BM	fst	6f	:223	:454	1:101	3↑ⒻClm 7000	8	1	2hd	1hd	1hd	11	Castanon A L	LBb	116	9.80	89-08	Shady Lace1161MissBereta116hdKnoluLittle1111	Held gamely	9
7Dec90- 7BM	fst	6f	:221	:444	1:101	3↑ⒻClm 9000	8	2	3nk	31½	76	63½	Ochoa A	Lb	115	44.60	85-10	Off ShoreFlo116hdHowie'sChoice111nkScare116nk	Wide, tired	10
18Nov90- 2BM	fst	6f	:223	:45	1:10	3↑ⒻClm 6250	5	9	96½	98	65½	53½	Kaenel J L	LB	117	15.40	86-07	ConvivialMiss111½LdyChrmin116nkMgicDy1162½	Wide stretch	11
7Nov90- 4BM	fst	6f	:221	:45	1:103	3↑ⒻClm 8000	10	4	46½	56½	54½	52¾	Kaenel J L	LB	117	25.00	84-12	Kryn'sLuck116½FrenchHmmer116nkDine'sTempo1161	No rally	12
20Oct90- 5BM	fst	6f	:221	:451	1:101	3↑ⒻClm 6250	2	6	57	45½	52½	33	Kaenel J L	LB	117	25.10	86-09	HereComesShady1162ConvivilMiss1111ShdyLce1173	Late bid	11
5Oct90- 9Fno	fst	6f	:213	:451	1:102	3↑ⒻClm 6250	8	2	3nk	31½	21½	32	Garcia E V5	LBb	111	3.30	87-09	Quickie Toes116½ Sucha Gal1161½ Shady Lace111½	Hung late	10

Speed Index: Last Race: (—) 3–Race Avg.: (—) 12–Race Avg.: (—) Overall Avg.: -4.2
LATEST WORKOUTS Jan 16 GG 3f fst :361 H

14 Dec- Running on 7 days rest, Shady Lace captures a whopping $21.60 payoff.

4 Jan- Attempting to duplicate the previous win, trainer Cametta again runs his horse on 7 days rest. The mare is beaten one length in a driving finish.

We're addicted to $20+ payoffs and will continue to watch for Otis Cameta's entries.

Nobody wins 'em all. But in your search for the key horse, your chances of finding one at a good price will be improved considerably with our hot horse criteria:

(1) The horse must be racing within 9 days, or less, of its previous race. Ten days or more is too long a wait.

(2) The horse must be racing in the same -- or lower -- class as in its last race. The horse cannot be moving up in class.

The Rested Horse

All human athletes must be rested from time to time. To maintain their competitive edge they must be given time away from their chosen profession. Staleness leading to poor performance is the result of overwork.

Except for winter ball in Latin venues south of our border, baseball players are given a winter respite. Both professional and collegiate football players enjoy a vacation period in late winter and early spring. And Joe Louis' "Bum of the Month" campaign aside, very few top-rank boxers fight more than two or three times per year.

The racing thoroughbred is much like his human counterpart. Eventually he must be rested or suffer the consequences. His performance, too, will tail off as the number of his starts begins to pile up. He is really not running slower, he's just growing stale from overwork.

With year-around racing now a *fait accompli*, the pressure is now on the owners and trainers for more races from each horse. The constant jump in the size of the purses is an added spur. More and more animals are being overworked, run into lethargy, raced out of condition.

So, what's a horseman to do?

Only the wealthiest of owners can afford a farm where their runners can be rested and revitalized. Only those same wealthy owners can afford to keep their stock idle for extended periods of time; periods when they might otherwise be earning substantial purses.

A compromise is usually worked out by owners and trainers falling outside the wealthy category. For most, the economics of the racing business today pushes them to maximize a horse's contribution to the overhead. Depending upon many factors, including facilities, location, and so on, it can cost $10,000 - $20,000 annually to care for and train a horse to compete for a share of whatever racing purses might be available. A race horse is expected to pay for its board, vet bills, and upkeep, and to justify it's owner's investment by racing.

With these everyday pressures to pay bills, it is not unusual to race a horse regularly, but with a lighter schedule from time to time, instead of forcing a layoff. Thus, a layoff is more likely to be required to heal an injury, or to avoid a potential injury, rather than to just provide a rest.

When the competent trainer suspects a horse is slipping, showing signs of fatigue, it is usually rested right in the barns at a local track. The horse will do a bit of jogging, maybe a gallop now and then. Primarily, it's a period of pampered rest and a break in the constant tension of competitive racing.

If the horse is injured, the most common problems are:

1). *BUCKED SHINS* (inflammation of the membrane around the cannon bone, located just above the horse's ankle). This injury takes about 4 1/2 months of recovery, including 90 days of rest, plus 30-45 days of workouts.

   Horses often run competitively after an injury of this type.

2). *CHIPS IN THE KNEE* usually involves about six months of recovery since anthroscopic surgery is normally required.

   Horses recovering from this injury are a *bad* bet in the first one or two races back.

3). *FRACTURES* are serious injuries but they can heal rapidly. A six-month layoff is normal.

   Horses with bone screws have been known to win races, but betting its first race back is risky.

4). *VIRAL INFECTIONS* are not uncommon when horses are exposed to "shippers," as in, for example, Florida.

   The seriousness and betting risks vary.

The average racing fan will rarely know the details about an injury, let alone be able to judge a horse's chances when it returns. However, as a general rule, bettors should be more wary of layoffs of six months, or more, than of layoffs involving 2-4 months.

Once the horse is rested and renewed to the trainer's satisfaction, the horse will commence a serious program of workouts leading toward a return to the racing ranks. Some trainers can bring a horse back to the track in A-1 condition for a strong run. Placed in the right spot, the horse will win at its very first call. Many trainers don't quite make it. They do, however, leave a trail behind.

While it is impossible in most cases to identify a horse ready to win at first call, we will consider those which meet our criteria. Horses that satisfy these rules can be considered legitimate key horse candidates:

1). The horse must have been rested for a least 45 days. We must be certain that the animal has had a meaningful rest. Understandably, many owners are reluctant to keep their runners idle for more than 30-40 days. Their overhead continues to mount without any offsetting purse money. A hurried layoff is sometimes worse than none.

2). The horse must contend for the lead but finally lose its first race following the layoff. We must be convinced the trainer was trying to win that first race. This pattern suggests a strong second effort and a high winning percentage. It also suggests that the horse is well along in recovering if there was an injury.

The past performances given below illustrate the type of wagers we are seeking.

EXAMPLE: MY SONG FOR YOU

This 4-year-old filly ran her first two races which proved to be just short of disastrous. The horse was shelved for 56 days of R and R.

My Song For You — Dk. b. or br. f. 4, by Seattle Song—Too Bald, by Bald Eagle
BLACK C A — Br.—Northridge Farm (Ky)
Own.—Groves Carolyn T — Tr.—Gregson Edwin — 115
Lifetime 10 2 2 1 $60,325 — 1991 1 0 1 0 $7,800 — 1990 7 2 1 1 $52,525 — Turf 3 0 2 0 $17,025

30Jan91- 5SA	fm	1⅛ ⓣ	:462 1:104 1:481	ⒻAlw 39000	3 4 32½ 32 11½ 2hd	Black C A	B 116	3.40	83-17	FrsdFvort114hdMySngFrY1161GrndAwrd1151¾	Lost whip 1/16	9
30Dec90- 5SA	fm	1⅛ ⓣ	:463 1:11 1:473	3↑ⒻAlw 42000	7 4 34½ 3½ 2hd 22¾	Black C A	B 116b	7.20	84-13	HghlndTd1122DHPndrg-Fr116DHMySngFrY116hd	No mishap	11
30Dec90-Dead heat												
30Nov90- 7Hol	fst	1	:45 1:094 1:344	3↑ⒻAlw 34000	2 2 1½ 2½ 32½ 57¾	Black C A	B 118	3.60	82-19	CscdnGld1151½WrCndrss1131½ErthAnl1122	Lugged out early	8
4Nov90- 7SA	fst	1	:454 1:101 1:353	3↑ⒻAlw 35000	3 2 21 1hd 11½ 14½	Black C A	B 119	3.70	89-10	MySongForYou1194½FrncSoir1151½DncingLndsy122hd	Driving	6
13Oct90- 9SA	fst	6f	:213 :441 1:092	3↑ⒻAlw 32000	5 7 88½ 87½ 74½ 53½	Black C A	B 117	34.40	86-16	CntnnlTm1171½DHFrncSr114DHMdclMrvl117no	Bumped start	8
11Apr90- 8SA	fm	1⅛ ⓣ	:463 1:104 1:472	ⒻⒷPrvdncia	1 3 32 31½ 31½ 54¾	Desormeaux K J	113	27.40	83-10	Mtrco120noSomthingmrry1201¾Nijinsky'sLovr120½	Weakened	9
14Mar90- 3SA	fst	1	:47 1:114 1:38	ⒻMd Sp Wt	5 4 43 1hd 1hd 1hd	Desormeaux K J	117	3.40	77-23	MySongForYo117hdWrCmmndrss1121Orlnv1173½	Bumped late	8
24Feb90- 4SA	fst	1 1/16	:481 1:123 1:453	ⒻMd Sp Wt	1 1 11 1hd 1hd 32½	Desormeaux K J	117	7.90	72-22	Conts1172½ArlngtonEght117hdMySngFrY117hd	Checked early	10
30Dec89- 4SA	fst	6f	:213 :442 1:092	ⒻMd Sp Wt	6 5 54 57½ 79½ 79¾	Solis A	117	41.40	81-08	BYorBst1171½Phl'sIllson1172LttlLxrs1173½	Bumped hard gate	12
7Oct89- 4SA	fst	6f	:214 :444 1:104	ⒻMd Sp Wt	10 10 83 1215 1216 1225½	McCarron C J	117	14.10	58-14	PuppetShow1124MissTris1171MediclMrvel1171	Wide 3/8 turn	12

Speed Index: Last Race: 0.0 — 3-Race Avg.: -3.3 — 3-Race Avg.: -3.3 — Overall Avg.: -5.3
LATEST WORKOUTS ●Mar 2 SA 5f sly 1:023 H (d) — Feb 24 SA 6f fst 1:134 H — Feb 18 SA 5f fst 1:003 H — Feb 13 SA 5f fst 1:041 H

24 Feb- The filly turns in a strong, front running effort, finally finishing third, beaten by 2 1/2 lengths.

14 Mar- In her second race, My Song For You finishes first by a head. To our disbelief, she pays a welcome $8.80.

EXAMPLE: MARILYNS FIRST

After a win on the NorCal County Fair circuit, trainer Bryan Webb stabled his horse, prepping his animal for the Fall meet at Bay Meadows.

Marilyns First — Dk. b. or br. g. 6, by Star of Ėrin-Ir—Radiant Hope, by Petrone
MILLER D A JR — $6,250 — Br.—The Crisci Family Trust 3 (Cal)
Own.—Mtn Hi St-Pilet-Tg-Vlkmn — Tr.—Webb Bryan — 117
Lifetime 22 4 4 3 $27,849 — 1991 1 0 0 0 — 1990 2 0 0 0

2Feb91- 4GG	sly	6f	:213 :442 1:104	Clm 6250	8 5 45½ 48 716 721	Snyder B D5	LB 112	4.40	63-18	Mid'sMistk1172FirstToArriv1126GoldnStks1193	Through early	9
25Feb90-10GG	fst	1 1/16	:471 1:111 1:432	Clm 6250	9 5 44 68 1115 1119¾	Gavidia W	117	6.40	61-22	Scrpbook117nkNorthSeed1172Bsingstoke117no	Bumped start	11
5Jan90- 9BM	fst	1⅛	:47 1:113 1:502	Clm 6250	8 4 43½ 44 46 69½	Hansen R D	117	*2.10	78-15	Popular Day1186 Getthegone1161 DHDarion116	No excuse	11
2Dec89-10BM	fst	1⅛	:462 1:111 1:501	3↑Clm 6250	8 8 86¾ 84¾ 43½ 45½	Kaenel J L	117	*1.90	84-10	Popular Day1171 Little Argument112½ Coach Conway1174		12
3Nov89- 7BM	fst	1 1/16	:462 1:104 1:423	3↑Clm 12500	1 6 42 31½ 33 58	Kaenel J L	119	*3.00	76-21	Mc Gruff1171½ Green Street1173 Chancery Lane1172½		12
6Oct89- 3BM	fst	1⅛	:462 1:104 1:483	3↑Hcp 6250s	7 5 58 54 2hd 31	Kaenel J L	120	*1.90	87-14	DHRylRlty112DHNMnyDwn1151MrlynsFrst1207	Broke slowly	7
15Sep89- 6BM	fst	1¼	:47 1:364 2:013	3↑Hcp 6250s	1 3 32½ 21½ 13 14½	Hubbard N J	113	8.20	94-15	Marilyns First1134½ Proceeding1222 Optimum Flyer114no		9
1Sep89- 6BM	fst	1⅛	:453 1:10 1:492	3↑Alw 6250s	4 1 32 42 41½ 23	Hubbard N J5	113	3.80	81-16	Hamilton House1173 Marilyns First113hd Sentinel Star117¾		6
15Jly89- 6Sol	fst	1 1/16	:473 1:114 1:444	3↑Clm 6250	9 3 1hd 12 15 18	Hubbard N J5	112	2.20	75-16	MrilynsFrst1128CutousEgl1191½BoldSongo1172	Bumped start	10
30Jun89-13Pln	fst	170	:47 1:121 1:434	3↑Clm 6250	7 3 32 2hd 31½ 310½	Hubbard N J5	112	*1.90	64-18	Cautious Eagle1179 Fun Is First1171½ Marilyns First1123		9

Speed Index: Last Race: -17.0 — 3-Race Avg.: -10.0 — 9-Race Avg.: -5.8 — Overall Avg.: -7.2
LATEST WORKOUTS Mar 3 GG 6f sly 1:214 H (d) — ●Feb 17 GG 5f fst :593 H — Feb 1 GG 3f fst :38 H — Jan 27 GG 5f fst 1:00 H

1 Sep- Idle for 47 days, the 6-year-old gelding pushes the pace.

15 Sep- Despite that second place finish--a previously mentioned flag to a coterie of bettors--the horse leaves the gate at unbelievable odds of $8.20. The gelding wins easily, paying $18.40 to knowledgeable holders of winning tickets.

EXAMPLE: SHOWERSTIME

Always trying hard on the front end, the 6-year-old mare went down for a 7-month hiatus after her losing race on 1 Jun.

Showerstime — Ch. m. 6, by Forget the Showers—Lovertime, by Old Time Nonsense
FLORES D R — $10,000 Br.—Steele V M (Cal)
Own.—Westerlund L E & Patricia L — Tr.—Eurton Peter — 117
Lifetime 29 6 6 3 $87,025 — 1991 3 1 1 0 $9,900 — 1990 10 1 2 2 $16,100

7Mar91- 1SA	fst	6f	:22	:451	1:111	ⒻⓈClm 10000	8	1	11½	12½	11½	23	Flores D R	LBb	117	*1.90	77-16	Cee'sVeryOwn1153Showerstime117¾SueForLibl1102	Set pace	12
6Feb91- 4SA	fst	6f	:214	:45	1:11	ⒻClm 12500	3	2	1½	1hd	21½	65	Stevens G L	Lb	119	*3.20	76-16	ZltnJnn1151½RsonToB114½LoosInPrds116nk	Lugged out early	12
17Jan91- 5SA	fst	6f	:213	:45	1:102	ⒻClm 12500	9	1	32½	21	21½	1no	Stevens G L	LBb	115	*1.40	84-12	Showerstime115noKhalMeADeb1154½ArchdleRod107½	Gamely	12
31Dec90- 1SA	fst	6½f	:214	:451	1:174	3+ⒻⓈClm 12500	10	1	1½	1hd	1hd	23	Stevens G L	LBb	115	18.30	78-15	Feverfew1153 Showerstime1152 Lou's Fast1152	Held 2nd	12
1Jun90- 1Hol	fst	6f	:222	:46	1:12	ⒻClm 10500	4	1	1hd	1½	21	107½	Stevens G L	b	114	9.80	72-15	Gold Decor116nk Donalda117nk Cherokee Kiss116½	Faltered	10
10May90- 5Hol	fst	6f	:213	:45	1:103	ⒻClm 10000	10	1	21	2½	21½	65¼	Black K	b	117	2.90	82-08	Lift Ticket117hdClassieDebonair1181½Startling1161	Weakened	12
27Apr90- 5Hol	fst	6f	:221	:452	1:103	ⒻClm 18000	8	1	1½	1hd	1hd	65¾	Black K	b	119	25.90	81-11	CookBr116hdSh'sSmokn116nkColClrWtr117½	Wide lane, tired	9
28Mar90- 1SA	fst	6f	:22	:46	1:111	ⒻⓈClm c-12500	8	2	1½	11½	2hd	34¾	Stevens G L	b	116	4.30	75-23	LightstRy1163½SuForLibl1111½Showrstim1162	Weakened late	11
11Mar90- 1SA	fst	6f	:214	:453	1:121	ⒻClm 12500	9	2	42	33	42½	69¼	Stevens G L	b	116	3.60	66-14	CookieBr1162½Chro'sBounty1161ConvivilMiss1163½	Gave way	12
16Feb90- 4SA	fst	6f	:22	:453	1:113	ⒻClm 12500	9	2	2hd	11½	11½	21	Stevens G L	b	116	4.30	77-21	GoldDecor1161Showerstime116hdCookieBer1151½	Clear, tired	11

Speed Index: Last Race: -7.0 — 3-Race Avg.: -6.3 — 10-Race Avg.: -8.1 — Overall Avg.: -8.1
LATEST WORKOUTS Jan 29 SA 4f fst :483 B

31 Dec- Showerstime comes back running, leading the race deep into the stretch. At odds of $18.30, she finishes second, three lengths off the winner.

17 Jan- Forcing the pace all the way, the horse drives for the wire, winning by a head. Her previous finish drew heavy support from the "finished second last out" bettors. A $4.80 payout is still just a tad better than a thumb in the eye.

Earlier we pointed out the importance of solid owner-trainer rapport; how the success of the trainer depends upon the trust of his owners. Bill Mastrangelo seems to be a fortunate trainer in this regard.

EXAMPLE: IRISH BULLDOG

Like many before them, the owners of this 3-year-old gelding first tried their runner at Hollywood Park, the Mecca of West Coast racing.

7 Jun-   After losing by 15+ lengths, trainer Mastrangelo moved the
            horse north to Bay Meadows where the competition would be
            less severe.

30 Aug-   Rested for 84 days, Irish Bulldog runs in front most of the
            distance, ending in third place, beaten off by four lengths. This
            is the past performance line we're always looking for.

13 Sep-   Driving all the way, the gelding pulls out at the wire, winning
            by one length. The win pay is $7.60.

EXAMPLE: HEY SISTER

Sometimes even the trainer must be convinced, especially when he is also
the owner. Savvy Jerry Dutton needed only one race to realize his filly was
overmatched in maiden allowance races.

After the defeat on 18 Sep, the horse was held out of the racing wars for
nearly seven months.

11 Mar–   Entered where she fits well, Hey Sister is made a 7 to 5 favorite.
            She turns in a powerful effort, finishing fourth, out just 2
            lengths.

28 Mar–   Perhaps due to that fourth place finish, the filly is sent from the
            gate at odds of 4 to 1. As expected, she wins and pays the
            overlay price of $10.00.

While we welcome every ten dollar payoff we can garner, twenty dollars is
twice welcome. While most of the odds generated by this criteria are of a
modest nature, there are enough boxcar prices to satisfy even the pie-in-the-
sky longshot seeker.

EXAMPLE: BE A ROADSTER

There is nothing like a poor finish to prompt a jump in future odds. Two
such finishes will virtually gaurantee a big price.

Be A Roadster												
GONZALEZ R M		Ch. g. 6, by Don B—Gurly's Secret, by Terrang						Lifetime	1991	1	0	0	0	
Own.—Manlove & Mason		$8,000	Br.—Kruljac & Kenly (Ariz)						38 6 5 6	1990	13	3	2	3	$19,538
			Tr.—Mason Lloyd C					**117**	$41,782	Turf	1	0	0	0	

After running that horror on 12 Oct, trainer Mason knew his horse was
over-raced, fatigued.

6 Dec–   Coming off a 55-day break, the 6-year-old gelding turned in a
            race line dear to our hearts. Setting the pace much of the way,
            Be A Roadster finished ninth, eight lengths behind. Perfect!

23 Dec–   Shunned by handicappers of many schools, the gelding goes
            postward sporting odds of 9 to 1. As we projected, he sets the
            early pace and leads all the way to the finish line. These juicy
            $20.00 payoffs do come up once in a while. Apply knowledge-
            able attention to the applicable past performance lines. Always

note those dates. It takes only a few $20.00 mutuels to keep a bettor solidly in the profit column.

For the happy traveller, you will discover that this spot play pattern is valid nationwide, from Aqueduct to Golden Gate.

EXAMPLE: DAIMON

26 Nov-   After watching his filly beaten by nearly 30 lengths, tainer Bill Turner wisely decided she was not ready for her racing debut.

27 Feb-   Ninety days later the horse is more than ready. Only a bump in the stretch keeps her from winning at 11 to 1.

4 Mar-   Turner has tipped his hand. Daimon romps in by six lengths at odds of 8-5. The nearest thing to a lock that we've seen in many races.

EXAMPLE: SENIOR HOUSE

Following a maiden win and a miserable effort in the Juvenile Mile, the gelded son of Leroy S spends the winter resting and readying for the spring and summer meet at Longacres.

```
Senior House                    B. g. 3(Apr), by Leroy S—Indecent, by Solari
    HANSEN R D                   Br.—Oak Crest Farm (Wash)              1990  9  2  2  0        $18,140
                         119     Tr.—Chambers Mike        $20,800       1989  2  1  0  0         $2,750
 Own.—Anderson & Mallck          Lifetime   11  3  2  0      $20,890
 28Oct90-3BM  1⅛ :464 1:102 1:412ft   4  LB117  63½ 64½ 68½ 59½   Hansen R D 2   25000  04-95 GoldenHope,ChrokPony,RcingDy 6
 50ct90-10BM  1⅛ :46 1:11 1:442ft   6½  LB117  67  42½  2½  1½    Hansen R D 4   20000  75-28 SeniorHous,DwPoint,FrdomAgin 10
 16Sep90-9BM  1  :461 1:11 1:37 ft  9-5  LB117  63½ 53½  34  44½   Hansen R D 5   16000  81-11 Chilly Water, Nauty Jeff, Bular 8
    16Sep90—Hand timed
 26Aug90-3L ga  1  :464 1:114 1:382ft  *9-5e LB117  76½ 712 810 810½  Hansen R D 2   25000  58-20 MjesticNsr,AbergwunDuk,SfToSy 8
 3Aug90-5L ga  1⅛ :471 1:123 1:461ft  *3½e LB120  75½ 65  55½ 2nd    Corral J R 2   20000  73-29 FoolishWy,SniorHous,TblForSix 12
 13Jly90-9L ga  1⅛ :461 1:111 1:44 ft  17  B 118  70  89½ 816 811    Kaenel J L 2   80000  73-24 fBarramundi,PortRinbow,Lepnto 8
 6Jly90-9L ga  6f :222 :454 1:101ft  14  B 118  77  76  714 614    Kaenel J L 7   40000  75-21 Spnooch,CctmplSwrd,Gnnrs MtMrt 7
 20May90-9L ga  1  :481 1:124 1:382ft   4  114  42  3½  2nd 11½    Fox W I Jr 1   c25000  77-24 SnorHous,TblForSx,MckMcDonld 7
 9May90-5L ga  1⅛ :473 1:122 1:453ft  10  114  22  23  22  21     Fox W I Jr 5 fⒷ 20000  75-28 NoWyMistr,SniorHous,ChoicAnnl 9
    9May90—Steadied early
 8Oct89-10Pla  1  :471 1:12 1:374ft  10e  121  64½ 65½ 912 920    RnnkrL 2 Juv Mile H  68-18 MilitryHwk,GoSeeSm,ShrpEvent 10
 Speed Index: Last Race: -11.0     3-Race Avg.: -5.3     9-Race Avg.: -5.4     Overall Avg.: -5.3
 Nov 18 BM 5f ft 1:023 H        Nov 12 BM 5f ft 1:032 H        Oct 17 BM 5f ft 1:001 H        Sep 29 BM 5f ft 1:03 H
```

16 May- Pushing the pace from gate to wire, Senior House finishes a one-length second.

26 May- Unbelieveable. The horse wins, as expected -- and pays $10.00.

The First Race and (Almost) Ready

As a corolary to the previous section, here we are dealing with younger horses making their racing debut. Some horses win the first time they are raced. An Old Touts Tale holds there are some trainers who are experts at winning the first time they race a newcomer. If this is true, we've yet to identify one consistent enough for profitable wagering. We never bet either a trainer or a jockey by name only. Not even those jockey/trainer "magic combos" sought out by a small band of racegoers.

As with the rested horses discussed earlier, we will closely watch the newcomers in their initial races. Those which set or push the pace deep into the stretch are worthy of a wager. As with the rested animals, the number of beaten lengths is of little import. In fact, in some respects, the greater the losing margin, the better for our odds.

For reasons best known to a multitude of assorted handicappers, the losing newcomer is instantly shunned. Even a horse favored to win the first time raced will go off at a good price, "the second time around."

EXAMPLE: TIZABEL

This Utley-trained 4-year-old filly was favored to win at her very first outing.

4 May-   Bumped at the start, the horse recovered, pushed the pace and finished fourth, more than three lengths behind. The pattern we love to spot.

6 Jun-   Now scorned by the crowd, Tizabel scores her win by one length. She rewards her backers with a $14.80 mutuel pay.

EXAMPLE: JOYFUL SCORE

Carla Gaines -- yes, there are many successful lady trainers-- may have a money machine in this 3-year-old gelding.

22 Dec-   Mistake at the start, the horse fights for the lead, finally finishing in third place.

3 Jan-   Maybe it was a "bad" trip. Maybe the pace was wrong. What-
           ever the reason, Joyful Score is ignored by several schools of
           handicapping. She wins and pays $16.40.

There are times when a trainer (owner?) will destroy the odds on a horse by
being over anxious to win a purse. Who is to say he is wrong? He is
gambling.

EXAMPLE: BOOM BOOM BOUNTY

The stable collected a purse but lost a good gelding who will soon be
winning in the allowance classification.

9 Nov-   Favored to win, the horse runs a strong second before giving
           way. Our ideal spot play.

13 Dec-   Doing everything possible to guarantee a purse, the trainer drops
           his charge nearly 50% in class: Md60000 to Md32000. The
           public quickly bets the promising gelding down to prohibitive,
           even-money odds. Boom Boom Bounty wins easily and is
           claimed by another barn.

Horses running their first race will always be flashing a win signal at tracks
everywhere.

EXAMPLE: THE IRON COUNT

```
The Iron Count              B. g. 3(Feb), by Native Uproar—Riviera Princess, by Traxton King
                            Br.—McMillin Brothers (Ky)                 1990  2  0  0  0
   BERRIO O A           1115  Tr.—Page Gary          $32,000           1989  4  1  0  0           $2,224
Own.—Schaffer & Woolsey Jr        Lifetime    6  1  0  0    $2,224
26Apr90-5Hol  6f :22 :45 1:10 ft   43 116  53 32 54½ 71⁰⅓  Garcia J A⁵    32000 88-10 PrinceGrenstr,InspirtionlWs,FirBck 8
 26Apr90—Bobbled at break
8Apr90-7SA   6f :21⁴ :45³1:10 ft   72 120  1ʰᵈ 53 6¹² 6²⁸  Cedeno E A²  Aw34000 58-17 Profit Key,Jacodra,TalentedPirate 6
3Aug89-11SR  5½f :22² :45⁴1:04¹ft  2⁴ 117  2¹ 2¹½ 37 5¹⁴  CblleroR² Rdwrd Empr 76-13 WoodSprt,MjortyWhp,BtchCmngs 10
25Jun89-6Rui  5½f :22¹ :46 1:06⁴ft 4⁴ 118  1ʰᵈ 1ʰᵈ 3¹ 46½  CunninghmV 2 Aw3500 76-13 BrnnGmmt,ChsnoThDrm,BldBlchry 9
22Apr89-6Sun  4½f :22⁴ :47³  :54 ft  2½ 120  6  1ʰᵈ 1½ 1ⁿᵏ  Martinez A J 2⁰ Mdn 82-10 ThIronCount,HyLuckyEln,GvrMnk 10
 22Apr89—Veered in start
10Mar89-5Sun  4f    :22¹ :47²ft    2⁵ 118  2  1¹ 1½ 4³  Cunningham V 2⁰ Mdn 86-13 Mr. Langolf, Breezy Cox, LadsEgc 10
 Speed Index: Last Race: –10.0   3-Race Avg.: –15.3  6-Race Avg.: –8.5   Overall Avg.: –8.5
9Apr 3Fpr 3f ft  :36⁴H        Mar 25 SA 6f ft 1:14³ H        Mar 18 SA 4f ft :49 H
```

While passing over this horse when it was entered in a race at Hollywood
Park, we noted the trainer's maneuvering at Sunland Park. Sunland is a
terrific "small purse" track. A suburb of El Paso, the track is just over the
state line in New Mexico. The grandstand is comfortably air-cooled against
the heat of the Southwest.

31 Mar-   Leading at every call, the youngster places fourth in a blanket
           finish.

22 Apr-   It's surprising how a fourth place finish turns off the bettors.
           Alas, we weren't on hand to cash a ticket when The Iron Count
           wins, paying $7.50 to his knowing backers.

The Green Baby

One variation of our ready-to-run theme is what we call the "green baby."
This is a 2-year-old that was placed on the track a little early. The trainer,
realizing it, returns the animal to the pastures until it matures into a stronger
3-year-old. The horse is then brought back for another try, usually several
months later. It often wins on first calling -- but not always. When it
doesn't, it qualifies for this section and should thus be regarded as an
improving horse and a key candidate.

EXAMPLE: CHIEF BUCKAROO

It was clear to Chief Buckaroo's first trainer that this promising son of the
top sprinter, Buckaroo, was brought to the track a little too early. When a

green baby returns to the track, it is almost always stronger and a better runner than when it was younger. After failing to win as expected after the 8-month rest, the pattern suggests a big win next time. Unfortunately, everybody in South Florida sees it.

Chief Buckaroo — Ch. g. 3(Apr), by Buckaroo—August Days, by In Reality
$6,500 Br.—Regal Oak Farm (Fla) — Tr.—Wise Charles G — 108^7
Own.—Leff Marilyn & Marcus
Lifetime 6 3 0 1 $14,754 — 1991 5 3 0 1 $14,654 — 1990 1 M 0 0 $100

11Sep91- 5Crc	fst	6f	:22^2	:46	1:11^4	3↑Clm 16000	4	3	2^{hd}	2^1	2^1	4^5	Moore B G	113	*2.30	86-16	Foolish MacDuff116^4 Chac-Mx109$\frac{1}{2}$ AHappyMan120$\frac{1}{2}$	Faltered	6
23Aug91-10Crc	gd	6f	:21^4	:45^3	1:12	Clm 11500	10	6	4$\frac{3}{4}$	1$^{1\frac{1}{2}}$	1$^{1\frac{1}{2}}$	1$^{1\frac{3}{4}}$	Moore B G	122	*2.60	90-11	ChiefBuckroo122$^{1\frac{3}{4}}$ReunitdAgin116^{no}KillDvilHill116$^{3\frac{1}{2}}$	Driving	11
4Aug91- 8Crc	fst	6f	:22	:46^1	1:12^4	Clm 17000	9	9	5$^{2\frac{1}{2}}$	2^1	1^3	1$^{1\frac{1}{2}}$	Moore B G	114	3.60	86-16	ChiefBuckroo114$^{1\frac{1}{2}}$MdeToCope116^{nk}PetitCeeCee108^1	All out	11
18Jly91- 3Crc	fst	6f	:21^4	:45^2	1:12^3	3↑Md 14000	8	1	1$^{2\frac{1}{2}}$	1^4	1^5	1^7	Lee M A	117	*.50	87-15	ChifBuckroo117^{7}TropiclHtwv115$^{2\frac{3}{4}}$MyHghRj113^{nk}	Ridden out	8
7Jly91- 4Crc	fst	6f	:22	:45^2	1:12^2	3↑Md 15000	9	1	1$\frac{1}{2}$	1$^{2\frac{1}{2}}$	1^3	3$^{1\frac{1}{2}}$	Lee M A	117	3.10	86-13	ContryThrll117$^{1\frac{1}{2}}$Shknh'sJ.R.113^{hd}ChfBckroo117$^{4\frac{1}{2}}$	Weakened	10
17Nov90- 2Crc	fst	6f	:22^1	:45^4	1:12	Md Sp Wt	9	4	2^1	3$^{2\frac{1}{2}}$	4^8	6^{13}	Lee M A	119	8.40	77-10	Kadiddy119^1 Scottish Ice119^6 Solid Sunny119$^{3\frac{1}{2}}$	Finished	9

Speed Index: Last Race: +2.0 3–Race Avg.: +1.6 6–Race Avg.: –1.1 Overall Avg.: –1.1

17 Nov- The horse begins racing in a MSW sprint as a baby, finishing 6th after pushing the early pace.

7 Jul- The odds are higher than expected as the horse is *dropped into the claiming ranks for the first time.* See the next section, "Maidens For Sale." It's an improved race, considering the layoff. The horse was rested, but not sharp enough to win, although it was part of the trifecta.

18 Jul- Once the gate opened Chief Buckaroo took command and never looked back. The greatest surprise that day was that the horse wasn't claimed. The ticket paid a modest $3.00.

The high success rate of this pattern should not be altogether surprising. The horse is now both stronger and more experienced, having already run competitively at least once. However, the handicapper must consider the return to be the beginning of another form cycle. This pattern appeared in the actual race example later (see "Maidens For Sale"). A second race example for this pattern appears in the section "Improving Newcomers."

Summary

Follow these simple rules to identify rested horses and you should materially improve your key horse selection process:

(1)   The horse has been rested for at least 45 days, or has just run for the very first time.

(2)   The horse must have contended for the lead throughout the race, losing out somewhere deep in the stretch. The number of beaten lengths frequently determines the horse's odds in its next (second) race -- the race we are betting.

Maidens For Sale

"Me? Bet on a maiden race? No way. Never. Not even with your money. Those dogs are inconsistent. It's a crime against nature."

This typical railbird can be found at most tracks, wandering about down near the finish line. Pontificating. Always expounding upon one or more Old Touts Tales for the benefit of everyone within earshot.

Consistent? Inconsistent? We once ran our own study of maiden races at two full race meets in Northern California. As we suspected, the maiden races proved to be among the most formful. Not yet war-scarred, maiden favorites won more often than the public choices in any other race category. The ultimate truth? Those maiden winners did not pay enough to produce a net profit over an entire race meet. So, our friend the railbird is right, but for the wrong reason.

We did confirm a second suspicion. This one based upon our own observation as well as the opinions of knowledgeable horsemen and a few astute race bettors. Once confirmed, the suspicion became our criteria for this chapter:

(1)   A maiden runner dropping into a claiming race for the very first time is a powerful key horse candidate, and usually at very good prices.

(2)   The horse's chance of winning seemed to be better if it finished its last race within a "respectable" distance, say fifteen lengths, of the winner (unless there was an excuse). Let's call fifteen lengths "somewhat competitive."

The rationale for this wager lies within the horsemen themselves. Successful owners and trainers are reluctant to maintain a horse not earning its keep -- plus a substantial profit. Animals incapable of competing in the rarefied atmosphere of allowance class racing are quickly dropped into claimers where they can earn purse money.

A poker player's nerves of steel can be a definite asset when wagering these maidens. The last running line often appears as an apparent disaster to the casual reader. The only reliable signal is that one, sudden drop into the claiming ranks for the very first time.

EXAMPLE: SPRING RAISED

Greg Gilchrist is one of those trainer who enjoys the full support and cooperation of his owners.

4 Nov-   It took just this 10 1/2 length loss to convince trainer Gilchrist his gelding was overmatched.

14 Nov-   Running for a price tag, Md32000, the horse wins by three lengths, returning a $12.40 mutuel.

EXAMPLE: SUPPORTING

This gelding was found wanting twice (23 Jun & 12 Nov) before being dropped into the claiming ranks.

Supporting Dk. b. or br. g. 5(Mar), by Kris S—Merry Sport, by Amasport
PEDROZA M A Br.—Meadowbrook Farms Inc (Fla)
Own.—Kessak & MeadowbrookFmsInc Tr.—La Croix David
115
Lifetime 7 1 0 1 $15,925 | 1991 3 0 0 0 $575 | 1990 4 1 0 1 $15,350

20Mar91- 9SA	fst	1	:462	1:104	1:362	Clm 25000	8	6	3½	2½	2½	54¼	Garcia J A	LBb	115	45.60	81-09	RestlessHnry115¾Dmlo115¾DimondbckDrgon1181½	Wide early	10
15Feb91- 7OP	fst	1	:464	1:131	1:412	Alw 20000	4	7	711	89¾	812	911¼	Gryder A T	Lb	117	9.40	57-32	ProprAcktn117hdHngngCrv122noGhtlGrg114no	Stumbled start	11
2Feb91- 7OP	fst	1	:454	1:113	1:384	Alw 20000	9	1	11½	2hd	78½	917½	Kutz D	Lb	114	*1.70	63-19	Megachief117nk Don'tAxeFoolish1115½SirRegis1144	Gave way	9
19Dec90- 8BM	my	1	:463	1:113	1:363	Alw 21000	1	1	11	22	26	312	Gonzalez R M	Lb	117	5.10	76-20	Mister Flyer11710 Condylar1172 Supporting1171½	Weakened	6
29Nov90- 4Hol	fst	1 1/16	:454	1:112	1:461	Md 50000	7	1	11½	13½	14	13½	Flores D R	LBb	118	7.80	69-20	Supporting1183½PeaceOfNsk1181Steppco118nk	Troubled start	8
12Nov90- 6Hol	fst	6½f	:214	:444	1:163	Md Sp Wt	2	4	42	810	1126	1139¾	Solis A	Lb	119	7.00	52-11	CienFuegos1196½MjorLunch1191¾TrucFlo119hd	Bumped start	11
23Jun90- 2GG	fst	5f	:211	:443	:572	Md Sp Wt	2	5	32½	32	34	44	Steiner J J		118	11.30	94-09	Bluegrass Law1181½ SailorGordon1182YouBlew118½	Even late	9

Speed Index: Last Race: (—) 3-Race Avg.: (—) 12-Race Avg.: (—) Overall Avg.: -12.5
LATEST WORKOUTS Apr 17 Hol 6f fst 1:151 H Apr 8 Hol 4f fst :481 H Mar 17 Hol 4f fst :501 H Mar 11 Hol 4f fst :49 H

29 Nov- Racing for a $50000 tag, Supporting wins easily, rewarding his backers with a handsome $17.60 payoff.

A card-playing friend studied the past performance lines of these two winners and showed the anticipated reaction.

He whistled.

"Betting on these horses is akin to re-raising a raiser with a four-flush showing."

The following two horses illustrate the validity of our pattern despite the interesting changes of jockeys.

EXAMPLE: THE MILLER TRICK

The Miller Trick B. g. 3(Jan), by The Miller (Fra)—Irma L'Douce, by L'Natural
GONZALEZ R M $10,000 Br.—McElhinney Mr-Mrs L C (Cal)
Own.—McElhinney L C Tr.—Larsen Lavar
117
Lifetime 9 1 1 0 $17,050 | 1991 3 0 0 0 | 1990 6 1 1 0 $17,050

18Apr91- 7SA	fst	1	:463	1:12	1:381	Clm 25000	6	6	65	89	914	919¾	Patton D B	LBb	115	55.00	56-25	DelawareDrive115nkCalifornian115nkTheCleners1157	4-wide 7/8	9
12Apr91- 5SA	fst	6½f	:222	:453	1:171	Clm 25000	3	11	128½	118½	1112	1115¼	Meza R Q	LBb	115	71.00	68-15	Fiesta Fair116½ Lazarito-Mx115¾Capirazza1152	Impeded start	12
29Mar91- 5SA	fst	6f	:22	:45	1:10	Clm 32000	4	5	54½	66½	68	611½	Meza R Q	LBb	115	12.60	74-14	Sonnys Rainbow1164 Damelo115½ Big BangBeau115hd	Outrun	7
5Sep90- 3Dmr	fst	6f	:22	:451	1:101	Clm 62500	7	5	41½	52¾	67½	69	Meza R Q	Lb	118	6.70	80-12	RichMinute115hdL'DeeDsco1132½TrulyRoyl1173	Bumped start	8
16Aug90- 11Bmf	fst	6f	:223	:454	1:102	Mid Pensla	1	4	53½	65½	48½	48	Steiner J J	LBb	114	4.20	80-17	Crystal'sGame1212Chrmonnier1142Cpt.CnDo1154	Steadied 3/8	6
23Jly90- 4Hol	fst	6f	:224	:453	1:111	Md 50000	4	4	3½	2hd	1hd	11	Meza R Q	Lb	118	7.20	84-11	The MillerTrick1181SuperJuice116½SuttonSpecial1181	Driving	9
7Jly90- 6Hol	fst	5½f	:22	:451	1:044	ⓈMd Sp Wt	2	3	65	67¾	69	79¾	Pincay L Jr	Lb	117	9.40	84-06	Apollo1171 Warfare Prince1171½ Pillaring1173	No threat	9
18Mar90- 3GG	fst	5f	:212	:451	:58	Md Sp Wt	11	6	41	2½	21	22	Steiner J J	b	118	14.40	93-11	SilentPle1182TheMillerTrick1185Cliche'sScrt118no	Wide early	11
4May90- 3GG	fst	4½f	:22	:46	:522	Md Sp Wt	3	2		814	712	65¾	Steiner J J	b	118	8.00	87-16	StrDPc118½RvrRodTom1184WlcomFrtnt118½	Rank early, wide	8

Speed Index: Last Race: -19.0 1-Race Avg.: -19.0 1-Race Avg.: -19.0 Overall Avg.: -7.4
LATEST WORKOUTS Apr 7 SA 3f fst :392 H Mar 23 SA 6f fst 1:144 H Mar 17 SA 5f fst 1:033 H Mar 10 AC 6f fst 1:14 H

18 May- Following a troubled debut, the 3-year-old gelding runs a fine race, finishing second. That race earns the animal a trip to Hollywood Park for a try with the top runners on the West Coast.

7 Jul- Even with Lafitte Pincay aboard, the horse is badly outrun.

23 Jul-   Entered in a Md50000 sprint, The Miller Trick wins by one
            length. Savvy holders of winning tickets are rewarded with a
            $16.40 payout.

EXAMPLE: FLYING IVAN

Trainer Caganich - another nice lady - didn't wait long to turn her 4-year-old
filly into a money winner.

11 Oct-   After watching her charge finish far up the track, she drops it
            into a maiden race with a $45,000 price tag. With Lafitte
            Pincay riding, the distaffer wins, paying $12.80.

Most of the horses in this chapter pay very good prices for their wins. This
is due to the poor showing of each immediately preceeding that first drop
into a claiming race. A rare exception does occur from time to time.

EXAMPLE: RAINBANK

Tested three times in the non-claiming ranks, the filly is a consistent
also-ran.

22 Apr-   Running as a top-priced claimer, Rainbank is spotted and bet
            down by the public. She wins by 7 1/2 lengths, paying a paltry
            $5.20.

EXAMPLE: SILVEYS TOUCH

Jerry Hollendorfer, one of the nation's most successful trainers, does not wait for a horse to slowly find its true level of competitive racing.

Silveys Touch
B. f. 4, by Silveyville—Kiss Me Mel, by Fleet Mel
$6,250 Br.—Qvale K M (Cal)
Tr.—Hollendorfer Jerry
116
Lifetime 1990 1 0 0 0
3 1 0 0 1989 2 1 0 0 $3,575
$3,575

Own.—Qvale K M
28Jan90- 5GG fst 1 :45³ 1:10³ 1:37 ④Clm 16000 7 4 55¼ 64¼ 79¾ 7¹⁴ Judice J C 116 8.40 66-14 More Torque116¼ Holiday Ranch116³ LookHereAMinute111½ 9
14Dec89- 1BM fst 1 :46⁴ 1:12⁴ 1:40¹ ⑥Md 12500 10 9 7⁷ 44¼ 3¹½ 1ⁿᵏ Hansen R D 117 *1.00 71-26 Silveys Touch117ⁿᵏ Queen Nambi117¾ Fantaskra117¼ 10
12Nov89- 6BM fst 6f :22² :45⁴ 1:11 ⑥Md Sp Wt 4 7 7⁸¼ 7⁹¾ 7¹² 7¹⁵ Hansen R D 117 5.30 72-08 Puff O Luck117⁴ Dalmation Princess117³ OurMissBrush117¹ 7

Speed Index: Last Race: -20.0 1-Race Avg.: -20.0 1-Race Avg.: -20.0 Overall Avg.: -14.3
LATEST WORKOUTS Feb 18 GG 6f fst 1:15 H Feb 11 BM 6f gd 1:17¹ H Feb 6 BM tr.t 6f fst 1:19² H Feb 1 BM 5f fst 1:03² H

12 Nov-   Shortly after this dead-last finish, Hollendorfer drops the filly to the bottom of the beginner's barrel: a race for 12500 maidens.

14 Dec-   Quick to recognize the ploy - that steep drop in class- the public promptly installs Silveys Touch as the even money favorite. The trainer collects a purse and launches another horse on what he hopes will be a profitable career. Ticket holders settle for a $4.00 mutuel.

The only thing worse than short-odds favorites are losers. We have our share of these, too.

EXAMPLE: BOBBI'S BLUE BLOOD

The four-year-old is sent against classier runners on two consecutive occasions. No go. Ninth place finishes both times.

Time for a change.

Bobbi's Blue Blood B. f. 4, by Impressive--Joyous Voyage, by Daryl's Joy
BAZE R A $6,250 Br.—Bach M W (Cal)
Own.—McVey-Pearson-Smith Tr.—Arterburn Lonnie
121
Lifetime 9 2 3 1 $18,000 — 1990 3 0 1 1 $4,350 — 1989 6 2 2 0 $13,650

9Nov90-	9BM	fst	6f	:221	:45	1:104	(F)Clm 16000	12	2	2hd	11	1hd	89¾	Warren R J Jr	LB	116	*2.00	79-14	Alicia's Girl116¾ Running Event1112 Fatease116hd	Stopped 12
25Oct90-	6BM	fst	6f	:221	:45	1:103	(F)Clm 20000	5	4	52½	31½	23	31½	Warren R J Jr	LB	116	3.10	85-13	Asqute1111ShivrsSvr116½Bobbi'sBluBlood1162	Evenly stretch 9
7Oct90-	7BM	fst	6f	:223	:451	1:122	(F)Clm 16000	3	4	42½	31	2½	22	Warren R J Jr	LB	116	3.40	76-20	Fltsvll1162Bobb'sBlBlod1161½HwDltKnw113nk	Stumbled start 9
23Nov89-	6BM	fst	6f	:221	:453	1:104	(F)Clm c-16000	5	2	1hd	11	12	1½	Frazier R L		116	*2.50	88-12	Bobbi's Blue Blood116½ Icy Answer1163 Holiday Ranch116hd	9
28Oct89-	2BM	fst	6f	:223	:46	1:103	(F)Md 20000	2	5	51½	51½	2hd	14½	Frazier R L		117	*2.00	89-07	Bobbi'sBlueBlood1174½AWitchInTime1173Planter'sLdy117nk	12
8Oct89-	2BM	fst	6f	:221	:45	1:101	(F)Md 20000	6	4	3½	22	21	23	Frazier R L		117	2.40	85-13	GinTucci1153Bobb'sBluBlood1175ThnksPp1171	Bumped start 9
14Sep89-	7BM	fst	6f	:221	:451	1:11	(F)Md 20000	8	2	2hd	1hd	11	2nk	Frazier R L		117	11.90	84-15	OldnFvr117nkBobb'sBlBld117[illegible]Btgns'Ldy117	Bumped 3-1/2 10
27Aug89-	6BM	fst	6f	:221	:45	1:102	(F)Md Sp Wt	4	3	1½	1hd	32½	915	Frazier R L		117	22.30	72-18	Bargain Doll1174½ Silk Puff117½ Doyle's Daughter117½	11
1Aug89-	6SR	fst	5½f	:223	:461	1:052	(F)Md Sp Wt	2	5	21	2½	33	910¾	Hamilton M		117	24.40	80-15	Nat's Sallie117½ Belle Of St. Marys1171½ Kulei1171	10

Speed Index: Last Race: -7.0 3-Race Avg.: -4.3 9-Race Avg.: -6.0 Overall Avg.: -6.0
LATEST WORKOUTS Aug 15 BM 6f fst 1:151 H Aug 8 BM 6f fst 1:133 H Aug 2 BM 5f fst 1:032 H Jly 27 BM 5f fst 1:034 H

14 Sep- The filly is entered for a $20,000 price tag. Her odds are nearly 12-1. Ideal conditions. We're drooling. She runs a great race, contending for the lead all the way. She's beaten a neck at the wire. We lose a heart stopper. Our approach is correct, the horse's execution is a neck short.

To ease the pain of a loss, we like to recall another Old Tout's Tale.

This one concerns the veteran handicapper sitting high in the grandstand. Clutched in his hand is a sheaf of $50.00 win tickets on a front runner he considers a "lock."

Leading by seven lengths, the speed horse loses his jockey just fifty yards short of the wire. The tickets slither through the old bettor's fingers as he slips quietly into the next world, arriving in a line at the Pearly Gates.

As the clouds clear away, he awakens to listen as a doctor lists his qualifications for admission.

"Look, St. Peter, I'm a doctor. I have healed the sick, cured the lame."

"Yes, my son, you have also grown arrogant, unfeeling and greedy. You must spend some time down below."

The next supplicant is a lawyer.

"I have studied long and hard to master the law. To serve the cause of justice, to protect the rights of all mankind."

St. Peter stares the man in the eye.

"You have also borne false witness, suborned perjury and coveted all thy neighbors possessions."

The haloed gatekeeper shakes his head in sorrow.

"You will be spending much time down below."

The handicapper hears all of the discussion and turns away to follow the other two.

St. Peter calls him back to the gate.

"Why do you follow those two, my son?"

"I don't have their education and training. I have never done a great deal for my fellow man. I'm probably due for a long stay down below."

"One moment, my son. What was your earthly calling?"

"Me? I was a handicapper."

"You mean you tried to pick the winners of horse races?"

"Yes, that's correct."

"Even before the race was run?"

"Oh yes, even before the race was run."

St. Peter shakes his head in disbelief and breaks into a broad smile. He swings back the Pearly Gates.

"Come right in, my son, you've been through Hell already!"

With that dash of cold water, we can now get back to those nice odds paid by our maidens dropping into a claiming race for the very first time.

EXAMPLE: NASTY TEMPTATION

The filly was well backed when beaten off by nine lengths at Golden Gate Fields. The horse was rested, then pointed for another try in Southern California.

19 Sep-   Running at Fairplex, the horse places second by a head.

7 Oct-   Competing against the big-time runners at Santa Anita, Nasty Temptation is beaten off by eight lengths. Now the stage is set for our betting action.

23 Nov-   Dropped into a Md50000 race, the horse wins, paying $14.00.

That's a good price, to be sure. Yet, it can be better! This pattern can pay off, even when the distance is changed, as in this next example.

EXAMPLE: SULTAN KUDARAT

Three strikes and you are out. Trainer Seguin gave his colt three shots at the brass ring. The last two times the odds were in triple digits.

Sultan Kudarat
ST. MARTIN E — 115
Own.—Asistio & Resurreccion

Ch. c. 3(Mar), by Green Forest—Cameo Native, by Raise a Native
Br.—Clay A G & R N (Ky) — 1990 3 1 0 0 $11,000
Tr.—Seguin Yves M — 1989 1 M 0 0
Lifetime 4 1 0 0 $11,000

22Feb90-4SA	1⅛	:474	1:123	1:532ft	13	117	11½	11½	16	15	Meza R Q6	M32000	69-23	SultnKudrt,PssMeLypheor,Tribe	12
28Jan90-6SA	6f	:214	:45	1:112ft	136	118	87¾	912	915	913¾	Mongil W1	Mdn	65-19	SqurCrk,LIBtO'Lrcny,NtsStGorgs	9
6Jan90-6SA	6½f	:212	:441	1:16 ft	100	118	89	78½	79½	711	Toro F7	Mdn	79-09	IndinWind,LtdEdition,SqureCrk	12
17Dec89-3Hol	1 1/16	:472	1:12	1:432ft	11	117	31	44	716	724½	Toro F7	Mdn	58-14	TightSpot,Carrie'sGlory,HwiinPss	7

17Dec89—Broke slowly

Speed Index: Last Race: (—) 3-Race Avg.: (—) 12-Race Avg.: (—) Overall Avg.: -16.0
Oct 31 Hol 1 ft 1:411 H Oct 25 Hol 6f ft 1:134 H Oct 19 Hol 5f ft 1:014 H Oct 13 Hol 4f ft :492 H

22 Feb- Trainer Seguin knows what he is doing even if the public misses out. At that low price tag of M32000, the young colt coasts home by five lengths. Winning tickets pay $28.00.

East Coast. West Coast. It makes no difference! Our maiden pattern appears regularly on every race program.

EXAMPLE: TOP BRASS GIRL

As our pattern demands, our filly was tried and found wanting at Arlington Park.

Top Brass Girl
GARCIA J A — $32,000 — 114
Own.—CatalanoCatino&DoubleDownSt

Ch. f. 4, by Barachois—Admiral's Affair, by Admiral's Voyage
Br.—Appleton A I (Fla)
Tr.—Catalano Wayne M
Lifetime 19 2 5 3 $32,462
1991 2 0 0 0
1990 17 2 5 3 $32,462
Turf 8 1 2 1 $13,486

10Feb91- 5SA	fm *6½f	ⓣ:214	:441	1:141		ⒻAlw 36000	9	1	3nk	31	108¾	1012	Velasquez J	LBb	116	43.20	76-12	Nrdcn-Ir114¾CpprWn-NZ1151¾FrchLc-NZ1151	5-wide stretch	11
18Jan91- 5SA	fm *6½f	ⓣ:214	:441	1:141		ⒻAlw 38000	2	6	41¾	3½	62¾	84½	Velasquez J	LBb	116	66.10	83-12	Sh'sAV.P.116nkWkBtty116½FrnchLc-NZ115nk	Drifted out 5/16	10
30Dec90- 5SA	fm 1⅛	ⓣ:463	1:11	1:473	3↑	ⒻAlw 42000	3	1	13	1hd	84¾	1011¾	Delahoussaye E	LBb	116	27.80	75-13	HghlndTd1122DHPndorg-Fr114DHMySongFrY116hd	Faltered	11
30Nov90- 9Haw	fst 170	:473	1:132	1:462	3↑	ⒻAlw 13500	11	2	1½	11½	11½	11½	Guidry M	b	113	2.40	64-37	Top Brass Girl1131½ Talculus1113½ Satin Purse112¾	Driving	12
12Nov90- 6Haw	fm 1	ⓣ:471	1:132	1:394	3↑	ⒻAlw 17100	3	3	42½	42	74½	42	Guidry M	b	113	3.90	67-31	SpendNickel1132MissTerr118hdMndSmith113no	Lacked room	9
5Nov90- 6Haw	sly 170	:463	1:131	1:453		ⒻAlw 19665	5	6	68¼	76¾	32	36¼	Guidry M	b	114	8.20	62-32	PositivAngl1175CocktilsnSpn1211½TopBrssGrl114hd	Late rally	8
5Nov90-Originally scheduled on turf																				
7Oct90- 7AP	sly 1⅛	:492	1:154	1:554	3↑	ⒻAlw 16000	2	1	14	1½	522	531	Fires E	b	112	2.70	32-39	DebbDoll11212½SuretoPlese1163½MndSmith1162	Nothing left	6
24Sep90- 6AP	fm *1	ⓣ:474	1:121	1:372		ⒻClm c-25000	9	5	41½	31	2hd	2no	Romero R P	b	118	*3.30	— —	StllWorthWhl116noTopBrssGrl1185Dnn'sShs118½	Just missed	10
26Aug90- 3AP	gd *1 1/16	ⓣ:483	1:15	1:484	3↑	ⒻMd 40000	4	5	45	43½	1hd	13½	Sellers S J	b	115	3.20	— —	Top Brass Girl1153½ Tanjee Miss118½ Marbesa1154½	Handily	9
4Aug90- 6AP	yl *1⅛	ⓣ:492	1:143	1:542	3↑	ⒻMd Sp Wt	6	3	21½	21½	3½	310½	Sellers S J	b	115	4.10	— —	PalaceChill1158½TanjeeMiss1222TopBrssGirl1153	Lacked rally	10

Speed Index: Last Race: +1.0 3-Race Avg.: -11.3 3-Race Avg.: -11.3 Overall Avg.: -9.2
LATEST WORKOUTS Jan 27 SA 4f fst :471 H Jan 10 SA 4f gd :473 H

26 Aug- Perhaps the public sees only the third place finish and ignores the 10 1/2 length losing margin. Whatever the reason, the horse breaks from the gate at odds of 3.20 in her first claiming race. She wins by a few lengths and pays $8.40.

EXAMPLE: MAKE ENDS MEET

Trainer Tom Greene was in a hurry with this filly.

Make Ends Meet — Ch. f. 3(Apr), by Magesterial—Processionate, by Candy Spots
VELASQUEZ J — $25,000 — Br.—Penn F Jr (Ky) — 115 — Lifetime 9 1 1 1 $15,660 — 1991 4 0 0 1 $2,700 — 1990 5 1 1 0 $12,960
Own.—Elite Sales Inc — Tr.—Greene Thomas

14Mar91- 5SA	my	6f	:22	:453	1:112	ⒻClm 25000	9	9	1110	1015	713	714¼	Velasquez J	Bb	115	158.20	65-19	SpottdProspctor1154½Minnu1152½Quck'sSstr1152½	Wide early	11
28Feb91- 9SA	sly	6½f	:22	:454	1:182	ⒻClm 32000	1	6	68	67½	610	612¾	Velasquez J	Bb	115	43.90	65-20	Spring Ballerina1154½FightingMelissa114½Minnu1153½	Outrun	9
12Jan91- 4Lrl	gd	6½f	:223	:463	1:191	ⒻClm 25000	1	4	55½	45½	46½	49½	Miller D A Jr	b	114	3.40	72-23	Bold Juana1194½ Lady Ardis1142½ CarninetyNine1122½	Evenly	8
1Jan91- 9Lrl	fst	6f	:23	:473	1:132	ⒻClm 25000	2	3	52¾	44	45	39	Miller D A Jr	b	115	4.80	69-23	BttrsctchBby114hdTnGrsshppr1149MkEndsMt115hd	No threat	8
21Dec90- 8Lrl	sly	6½f	:224	:47	1:204	ⒻClm 25000	1	4	41½	42½	23	22½	Stacy A T	b	114	5.10	73-22	ProbblyGon1172½MkEndsMt1141ButtrscotchBby1145½	Rallied	9
8Dec90- 9Lrl	fst	6f	:223	:464	1:134	ⒻClm 25000	2	3	64½	68	57	53½	Miller D A Jr	b	115	*2.90	72-16	Rchel'sTurn1141½Dnielle'sDrling1091½ErlyMessg114¾	Checked	10
11Nov90- 9Lrl	fst	6½f	:221	:46	1:191	ⒻAlw 17000	4	5	65	66½	65	76½	Miller D A Jr	b	115	11.60	76-14	Aca Joy1142¾ All Told1141½ Miss Champagne114½	Bumped	8
9Oct90- 7Lrl	fst	6f	:23	:472	1:131	ⒻMd 50000	5	2	1½	1hd	12	1¾	Miller D A Jr	b	119	4.20	79-17	MakeEndsMeet119¾GoldRusher1191PrincessKtie119¾	Driving	9
2Oct90- 6Lrl	fst	6f	:222	:47	1:123	ⒻMd Sp Wt	1	6	41½	32½	24	48	Miller D A Jr	b	119	7.30	74-15	HrComsSusi1197SocilLunch119¾MissChmpgn119nk	Weakened	9

Speed Index: Last Race: (—) 3-Race Avg.: (—) 12-Race Avg.: (—) Overall Avg.: -9.5
LATEST WORKOUTS Feb 16 Hol 5f fst 1:034 H ●Jan 30 Lrl 4f fst :483 H

2 Oct- The filly makes her racing debut in a non-claimer, finishing in fourth place.

9 Oct- *Seven days later* the animal is running for a price tag of $50,000. *Two* reasons for us to bet on the horse. As we anticipate, she wins the race. To our pleasant surprise she pays $10.40.

EXAMPLE: SARATERN

This young lady has two tries in the non-claiming ranks before going for a price tag.

Saratern — Ch. f. 3(May), by Arctic Tern—Sarawitha, by Sir Ivor
Br.—Hudson E J (Ky) — 1990 6 1 0 0 $8,760
Own.—Dehechavarria L — 115 — Tr.—Shahinian Steven A — $14,000 — 1989 2 M 0 0 $475
Lifetime 8 1 0 0 $9,235 — Turf 6 0 0 0 $475

19Sep90-9Bel	6f :223 :463 1:123ft	8½	118	89½	66½	33½	11½	MrqzCHJr 4	ⒻM35000	76-18	Srtrn,Prodpromsdldy,InWnMmnt	9
30Jly90-5Bel	1⅛ Ⓣ:49 1:3642:02 fm	20	116	53½	613	715	714½	Rogers K L 7	ⒻMdn	75-06	CzzyB.,Mrs.Fletcher,LittleSciolo	11
18Jly90-5Bel	1 1/16 :471 1:124 1:452ft	—	116	42½	44½	48	48½	Rogers K L 3	ⒻMdn	66-22	NorthrnDm,WntrCrwn,HrrhAtLst	7

18Jly90—Raced for Purse money only

9Jly90♦3Compiegne(Fra)	a1⅛ 1:504gd	29	115	Ⓣ	95½	JnprrN	PrixParisTurfHcp	Le Scoot, Jazzinski, Lyphesan	16
21Jun90♦6Longchamp(Fra)	a1 1/16 1:503yl	59	122	Ⓣ	715	BnstO	ⒻPrix Fould (Mdn)	ReinedesIrles,PlesntRiver,LdyofPrsi	9
16Feb90♦3Cagnes(Fra)	a1⅛ 2:044gd	—	118	Ⓣ	19	ChilleL	Prix de Castellane	RubisChsn,BllissimMusc,DrKldoun	20
1Dec89♦4StCloud(Fra)	a1 1:492yl	21	123	Ⓣ	812	BdelA	ⒻPrix Clyde(Mdn)	Mabville, Anitraline, Caprarola	10
12Nov89♦6Rouen(Fra)	a1⅛ : yl	—	119	Ⓣ	46½	CllL	ⒻPrixLiberteDimnch(Mdn	TellTaleHeart, Kalapa,ChicaBonita	14

12Nov89—No time taken
Speed Index: Last Race: -12.0 1-Race Avg.: -12.0 1-Race Avg.: -12.0 Overall Avg.: -12.3
Sep 6 Aqu 5f ft 1:042 B Aug 31 Aqu 3f ft :40 B

19 Sep- Saratern makes her claiming race debut a winning one. She pays $19.00.

To avoid overlooking wagers in this category, the bettor should quickly double-check each maiden claiming race on the program. Any horse dropping into maiden claiming ranks for the very first time (usually from a maiden special weight) deserves special attention. It could be a powerful key horse candidate.

Remember, this situation does not include first-time starters that begin their racing careers as claimers. All of the horse's prior races had to have been non-claiming contests.

Here is a full-race example. This was a $10,000 Maiden Claiming race for 3- and 4-year-old fillies at Hialeah on November 29.

5 HIALEAH START 6 FURLONGS HIALEAH FINISH

6 FURLONGS. (1.08) MAIDEN CLAIMING. Purse $5,500. Fillies. 3- and 4-year-olds. Weights, 3-year-olds, 120 lbs. Older, 122 lbs. Claiming price $10,000; for each $500 to $9,000, allowed 2 lbs.

Chelsea's Bid — B. f. 3(Mar), by Spectacular Bid—Fully Funded, by Red Wing Bold
$9,000 Br.—Serafino P & R (Fla) Tr.—Azpurua Lee J Jr — 116
Own.—Belly B
Lifetime 14 0 2 2 $6,616 | 1991 12 M 2 2 $6,616 | 1990 2 M 0 0 | Turf 1 0 0 0 $170

x 9Nov91- 1Crc fst 6½f :223 :472 1:212 3↑ⒻMd 10000 10 1 33½ 31½ 51½ 53¼ St Leon G 121 2.60 74-12 LydinPrincss121¾Lurn'sLov121hdWildBlossom1212½ No threat 10
3Nov91- 1Crc fst 6½f :223 :47 1:204 3↑ⒻMd 10500 3 5 21 2½ 21½ 21 St Leon G 117 *1.20 80-14 PumpkinStrshin1171Chls'sBid1172LydinPrincss117no 2nd best 6
24Oct91- 5Crc fst 7f :231 :47 1:28 3↑ⒻMd 14000 8 2 11½ 11 21½ 34¼ Hernandez R C7 113 *.90 71-14 Mood'sIde1164PssOnBlessings109nkChls'sBid113hd Weakened 8
10Oct91- 4Crc gd 7f :231 :474 1:274 3↑ⒻMd 14000 6 4 1hd 11 1½ 23 Verenzuela J L 116 2.00 73-19 OurCrdiologist1203Chelse'sBid1162SweetGreek115nk 2nd best 8
25Sep91- 6Crc gd 1⅛ Ⓣ 1:52 3↑ⒻMd Sp Wt 7 3 33 11 21½ 56 Verenzuela J L 118 14.60 52-38 CndyKiss1181½SeeSingulr118¾Allie'sSuperPet118hd Weakened 10
11Sep91- 7Crc fst 170 :482 1:14 1:471 3↑ⒻMd Sp Wt 4 1 11 1hd 2½ 35¼ Verenzuela J L 118 23.40 71-15 Number'sOnly1181Nomd'Amour1184¼Chls'sBid1182 Weakened 7
28Aug91- 5Crc sly 1⅛ :483 1:151 1:573 3↑ⒻMd Sp Wt 1 1 1hd 21 48 410 Verenzuela J L 117 20.20 60-22 Cozie Keri117nk Nom d'Amour117¾ Astute1129 Faltered 6
28Aug91-Originally scheduled on turf
17Aug91- 4Crc fst 170 :47 1:143 1:47 3↑ⒻMd Sp Wt 4 3 44½ 58 714 715½ Verenzuela J L 117 40.80 62-22 Little Pigeon117hd Lauren'sLove1172Nomd'Amour1172 Faded 9
3Aug91- 3Crc fst 7f :223 :453 1:271 3↑ⒻMd Sp Wt 6 1 31½ 58 614 79¾ Matules L S5 113 29.40 69-15 MissMaud1184¾Jaguarette1181Luren'sLove1181½ Early speed 8
24Feb91- 6Tam fst 7f :23 :464 1:253 ⒻMd Sp Wt 10 2 66¾ 76¾ 516 616¾ Rivera J A II 118 12.80 70-14 StrkMGntly11810½BoldPstol1181½ChldActr1111½ No response 10

Speed Index: Last Race: -14.0 3-Race Avg.: -11.6 6-Race Avg.: -12.5 Overall Avg.: -13.3

Delightful Book — Dk. b. or br. f. 4, by Marl's Book—Delldust, by Dust Commander
$10,000 Br.—Murty Farm (Ky) Tr.—Van Sant Edgar I — 122
Own.—Van Sant E L
Lifetime 1 0 0 0 | 1991 1 M 0 0 | 1990 0 M 0 0

29Sep91- 4Del fst 6f :22 :453 1:122 3↑Md Sp Wt 3 6 67¾ 610 611 611¾ Lizarzaburu P M 119 6.80 73-14 TuffTurf1221½SibilntSounds1224SouthrnGunnr1223 No factor 8

Speed Index: Last Race: -13.0 1-Race Avg.: -13.0 1-Race Avg.: -13.0 Overall Avg.: -13.0

LATEST WORKOUTS Nov 23 OTC tr.t 4f fst :524 B Nov 1 Del 6f fst 1:18 B ●Oct 21 Del 4f fst :501 B

My Kim — Ro. f. 3(Mar), by Interdicto—Princess Kim, by Noble Michael
$10,000 Br.—Loring B Dean (Fla) Tr.—Loring B Dean — 120
Own.—Loring B Dean
Lifetime 8 0 0 0 $340 | 1991 4 M 0 0 $340 | 1990 4 M 0 0

19Nov91- 1Hia fst 6f :224 :471 1:142 3↑ⒻMd 9000 2 3 31½ 21 44½ 44 Lombardo A A b 116 76.20 66-19 EccoLa1123MoreSweaters109¾CongressGranj116nk Weakened 11
x 11Nov91- 7Hia fst 6f :222 :454 1:12 ⒻClm 9000 4 9 97¼ 1213 1222 1222¾ Sebreth Z O5 b 107 76.80 59-16 JerryChesnut1121HopeforMyLdy112hdNeecyBby1141½ Outrun 12
21Feb91- 2TP gd 6f :221 :46 1:121 ⒻClm 7500 7 3 78 710 719 722¾ Knott R L LBb 113 37.30 61-13 Strwbrry'sBst1191½LxingtonWitch1162½SssySunn1168 Outrun 7
27Jan91- 1TP fst 6f :221 :46 1:13 ⒻMd 7500 8 6 41 63¼ 67¾ 88¼ Tsuchiya K LBb 122 16.50 72-12 Lytonmbby122noCrolnNl1223½JunkmlMss122¾ Broke awkward 12
20Dec90- 1TP fst 6f :223 :463 1:141 ⒻMd 17500 9 6 74½ 86¼ 914 917½ Troilo W D Bb 122 23.50 56-13 DanzigsFshion122¾SprklingCounters1224MissChoy1221½ Tired 12
20Nov90- 3CD fst 6f :221 :47 1:131 ⒻMd 25000 1 2 62¾ 65 89 912¾ Sanders J L5 B 111 65.00 67-15 Clrk'sGp1186EtchdnCncrt1162MyWnngWys116½ Brief speed 11
21May90- 4AP gd 5f :234 :464 :594 Md Sp Wt 5 2 710 715 727 729¾ Allen R D Jr 115 46.00 61-11 Ever a Lady115noGreeneWithanE118¾BlackJim1187 No factor 7
11Apr90- 3Kee gd 4½f :223 :464 :532 ⒻMd Sp Wt 5 11 1112 1115 1118½ Lopez R D 117 48.80 75-09 HilSecreto117nkFlshingEyes1171FlyRod117½ Ducked out start 11

Speed Index: Last Race: -15.0 3-Race Avg.: -22.0 8-Race Avg.: -21.8 Overall Avg.: -21.8

General Spotlight — Dk. b. or br. f. 4, by Spot Light—General Quality, by Prince Roger
$9,000 Br.—Joseph N. Lococo (Ky) Tr.—Lococo David B — 108 10
Own.—Lococo J N
Lifetime 1 0 0 0 $55 | 1991 1 M 0 0 $55 | 1989 0 M 0 0

9Nov91- 1Crc fst 6½f :223 :472 1:212 3↑ⒻMd 10000 1 10 1029 1033 1024 1025¼ Russell W B10 L 112 28.60 52-12 LdnPrncss121¾Lrn'sLv121hdWldBlssm1212½ Poor st threw hd 10

Speed Index: Last Race: -36.0 1-Race Avg.: -36.0 1-Race Avg.: -36.0 Overall Avg.: -36.0

LATEST WORKOUTS Nov 1 Crc 3f fst :392 Bg Oct 27 Crc 3f sly :393 Bg Oct 21 Crc 5f sly 1:062 B Oct 15 Crc 4f fst :53 B

Wild Blossom

Ch. f. 3(Apr), by L'Emigrant—Stem, by Damascus
$9,000 Br.—Bradley M. Shannon & H & R Stable (Ky)
Tr.—Bracken James E
116
Lifetime 9 0 1 2 $2,510
1991 9 M 1 2 $2,510
1990 0 M 0 0
Turf 1 0 0 1 $360
Own.—H & R Stable

9Nov91- 1Crc fst 6½f :223 :472 1:212 3+ⒻMd 10000 2 6 67½ 65½ 61½ 3½ Ramos W S b 121 5.20 77-12 LydinPrincess121½Luren'sLov121hdWildBlossom1212½ Rallied 10
24Oct91- 5Crc fst 7f :231 :47 1:28 3+ⒻMd 12000 7 3 31½ 32½ 46 66½ Castillo H Jr b 116 3.60 69-14 Mood'sIdea1164PassOnBlessings109nkChelse'sBid113hd Faded 8
10Oct91- 4Crc gd 7f :231 :474 1:274 3+ⒻMd 16000 5 3 31 21 69 59¾ St Leon G b 120 *1.60 66-19 OurCrdiologist1203Chelse'sBid1162SweetGreek115nk Faltered 8
27Sep91- 7Crc fst 6f :222 :471 1:142 3+ⒻMd 18000 6 7 64 53 44 21½ St Leon G b 115 8.50 76-21 AnotherGrt1191½WildBlossom115½OurCrdiologist119¾ Rallied 8
25Jly91- 5RD fm 5f Ⓣ:22 :453 :574 3+ⒻClm 10000 8 6 55½ 46 3nk 3nk Sexton R D B 113 30.70 93-05 Alli Honors117hd Alkene111hd Wild Blossom113no Stride late 10
25Jun91- 4CD fst 1$\frac{1}{16}$:48 1:142 1:482 3+ⒻMd 17500 9 3 55½ 66½ 711 812½ Parsley J R7 B 102 81.40 60-21 EustaciaVye1092MemoriesofDelta1172BionicBeuty109¾ Tired 12
15Jun91- 1CD fst 6f :214 :464 1:134 3+ⒻMd 12500 7 7 910111010 13 912¾ Bruin J E B 114 54.90 65-14 Big Nose Kate1181 Battle Hat1091½ Ms.TeresaV.112hd Outrun 11
31May91- 3CD fst 6f :221 :472 1:142 3+ⒻMd 12500 10 8 94 75½ 76 810 Parsley J R7 B 104 44.00 65-10 Charming Me1122 Battle Hat111hd Major Maui108¾ No factor 12
20Apr91- 4Kee fst 7f :224 :46 1:234 ⒻMd Sp Wt 4 9 94½109½10201032¾ Sunseri J J B 119 31.20 58-11 Curtains Drawn1198 RoyalProtocol1192K.OneDia119hd Outrun 10

Speed Index: Last Race: −11.0 3–Race Avg.: −14.3 7–Race Avg.: −17.5 Overall Avg.: −16.0
LATEST WORKOUTS Nov 23 Crc tr.t 4f fst :52 B Oct 17 Crc 4f fst :52 B Oct 4 Crc 5f sly 1:02 H

More Sweaters

Dk. b. or br. f. 3(Apr), by Treatise—Suzanne Jay, by Noble Jay
$9,000 Br.—Radice Steve S (Fla)
Tr.—Cadahia Cayetano B
116
Lifetime 14 0 2 1 $3,800
1991 13 M 2 1 $3,745
1990 1 M 0 0 $55
Own.—Cadahia & Gonzalez

19Nov91- 1Hia fst 6f :224 :471 1:142 3+ⒻMd 9000 3 8 119½106½ 54¾ 23 Sebreth Z O7 b 109 7.40 67-19 Ecco La1123 More Sweaters109¾CongressGranja116nk Rallied 11
9Nov91- 1Crc fst 6½f :223 :472 1:212 3+ⒻMd 10000 7 7 89 78 72¾ 43 Sebreth Z O7 b 114 5.70e 75-12 LydinPrincss121½Lurn'sLov121hdWildBlossom1212½ Late rally 10
29Oct91- 3Crc fst 6½f :224 :47 1:21 3+ⒻMd 10000 2 6 65½ 57½ 33½ 23½ Sebreth Z O7 b 113 6.30 76-13 Office Lady1203¾ More Sweaters1134Posada'sGirl1201 Rallied 7
23Oct91- 4Crc gd 6f :222 :464 1:142 3+ⒻMd 10000 8 12 128½ 99¾ 67 65¾ Sebreth Z O7 b 113 21.60 72-17 Robrt'sRisk1201CocktilHour115¾BucksSilvrBll1204 No threat 12
18Oct91- 1Crc fst 7f :224 :472 1:282 3+ⒻMd 10000 5 3 79 67½ 55 34 Sebreth Z O7 b 113 147.60 69-18 ArbyVixen1154BonnieBlueBird113hdMoreSwtrs1132 Late rally 9
20Sep91- 1Crc fst 6f :223 :464 1:132 3+ⒻMd 10500 1 8 31½ 57¾ 812 813½ Bultron J D b 115 60.60 69-18 MariaDancer1152¾Roberta'sRisk1152½Sitzmrk'sToy1143 Faded 11
16Aug91- 5Crc fst 170 :494 1:154 1:473 3+ⒻMd 10500 2 3 33½ 76½ 57½ 59¾ Bultron J D b 113 57.10 65-15 Chelsea'sGold1133¾Lover'sQuest117nk Wo... Ide1084 Faltered 7
31Jly91- 1Crc gd 7f :224 :464 1:281 3+ⒻMd 10000 6 7 83 108½1218 1215¾ Bultron J D b 117 61.50 58-15 BeProudst117¾Chls'sGold1172BlckRob117nk Showed nothing 12
25Jly91- 6Crc fst 170 :491 1:154 1:472 3+ⒻMd 12500 1 2 1hd 45½ 713 913½ Reyes A R7 b 108 173.20 62-20 FrNrthSng1152¾Lvr'sQst1122¾PssOnBlssngs1101¾ Early speed 12
5Apr91- 3GP fst 1$\frac{1}{16}$:484 1:14 1:464 ⒻMd 20000 2 10 1013 1022 1030 939 Halimi J b 116 152.30 40-15 WhyBeNormal1206BabyScarface1203Collbortion1204 No rally 11

Speed Index: Last Race: −14.0 3–Race Avg.: −12.6 7–Race Avg.: −14.5 Overall Avg.: −18.5

Drive Time Queen

Ch. f. 3(Apr), by Interdicto—Royal Worden, by Worden
$9,000 Br.—Revels Paul M (Fla)
Tr.—Guerrera Robert J
116
Lifetime 1 0 0 0 $55
1991 1 M 0 0 $55
1990 0 M 0 0
Own.—Neill K

3Oct91- 1Crc fst 6f :232 :474 1:143 3+ⒻMd 10000 10 8 41 915 1015 1017 Castillo H Jr 120 42.00 60-23 NughtyPlsur1202¾CocktilHour1152LydinPrncss1201 Gave way 12

Speed Index: Last Race: −17.0 1–Race Avg.: −17.0 1–Race Avg.: −17.0 Overall Avg.: −17.0

Astute

Dk. b. or br. f. 3(Mar), by Triomphe—Gallant Trial, by Gallant Man
$10,000 Br.—Erwin E & Janet (Fla)
Tr.—Monteiro Arthur
115[5]
Lifetime 13 0 1 1 $6,600
1991 13 M 1 1 $6,600
1990 0 M 0 0
Turf 2 0 0 0 $310
Own.—Bishop Beth & Mankowitz

15Nov91- 8Hia fst 1⅛ :472 1:121 1:522 3+ⒻAlw 14000 2 10 1018 712 69½ 512½ Santos C M7 107 24.00 62-24 NickleBlus1174LittlPigon1195½Expnsivnss1142 Mild bid inside 10
15Nov91-Originally scheduled on turf
22Oct91- 6Crc fst 1⅛ :493 1:16 1:573 3+ⒻMd Sp Wt 7 8 814 77½ 49½ 27 Ramos W S 119 3.70 63-21 Real Elaine1197 Astute1191½ See Singular1191½ Rallied 8
22Oct91-Originally scheduled on turf
25Sep91- 6Crc gd *1⅛ Ⓣ 1:52 3+ⒻMd Sp Wt 5 10 1014 97½ 713 710½ Ramos W S 118 16.80 47-38 CndyKiss1181½SeeSingulr118¾Allie'sSuprPt118hd Never close 10
11Sep91- 7Crc fst 170 :482 1:14 1:471 3+ⒻMd Sp Wt 1 7 711 710 68 69¾ Matutes L S5 113 11.90 67-15 Nmbr'sOnly1181Nomd'Amor1184¾Chls'sBd1182 Showed little 7
28Aug91- 5Crc sly 1⅛ :483 1:151 1:573 3+ⒻMd Sp Wt 6 6 616 615 34 31 Matutes L S5 112 26.40 69-22 Cozie Keri117nk Nom d'Amour117¾ Astute1129 Gamely 6
28Aug91-Originally scheduled on turf
24Aug91- 1Crc fst 7f :231 :471 1:27 3+ⒻMd 25000 10 1 5¾ 66½ 611 513½ Daigle E T7 111 20.70 66-15 Dancin'Sunset1182Number'sOnly1111CaitlinAdir1189 Faltered 10
25Jly91- 6Crc fst 170 :491 1:154 1:472 3+ⒻMd 12500 10 3 51½ 35¾ 36½ 46½ Daigle E T7 109 91.20 69-20 FrNrthSng1152¾Lvr'sQst1122¾PssOnBlssngs1101¾ No late bid 12
19Jun91- 5Crc gd *1⅛ Ⓣ 1:522 3+ⒻMd Sp Wt 2 3 45 54 713 512 Lester R N 114 47.50 44-44 Tra La Dot1161 HostileFleet1141½Allie'sSuperPet114½ Outrun 9
30May91- 1Crc fst 1 :492 1:163 1:451 3+ⒻMd 10000 8 10 1020 1022 821 614½ Sweeney K H b 113 24.80 52-25 Hexed106hd Trebea113nk ⒹChelsea's Gold113nk Outrun 10

Speed Index: Last Race: −19.0 1–Race Avg.: −19.0 1–Race Avg.: −19.0 Overall Avg.: −15.2
LATEST WORKOUTS Nov 7 Hia 5f fst 1:014 H

Congress Granja

Dk. b. or br. f. 3(May), by Big Burn—Congress Flier, by Congress
$9,000 Br.—George Julian & Elsie Julian (Fla)
Tr.—Julian George
116
Lifetime 6 0 0 1 $845
1991 6 M 0 1 $845
1990 0 M 0 0
Own.—Tobia & Julian

19Nov91- 1Hia fst 6f :224 :471 1:142 3+ⒻMd 9000 6 11 85½ 85½ 34 33¾ Gaffglione R 116 59.60 66-19 EccoLa1123MoreSweaters109¾CongressGranj116nk Late rally 11
29Aug91- 1Crc fst 7f :231 :472 1:28 3+ⒻMd 10000 2 10 96½ 99¾ 1014 1018¾ Kornmeyer L J 118 66.30 56-17 Nationalist1182 NaughtyPleasure113¾Mood'sIdea1183 Outrun 10
21Aug91- 1Crc fst 6f :222 :471 1:13 3+ⒻMd 10000 11 1 1011 98¾ 811 714¾ Matutes L S5 113 46.60 70-10 ChopChop1181½FineFortunte1183Robert'sRisk118½ No factor 11
10Aug91- 1Crc fst 6½f :23 :471 1:21 3+ⒻMd 10500 3 9 911 99¾ 66¾ 66 Martin C W 114 8.80 74-11 SmokeDnc1182Impostrss1221TooMuchNois1071 Showed little 9
4Aug91- 1Crc fst 6f :221 :462 1:133 3+ⒻMd 10000 5 9 911 918 713 59½ Martin C W 118 10.30e 73-16 JillJaime1182¾FineFortunte118hdNtionlist1186 Sluggish early 9
11Jan91- 4Crc fst 7f :223 :46 1:252 ⒻMd 30000 10 4 55½ 1025 1033 1038¾ Lester R N b 116 73.70 49-17 Secret Quest1208 WhyBeNormal116½Baldee120nk Early factor 10

Speed Index: Last Race: −15.0 3–Race Avg.: −18.0 6–Race Avg.: −19.0 Overall Avg.: −19.0
LATEST WORKOUTS Nov 23 Hia 4f fst :481 H Nov 9 Crc 4f fst :483 H Nov 1 Crc 6f fst 1:16 B Oct 27 Crc 5f sly 1:022 H

Giveasmile

B. f. 3(May), by Smile—Dansecompany, by Crimson Satan
$10,000 Br.—Polk Harold H (Fla)
Tr.—Standridge Steve W
120
Lifetime 4 0 0 0 $400
1990 4 M 0 0 $400
Own.—Polk H H

2Dec90- 4Crc fst 6f :22 :453 1:114 ⒻMd Sp Wt 9 4 55 46½ 411 511½ ArguelloFAJr10 b 110 36.60 79-10 RebeccBlue1207¾MissRsolut120¾AurorWinnrs1203 Wide tired 9
20Oct90- 4Crc fst 6f :221 :463 1:133 ⒻMd Sp Wt 2 9 98½ 89½ 77½ 610½ Felix J E 118 53.40 72-14 Cup ofCheers118hdFullofstuff1184½RebeccaBlue1183½ Outrun 10
29Sep90- 6Crc fst 6f :221 :463 1:141 ⒻMd Sp Wt 2 9 105½ 87½ 69 66½ Felix J E5 112 29.20 72-21 NationalSpirit1171½CupofCheers1171½MenMissy1171½ Outrun 10
12Aug90- 2Crc fst 6f :222 :463 1:13 ⒻMd Sp Wt 1 7 33 55 79½ 816 Felix J E5 111 13.80 69-14 Solly'sFolly1162½SunnyHwi1164FrNorthPort1161½ Early speed 10

Speed Index: Last Race: −11.0 3–Race Avg.: −10.6 4–Race Avg.: −12.2 Overall Avg.: −12.2
LATEST WORKOUTS Nov 16 Hia 3f fst :38 Bg Nov 10 Hia 5f fst 1:03 B Oct 29 Crc 5f fst 1:04 Bg Oct 17 Crc 3f fst :39 B

After entering the past performance data from the *DRF* into the *Winning at the Track* computer program, four contenders emerged from the printouts as indicated:

- GIVEASMILE (7 to 1 at Post Time)
- WILD BLOSSOM (4 to 1)
- CHELSEA'S BID (2 to 1)
- CONGRESS GRANJA (12 to 1)

This was the P/M Table from the *Winning at the Track* program:

Hialeah Park   FL   November 29
5th   Race   6 f

PP	Horse	Notes	Odds	Ability Factor	Pure Speed	Early Speed	Late Speed	MF	P/M RATING
1	ChelseasBid	85/81	6:1	438	86	285	750	1035	3018
2	DelightfulBook	82/75	10:1	429	75	264	719	983	2835
3	MyKim	87/73	20:1	399	79	285	728	1013	2899
4	GenlSpotlite	50/61	30:1	372	61	196	697	893	2610
5	WildBlossom	82/83	6:1	434	85	279	756	1035	3022
6	MoreSweaters	78/74	4:1	429	82	268	744	1012	2957
7	DriveTimeQueen	66/69	30:1	429	69	260	721	981	2796
8	Astute	79/78	8:1	439	78	230	768	998	2968
9	CongrssGranja	79/73	15:1	422	82	264	750	1014	2970
10	Giveasmile	85/88	15:1	441	88	285	752	1037	3038

This was the Display screen from the *Pace Analyst* module:

Race: 5   HIA   6 f

			Best Race			Second Best			
PP	Likely Pacesetters		Pole Speed	Last Qtr.	Late Speed	Pole Speed	Last Qtr.	Late Speed	P/M Rating
3	MyKim	87/73	87	172	728	83	171	723	2899
10	Giveasmile	85/88	85	182	752	80	180	745	3038
PP	Best-4 P/M Horses								
10	Giveasmile	85/88	85	182	752	80	180	745	3038
5	WildBlossom	82/83	81	183	756	77	185	744	3022
1	ChelseasBid	85/81	84	181	750	81	180	745	3018
9	CongrssGranja	79/73	70	191	750	75	185	739	2970
PP	Selection - Display								
2	DelightfulBook	82/75	82	172	719	0	0	0	2835
8	Astute	79/78	49	211	768	56	200	750	2968

After further analysis, Giveasmile was established as the "key horse" based on the following observations:

1. Clearly, there would be "no contest" between the two pacesetters, Giveasmile and My Kim. Once Giveasmile takes control of the pace as expected, the rest of the field would have to work hard to catch her.

2. Giveasmile's last race rating was an adjusted FIVE lengths better than the next-best figure available (an 88 Pure Speed vs. 83 for Wild Blossom). This is a substantial 5-length margin.

3. Two horses in this race (Giveasmile and Delightful Book) are RUNNING FOR A CLAIMING TAG FOR THE FIRST TIME EVER. We now have one more indication that Giveasmile should be our key horse selection.

4. One major question remains -- is this horse ready to run following the layoff? YES! Trainers are frequently successful when they bring a green baby back after performing badly as a 2-year-old ... older and wiser, as they say.

To repeat again, regarding point #3, whenever a horse is "somewhat competitive" in MSW company, a sudden drop into the claiming ranks for the first time is often enough to make it a threat in the race. Also, as a general rule, the payoff for this potential contender is usually directly related to how close it came to victory in its last race.

Finally, note that the 4-year-old Delightful Book, which failed to come up in the computer numbers, ran a respectable race as the results below indicate. By the same token, notice that My Kim had her chance earlier and failed, as did Wild Blossom in May. Of course, each lost by about 30 lengths without excuses which hardly qualifies as "somewhat competitive." Chelsea's Bid had better results when she had her chance (assuming this was the first time) last October after testing the grass.

The results of this contest were as follows:

Giveasmile led by three lengths over Drive Time Queen and My Kim at the second call point. She went on to win by 10 lengths. Congress Granja closed well in the stretch to finish a nose ahead of Delightful Book. Chelsea's Bid outlasted Wild Blossom for fourth.

FIFTH — $5500; 6 fur.; fil 3&4; clg $10,000-9000; winner $3300; time 22 2/5, 46 2/5, 1:11 3/5; winner b d 1988 by Smile—Dansecompany; trainer, Steve W. Standridge; owner, H.H. Polk.

PP-Horse, Weight	St	½	Str	Fin	Eqv
10-Giveasmile, 120	1	1-3	1-6	1-10	7.60
9-Cngrss Grnga, 116	6	7-1½	6½	2-no	10.00
2-Delightfl Bk, 122	7	4-1½	3½	3-1½	3.90
1-Chelsea's Bd, 116	10	9½	5½	4½	2.00
5-Wild Blssm, 116	5	6-1	7-1	5-2	3.90
6-More Swtrs, 116	8	8-2	8-1	6-nk	9.60
8-W-Astute, 120	2	5-hd	4-hd	7-nk	7.90
7-Drv Tm Queen, 116	3	2½	2-1	8¾	113.4
3-My Kim, 120	4	3-3½	9-2½	9-4½	16.30
4-Genl Sptlght, 108	9	10	10	10	116.3
11-Giveasmile (Cstlo)			17.20	8.20	5.40
10-Congress Granja (Gaffgine)				9.00	5.80
3-Delightful Book (Thibeau)					5.00

PERFECTA (11-10) paid $131.60
QUINELLA (10-11) paid $86.60
TRIFECTA (11-10-3) paid $2,404.20

It's easy to see why our "Maidens For Sale" key horse pattern can be a valuable tool for any handicappers who are willing to assume the higher risk/reward ratio that is typically found in maiden claiming contests.

"In Tough"

There are times to bet the young, improving horse, and there are definitely times to avoid them. There is one trainer decision that proves fatal at the betting window almost all the time. That is: A horse that has just won its maiden race and is now being moved into Allowance Company.

Horse racing is a sport known for its optimism. The owner has a runner that has a shot to win the Triple Crown if it can just stay healthy! The trainer is watching the filly improve day-by-day. If the track is dry for Saturday's race, she'll finally get the opportunity to show what she can REALLY do!

It's our observation that during the early stage of a horse's career, optimism abounds! The horse's first race was run on a sloppy track. He simply disliked the mud. In the second race, he seemed to stumble leaving the gate. Finally, he won the MSW contest by almost a length, even though there appeared to be a great deal of traffic throughout most of the race. Is he ready for this Allowance? The workouts have been good. The weather's clear. "You can bet on it," the optimists declare.

Oh, no you can't; not with any confidence! Unless this is a Rising Champion of the highest order -- and there are precious few of these -- you can usually bet against an animal moving into allowance company following its maiden victory. This is especially true if it was a maiden claiming win, even by a large margin. Sometimes a trainer is able to find a soft spot in a field of proven winners, but most can't.

EXAMPLE: ORIANE

Owner Arthur Hancock and trainer Schulhofer had to have been optimistic with this Bold Forbes filly. By going to the post in her first race with odds of less than 5 to 1, it's fair to say that the crowd thought highly of her too.

Oriane — B. f. 3(Mar), by Bold Forbes—Coulee Queen, by Bustine
Own.—Hancock Arthur B III — $45,000 — Br.—Hancock Arthur (Ky) — Tr.—Schulhofer Flint S — **114**
Lifetime 8 2 2 1 $49,640 — 1991 8 2 2 1 $49,640 — 1990 0 M 0 0

6Dec91- 6Aqu	fst	$1\frac{1}{16}$ ⊡	:48	1:13^{2}	1:46^{3}	3↑ⒻAlw 29000	4	2	3^{1}	2^{hd}	2^{hd}	1no	Antley C W	115	3.80	75-22	Oriane115^{no} Cozzinia115^{no} Tuned Way Up115$^{4\frac{1}{2}}$	Hard drive	6
25Nov91- 4Aqu	fst	1	:46^{3}	1:12	1:39	3↑ⒻAlw 29000	6	2	3^{2}	3^{2}	3$^{\frac{1}{2}}$	2$^{\frac{3}{4}}$	Antley C W	115	3.60	66-26	Maxamount115$^{\frac{3}{4}}$ Oriane115^{nk} Long Term115^{no}	Bumped 3/16	6
10Nov91- 1Aqu	fst	7f	:23^{1}	:46^{1}	1:24^{2}	3↑ⒻAlw 27000	3	6	4$^{2\frac{1}{2}}$	4^{8}	6$^{9\frac{1}{2}}$	6$^{17\frac{3}{4}}$	Santos J A	117	6.60	62-25	RunningShine115^{5}Streming115$^{\frac{1}{2}}$AbsolutelyGrt115$^{4\frac{1}{2}}$	No factor	6
17Oct91- 6Bel	sly	7f	:22^{3}	:46	1:24^{2}	3↑ⒻAlw 27000	3	2	3^{2}	3$^{1\frac{1}{2}}$	2^{3}	2$^{7\frac{1}{4}}$	Santos J A	119	19.60	75-19	Diable Rose116$^{7\frac{1}{4}}$ Oriane119^{1} All Power114$^{\frac{1}{2}}$	Held 2nd	6
7Oct91- 1Bel	fst	1	:48^{1}	1:12^{3}	1:38^{2}	3↑ⒻMd Sp Wt	7	1	1^{1}	1$^{\frac{1}{2}}$	1^{1}	1$^{\frac{3}{4}}$	Santos J A	119	2.10	78-25	Oriane119$^{\frac{3}{4}}$ Long Term119^{4} Skep119^{15}	Driving	7
25Sep91- 7Bel	sly	7f	:22^{2}	:46	1:24^{1}	3↑ⒻMd Sp Wt	5	2	4^{nk}	3^{3}	2^{3}	3^{6}	Santos J A	118	9.80	77-14	Diable Rose118^{6} Loudly Appealing118^{hd}Oriane118$^{1\frac{1}{4}}$	Willingly	8
13Sep91- 1Bel	fst	6f	:22^{1}	:44^{4}	1:09^{2}	3↑ⒻMd Sp Wt	5	5	3$^{3\frac{1}{2}}$	3$^{5\frac{1}{2}}$	5^{13}	7$^{24\frac{3}{4}}$	Santos J A	118	5.60	68-11	Absolutely Great118^{13} Diable Rose118$^{2\frac{1}{2}}$RogueGirl118^{3}	Faded	9
2Sep91- 4Bel	fst	7f	:22^{4}	:46	1:24	3↑ⒻMd Sp Wt	6	1	3$^{\frac{1}{2}}$	3$^{\frac{1}{2}}$	2$^{\frac{1}{2}}$	4^{2}	Santos J A	118	4.60	82-15	GnrllySwt118$^{\frac{3}{4}}$RoguGirl118$^{1\frac{1}{2}}$DibloRos118^{no}	Forced pace tired	7

Speed Index: Last Race: -3.0 3-Race Avg.: -2.6 3-Race Avg.: -2.6 Overall Avg.: -7.5

25 Sep- Oriane's third try occurred in the slop. At this point, even the bettors were beginning to lose the faith.

7 Oct- Entered in a mile race for the first time, everyone became a little more optimistic about her chances. She ran close to the pace in the early part of the September 25 contest, providing a sign of life. Then, finally victorious, she paid $6.20 to her patient backers.

17 Oct- Her support at the windows vanished when the rain made the track sloppy for her first race against prior winners. However, it was a respectable effort as she finished second. It was the proper level, however, as her subsequent win at Alw 29000 indicated.

EXAMPLE: ENVIED

We are fans of anything with four legs and Mr. Prospector as the daddy. After Envied's uneventful visit to New Jersey, the young lady was placed in a MSW 6f contest at Belmont.

Envied Dk. b. or br. f. 2(Apr), by Mr Prospector—Green Greek, by Green Ticket Lifetime 1991 5 1 0 1 $17,988
Own.—Garvin-Clay & Mooney Br.—Hermitage Farm Inc (Ky) 116 5 1 0 1
Tr.—Mott William I $17,988

23Nov91- 7CD	fst	6f	$:21^{2}$	$:45^{4}$	$1:11^{4}$	ⒻAlw 26960	8	5	$4^{2\frac{1}{2}}$	4^{1}	3^{1}	$4^{3\frac{1}{2}}$	Melancon L	LB	121	*2.50	85-17	Athenium$113^{\frac{1}{2}}$ Miss Candystripe$118^{1\frac{1}{4}}$ Flattery$121^{1\frac{1}{2}}$	No rally	10
19Oct91- 5Kee	fst	$6\frac{1}{2}$f	$:22^{4}$	$:46^{2}$	$1:19^{4}$	ⒻAlw 21600	6	1	$5^{1\frac{1}{4}}$	$5^{1\frac{1}{4}}$	$5^{5\frac{1}{4}}$	$5^{6\frac{3}{4}}$	Day P	B	121	*1.60	74-16	Frozen Rope$118^{\frac{3}{4}}$ Forewarn113^{no} Reply Paid118^{4}	Tired	7
26Sep91- 5Bel	sly	6f	:22	$:45^{4}$	$1:10^{3}$	ⒻMd Sp Wt	1	1	1^{1}	$1^{\frac{1}{2}}$	$1^{2\frac{1}{2}}$	1^{4}	Smith M E		117	4.50	87-16	Envied117^{4}Sleepwiththeenemy$117^{5\frac{3}{4}}$OnDumpling$117^{5\frac{1}{2}}$	Driving	9
1Sep91- 7Mth	fst	6f	$:22^{1}$	:46	$1:12^{2}$	ⒻMd Sp Wt	4	6	$10^{6\frac{3}{4}}$	7^{4}	$4^{3\frac{3}{4}}$	$3^{4\frac{3}{4}}$	Ferrer J C		117	8.70	74-18	CherokeeVail117^{nk}LuLu'sLullaby$117^{4\frac{1}{2}}$Envied117^{nk}	Some gain	11
23Aug91- 1Mth	fst	6f	:22	:46	$1:12^{2}$	ⒻMd Sp Wt	7	2	1^{hd}	2^{hd}	$3^{3\frac{1}{2}}$	$5^{13\frac{1}{2}}$	Gryder A T		117	14.90	65-12	Luramore117^{2} Come On Spring117^{3} Skip Star$117^{5\frac{1}{2}}$	Gave way	8

Speed Index: Last Race: (—) 3-Race Avg.: (—) 12-Race Avg.: (—) Overall Avg.: -7.2
LATEST WORKOUTS Nov 14 CD 4f fst :50 B Oct 29 CD 5f fst $1:01^{3}$ B

26 Sep- The demonstration of some early speed in the first race, coupled with the third place finish in its last, gave the bettors reason to hope and she won her maiden race by four.

19 Oct- Back home and ready to steal a purse, the Keeneland bettors thought enough of Envied to send her to the post as the favorite. Even leading jockey Pat Day couldn't make the difference.

EXAMPLE: BUCK SOME BELLE

Many bettors tend to place a great deal of faith in the last running line in the newspaper and will make a certain loser the favorite if the earlier race was respectable. Such was the case with Buck Some Belle, a nice looking 2-year-old filly by Kentucky Derby winner, Spend A Buck.

Buck Some Belle Dk. b. or br. f. 2(Mar), by Spend a Buck—Stanwich Miss, by Advocator Lifetime 1991 2 1 0 0 $16,140
Own.—Heatherwood Farm Br.—Crabtree & Lyster (Ky) 116 2 1 0 0
Tr.—Schosberg Richard $16,140

28Nov91- 6Aqu	fst	1	$:46^{3}$	1:12	$1:38^{1}$	ⒻAlw 29000	6	4	3^{1}	$3^{\frac{1}{2}}$	$6^{1\frac{3}{4}}$	$4^{5\frac{1}{2}}$	Cordero A Jr		116	*1.80	65-26	Contradiction$116^{\frac{1}{2}}$SnowTitle$116^{2\frac{1}{2}}$ApalcheeSunset$116^{2\frac{1}{2}}$	Tired	7
23Oct91- 4Aqu	fst	6f	$:22^{1}$	$:45^{3}$	$1:11^{2}$	ⒻMd Sp Wt	8	2	$2^{\frac{1}{2}}$	$2^{\frac{1}{2}}$	1^{hd}	$1^{1\frac{3}{4}}$	Cordero A Jr		117	19.00	84-13	BckSomBll$117^{1\frac{3}{4}}$WyofthWorld117^{3}CrslMdnss117^{hd}	Drftd drvg	9

Speed Index: Last Race: -9.0 1-Race Avg.: -9.0 1-Race Avg.: -9.0 Overall Avg.: -6.0
LATEST WORKOUTS Dec 12 Bel tr.t 4f fst $:49^{3}$ B Nov 24 Bel tr.t 4f sly $:49^{1}$ B Nov 18 Bel tr.t 5f fst $1:03^{2}$ B ●Nov 12 Bel tr.t 5f my 1:02 B

23 Oct- A very good effort in her initial 6f race at the "Big A" gave fans a solid reward at almost 20 to 1.

28 Nov-   Despite the drifting comment, fans decided the late October
           showing was impressive enough and made her post time
           favorite. Welcome to the big leagues missy!

EXAMPLE: DIXIE BRASS

When Dixie Brass surprised everyone with the big MSW win over the
sloppy Belmont surface, trainer Brida must have imagined a trip to Churchill
Downs to listen to My Old Kentucky Home!

Dixie Brass

		Dk. b. or br. c. 2(Mar), by Dixieland Band—Petite Diable, by Sham			Lifetime	1991 3 2 0 0	$30,600
Own.—Watral Michael		Br.—Rooker John W (Ky)		**117**	3 2 0 0	
		Tr.—Brida Dennis J			$30,600	
18Nov91- 1Aqu fst 6f	:22 :45¹ 1:10³	Alw 27000	1 4 2¹½ 2¹ 1ʰᵈ 1ⁿᵒ Mojica R Jr	117 2.90	88-18 DixieBrass117ⁿᵒBestDecorted118⁵¼Chpito119ⁿᵒ Drifted, drvng 5
23Oct91- 8Aqu fst 7f	:21⁴ :44 1:22³	Cowdin	2 5 42¼ 44 99½ 81¹¾ Migliore R	122 7.30	77-13 Salt Lake122⁴¼ Montreal Marty122ⁿᵏ Offbeat122¾ Bmpd st 9
23Oct91-Grade II						
25Sep91- 4Bel sly 6f	:22¹ :45¹ 1:10¹	Md Sp Wt	3 3 11½ 12½ 1⁷ 1¹¹ Mojica R Jr⁵	113 28.90	89-14 Dixie Brass113¹¹ Chapito118ⁿᵒ Meniscus118¹½ Kept to drive 12

Speed Index: Last Race: +6.0   3–Race Avg.: –0.3   3–Race Avg.: –0.3   Overall Avg.: –0.3
LATEST WORKOUTS   Dec 13 Bel tr.t 4f fst :47⁴ H   ●Dec 9 Bel tr.t 3f fst :35 H   Nov 27 Bel tr.t 3f fst :37 B   Nov 15 Bel 3f fst :36 H

23 Oct-   Talk about optimism! Dixie Brass is entered in the Grade II
           Cowdin and finishes the race pretty much as expected. The poor
           start excuse is reason enough to keep the optimism flowing, but
           the horse was "in tough," as they say.

18 Nov-   With Mojica, no longer an apprentice, back in the irons, Dixie
           Brass wins his first race against prior winners. The pace of this
           contest was very similar to his "loose on the lead" effort in
           September.

EXAMPLE: STARVIEWER

Trainers who take their maiden winners into an allowance race are not to be
blamed for poor judgment. Optimism is sometimes justified, and only a fool
would place a maiden winner into a claiming race when the horse's true
worth is not yet known. However, experience shows us that the chance of
the horse winning the allowance is very poor. Jumping from a "for sale"
race into an allowance is another matter, as Starviewer's chart shows.

Starviewer — Ch. c. 2(Apr), by Silent Review—Starlight Desire, by Dactylographer — Lifetime 6 1 0 1 $7,265 — 1991 6 1 0 1 $7,265

Own.—Rocca Carol — $25,000 — Br.—Corry Don (Fla) — Tr.—Imprescia Dominic Jr — 119

13Dec91- 5Hia	fst	6f	$:22^{1}$	$:45^{2}$	$1:11^{3}$	Clm 20000	6	4	2$1\frac{1}{2}$	3^{nk}	2^{1}	3^{3}	Ramos W S	L	119	*3.60	81-16	Rockfine113$1\frac{1}{2}$ Jet Haze119$1\frac{1}{2}$ Starviewer119^{nk}	Faded 12
1Dec91- 8Hia	fst	6f	$:21^{3}$	$:44^{4}$	$1:10^{2}$	Alw 17500	6	5	3^{3}	4^{3}	4^{4}	$7^{10\frac{1}{2}}$	Castillo H Jr	L	117	11.40	79-14	Seek AFortune119^{1}AlwaysSilver$119^{2\frac{1}{2}}$WayAbove117^{2}	Faltered 12
17Nov91- 4Hia	fst	6f	$:21^{3}$	$:45^{4}$	$1:11^{3}$	Md 25000	1	5	3^{4}	2^{hd}	1^{4}	$1^{3\frac{1}{2}}$	Lee M A	L	122	34.10	84-15	Strviewer$122^{3\frac{1}{2}}$PeerlessPerformer122^{5}ApplToUs118^{no}	Driving 12
18Oct91- 6Crc	fst	7f	$:22^{3}$	$:46^{2}$	$1:28^{1}$	Md 25000	3	8	$6^{4\frac{1}{2}}$	$9^{6\frac{1}{2}}$	10^{10}	$11^{13\frac{3}{4}}$	Lee M A	L	118	28.90	60-18	Angilla118^{hd} It's Joseph118^{3} Classy Groom$118^{1\frac{1}{2}}$	Faded 12
28Sep91- 3Crc	fst	6f	$:22^{1}$	$:46^{3}$	1:14	Md 25000	4	8	$6^{3\frac{3}{4}}$	$6^{4\frac{3}{4}}$	$5^{3\frac{1}{2}}$	$6^{2\frac{3}{4}}$	Castillo H Jr	L	113	22.50	77-14	Senor Bo$117^{\frac{1}{2}}$ TriGranPaw115^{nk}PositivePayoff117^{1}	No threat 8
25Jly91- 5Crc	fst	5½f	$:22^{3}$	:47	1:07	Md 30000	2	5	$1^{1\frac{1}{2}}$	1^{hd}	$5^{6\frac{1}{2}}$	$10^{13\frac{1}{2}}$	Gonzalez M A	L	112	34.70	78-15	MysticSwp116^{6}It'sOnRhythm116^{nk}ClsscIMn109^{hd}	Speed, tired 12

Speed Index: Last Race: -3.0 3-Race Avg.: -3.6 6-Race Avg.: -8.1 Overall Avg.: -8.1

LATEST WORKOUTS Nov 14 GP 5f fst 1:02 B

17 Nov- Trainer Imprescia enters the two-year-old colt into a maiden claiming contest at Hialeah where the level of competition is close to that of Calder Race Course. The horse wins over the faster surface by 3+ lengths paying a boxcar price.

1 Dec- Back to Hialeah again, the horse is entered against a field of quality winners. For Starviewer, this move represents a sharp jump up in class. Most bettors recognized it and kept him as a long shot.

The lesson here is simple. Handicappers should read the conditions of the race and know what the horse could be facing when a trainer places it in an allowance race immediately after winning its maiden contest. We are not "class" handicappers, but there are situations that demand attention. This is one of those situations.

EXAMPLE: ONE SWEET GAL

To say that the public at large is aware of the consequences of this trainer move is not correct. Happy Alter is one of the better trainers in the South Florida circuit. Both locals and snowbirds are never afraid to bet his barn. When he entered One Sweet Gal in a 6 furlong allowance sprint at Calder, kept the same winning jockey, and drew a better post position with a much smaller field, the bettors jumped in when it was clear to us that the horse had little or no chance to win.

B. f. 2(May), by Singular—Sweet Ricki, by Nain Bleu
$9,000 Br.—Siegel Jan & Mace & Samantha (Fla)
Tr.—Alter Happy
112
Lifetime 7 1 0 1 $7,350
1991 7 1 0 1 $7,350

4Dec91- 2Hia	fst	6f	:23	$:47^{2}$	$1{:}13^{2}$	ⒻClm 15000	3	4	1^{hd}	5^{2}	8^{8}	$9^{11\frac{3}{4}}$	Santos C M^{7}	105	11.10	63-25	First Courtship116^{2} Alice Key114^{1} Premier Gal$112^{2\frac{1}{4}}$	Faltered	12
16Oct91- 8Crc	fst	6f	$:22^{2}$	$:46^{4}$	$1{:}13^{4}$	ⒻClm 15000	7	1	1^{hd}	3^{1}	$7^{7\frac{3}{4}}$	$7^{10\frac{1}{2}}$	Castillo H Jr	114	5.20	70-18	LuckyThundr$109^{\frac{1}{2}}$BrgingThrough118^{2}LdyAlicO114^{3}	Gave way	9
5Jly91- 7Crc	fst	5½f	$:22^{2}$	$:46^{2}$	$1{:}06^{1}$	ⒻAlw 15800	4	2	3^{2}	$4^{4\frac{1}{2}}$	5^{9}	$6^{7\frac{3}{4}}$	Guerra A J^{5}	108	3.70e	87-11	SexySurgeon$114^{\frac{1}{2}}$SpinninOut$116^{2\frac{1}{2}}$LdyAlicO$114^{1\frac{1}{2}}$	Early factor	6
26Jun91- 4Crc	fst	5f	$:23^{1}$	$:47^{3}$	$1{:}00^{4}$	ⒻMd 27500	11	1	$1^{1\frac{1}{2}}$	1^{4}	1^{3}	$1^{1\frac{1}{2}}$	Guerra A J^{5}	109	16.30	92-13	OneSwtGl$109^{1\frac{1}{2}}$ⒹAppiToGlory$116^{1\frac{1}{2}}$OhMySllyBrns116^{3}	Driving	11
13Jun91- 5Crc	fst	5f	$:22^{4}$	$:47^{3}$	1:01	ⒻMd 25000	6	3	3^{1}	4^{3}	4^{4}	4^{6}	Nied D	116	*2.30	85-12	Ile d'Or$116^{2\frac{3}{4}}$ Snowdrop$114^{\frac{3}{4}}$ AppealToGlory$116^{2\frac{1}{2}}$	Early speed	8
30May91- 5Crc	fst	4½f	$:23^{3}$	$:48^{1}$	$:54^{4}$	ⒻMd 25000	8	3		2^{1}	2^{1}	$3^{2\frac{1}{2}}$	Nied D	116	4.10	87-09	It'sOutofHere116^{1}SpecilTle$116^{1\frac{1}{2}}$OneSweetGl$116^{2\frac{3}{4}}$	Weakened	9
8May91- 3Crc	fst	4½f	$:23^{1}$	$:47^{4}$	$:54^{3}$	ⒻMd 25000	8	3		$3^{2\frac{1}{2}}$	$4^{4\frac{1}{2}}$	$5^{4\frac{3}{4}}$	Nied D	116	5.60	86-16	BoundtoFly$111^{3\frac{1}{2}}$It'sOutofHere$116^{1\frac{1}{2}}$Maricarmen111^{no}	Outrun	8

Speed Index: Last Race: −12.0 3–Race Avg.: −8.6 7–Race Avg.: −3.7 Overall Avg.: −3.7

LATEST WORKOUTS Dec 17 GP 4f fst :49 B Nov 27 GP 5f fst 1:02 B Nov 19 GP 3f fst :37 B Nov 9 Crc 5f fst $1{:}02^{3}$ B

26 Jun- Maybe the move from Danny Nied, a solid, experienced jockey, to an apprentice was a no-no at the betting windows. One Sweet Gal wins the maiden claiming contest comfortably and everyone is shocked to see the $34.60 price.

5 Jul- *In only 9 days*, normally a positive, One Sweet Gal is placed in another sprint, an allowance contest. The bettors see an opportunity to make some money! Everything seemed to be normal to those who are not aware of this trap. Wham! Gottcha! Dead last!

The rule to this section is clear. If today's contest is an allowance, NEVER make any horse that just won its maiden race a key horse selection unless it's a sure-fire champion-to-be!

Improving Newcomers

The Maidens

Doctor Coue was speaking of the human condition when he formulated his theory of day-by-day improvement. He may never have seen a horse race, but his holistic approach aptly describes a specific horse and trainer combination.

In an earlier section we noted how some first-time starters come to the track razor-sharp and ready to win at first calling. While it's nearly impossible to identify a horse honed to win its racing debut, we do win many bets on those animals that signaled a near-readiness. See " The First Race and (Almost) Ready," page 55.

At the other end of the spectrum are those horses which must be raced into winning condition. No regimen of training and workouts will bring these thoroughbreds onto the track ready to win. Only actual racing will produce the necessary results.

We are constantly alert for the horse showing marked improvement between its first and second races. The first outing can be a big disappointment, but if there is noticeable progress in that second race...! The *third* contest is the one on which we put our money down. If the computer has already identified this contender as a key horse candidate, this pattern usually confirms it.

EXAMPLE: MAJESTIC CLASS

The 3-year-old colt makes his racing debut at Santa Anita in January.

LASIX—Mr. P. and Max, Soweto-Ir, What A Spell, Character-GB, Whadjathink.

Majestic Class Ch. c. 3(Feb), by Majestic Shore—Broadway Dolcie, by Broadway Forli Lifetime 1991 4 1 0 1 $22,2..
LOPEZ A D Br.—Arnold G R Sr (Ky) 4 1 0 1 1990 0 M 0 0
Own.—Thoroughbred Promotions Tr.—Sadler John W 114 $22,225 Turf 1 0 0 0 $1,8..

17Apr91- 8SA fm 1⅛ (T):493 1:133 1:49 (S)La Puente 7 2 21 2hd 41½ 53¾ Flores D R B 114 7.90 75-21 Soweto-Ir115½ Mr. P. AndMax114½TripleAlpha1141 Weakened
9Mar91- 6SA fst 7f :223 :453 1:23 Md Sp Wt 1 3 11½ 1½ 12 13½ Flores D R B 118 3.50 88-12 MjesticClss1183½ElTrvieso118½HevyRin1182 Lugged out early
10Feb91- 6SA fst 6½f :221 :451 1:162 Md Sp Wt 10 4 41¼ 42 42½ 32½ Flores D R B 118 8.00 85-10 Warfield118¾WhatAProspect1181¾MjesticClss118¾ Wide early
12Jan91- 6SA fst 6½f :214 :444 1:164 Md Sp Wt 6 6 85 97½ 89½ 58 Desormeaux K J B 118 13.70 78-17 NorthrnBu1181½Mr.Stlwrt1182BondngBck1184 6-wide stretch

Speed Index: Last Race: -4.0 1-Race Avg.: -4.0 1-Race Avg.: -4.0 Overall Avg.: -3.5
LATEST WORKOUTS Apr 29 Hol 5f fst 1:00 H Apr 10 SA (T) 1 fm 1:452 H Apr 4 SA 1 fst 1:423 H Mar 29 SA 6f fst 1:144 H

12 Jan- The horse runs fifth, beaten eight lengths.

10 Feb- Majestic Class runs third, beaten 2+ lengths.

9 Mar- Still running in the MSW class, the animal wins easily, and pays $9.00.

EXAMPLE: VARNEY

Trainer Allen Severinsen starts his 3-year-old runner in a sprint at Golden Gate.

Varney Gr. g. 3(Apr), by Dahar—Spectacular Lady, by Spectacular Bid Lifetime 1991 3 1 1 0 $7,950
CHAPMAN T M Br.—Paulson A E (Ky) 3 1 1 0 1990 0 M 0 0
Own.—Paulson A E Tr.—Severinsen Allen 117 $7,950

6Apr91- 2GG fst 1 :463 1:113 1:374 Md 20000 7 6 53½ 32 21 11½ Chapman T M Bb 118 4.60 76-23 Vrney1181½WelcomeFortunte1181Tetrod118½ Bobbled stretch
9Mar91- 2GG fst 1 1/16 :463 1:113 1:451 Md 16000 7 9 78½ 42½ 21 22 Lamance C Bb 118 2.90e 78-12 Merit Increase1182 Varney118½ Papa Oscar1185 Wide rally
7Feb91- 5GG gd 6f :222 :462 1:122 Md 16000 9 11 98 77½ 67 58½ Lamance C Bb 118 9.80 68-22 WinterResort1132VisionryWonder118nkHrToThr1164 Far wide

Speed Index: Last Race: (—) 3-Race Avg.: (—) 12-Race Avg.: (—) Overall Avg.: -9.5
LATEST WORKOUTS Apr 29 GG 5f fst 1:012 H Apr 24 GG 5f fst 1:013 H Apr 17 GG 4f fst :492 B Apr 3 GG 4f fst :49 H

7 Feb- The gelding is beaten by eight lengths.

9 Mar- The animal is much closer in its second race.

6 Apr-   Severinsen recruits Tommy Chapman, "the jockey's jockey" to
           ride Varney to a $11.20 win.

When he has a thoroughbred ready for that all-important third run, the
successful trainer will often mix in another move to further buttress the
horse's chances.

As one outstanding horseman explains:

"You have probably heard all of our complaints a dozen times. There's the
owner who comes in with a newly-acquired animal and tells the trainer: 'Believe me, Mac, this horse can run all day.' The trainer then looks over
to the poor, pathetic animal and mutters 'Alpo' under his breath."

The trainer draws a deep breath and continues.

"Then, there's the Old Trainer's Lament...

Doctors bury their mistakes. Lawyers hang their mistakes. But, trainers'
mistakes run dead last, right out there in front of God and everybody."

He pauses a moment and then becomes serious...

"Look, there are no sure things in horse racing. No cinches, no locks. The
capable trainer does everything possible to produce a win for his horse. A
rider switch here, a class drop there. The good ones know all the tricks --
and when and how to use them."

With the Improving Newcomers pattern, the trainer's work is there for all to
see and the horse's progress is usually obvious when you look for it.

EXAMPLE: MR. P AND MAX

Prominent trainer Bobby Frankel debuts his gelding at Hollywood Park.

Mr. P. And Max B. g. 3(Feb), by Nodouble—Bijou, by Seattle Slew
ORTEGA L E Br.—Trans Media Productions Pty Ltd (Ky)
Own.—Engelson D & M Tr.—Frankel Robert 114
Lifetime 5 1 1 1 $30,550 | 1991 3 1 1 1 $30,550 | 1990 2 M 0 0 | Turf 1 0 1 0 $15,000

17Apr91- 8SA	fm	1⅛	Ⓣ:493	1:133	1:49	⑧La Puente	5	1	11	1hd	1½	2½	Santos J A	LB 114	22.70	78-21	Soweto-Ir115½ Mr. P. And Max114½TripleAlpha1141	Sharp try	9
8Mar91- 5SA	fst	1 1/16	:462	1:104	1:434	Clm 50000	6	6	55	33	33	31	Santos J A	LB 115	15.00	83-17	PrncOfHn1151RcntArryl117hdMr.P.AndM1152	Veered in break	8
31Jan91- 4SA	fst	1 1/16	:47	1:121	1:443	Md 28000	1	3	32	33	22½	11	Santos J A	LB 115	6.00	80-13	Mr. P. And Max1151 Big Barton1172½ Sharkster1171½	Got up	12
31Dec90- 4SA	fst	1 1/16	:47	1:12	1:451	Md 32000	1	1	1hd	2hd	21½	88¼	Flores D R	B 118	8.10	69-21	DlwrDrv1182½LdngAccnt1181½SnrLnrd1181½	Bumped at break	11
7Dec90- 4Hol	fst	6½f	:22	:451	1:161	Md 32000	12	7	52½	43	68¾	614	Flores D R	B 118	8.80	80-11	Special Toy1131½CutOfReality1187½PlataPatter1183	Wide trip	12

Speed Index: Last Race: –1.0 1–Race Avg.: –1.0 1–Race Avg.: –1.0 Overall Avg.: –5.4
LATEST WORKOUTS Apr 25 Hol 4f fst :473 H Apr 14 SA 5f fst 1:034 H Apr 9 SA 6f fst 1:141 H Apr 3 SA 6f fst 1:143 H

7 Dec- The horse is beaten by 14 lengths.

31 Dec- Shipped across town to Santa Anita, Mr. P. And Max shows remarkable improvement. For a real insight, look at the pre-stretch calls: December 7, behind 8+ lengths. December 31, behind only 1 1/2 lengths.

31 Jan- Dropped in class from Md32000 to Md28000, the horse wins in a driving finish. The mutuel returns a handsome $14.00.

EXAMPLE: TRUCE PREVAILS

Jim Benedict mixes in a jockey switch to guarantee a purse for his improving colt.

Truce Prevails Ch. c. 3(Apr), by Truce Maker—Vigeff's Lady, by Vigors
WARREN R J JR $10,000 Br.—Fogelson Greer Garson (Cal)
Own.—John H Deeter Trust Tr.—Benedict Jim 117
Lifetime 4 1 0 0 $5,500 | 1991 3 1 0 0 $5,500 | 1990 1 M 0 0

8Feb91- 7GG	fst	1	:454	1:101	1:353	Alw 22000	6	6	79	78½	713	820	Warren R J Jr	LB 117	30.80	67-22	KeyRecognition1171½TripleAlpha1172BodyBubbles1125	Outrun	8
27Jan91- 7GG	fst	6f	:221	:452	1:112	Md 20000	11	3	43½	33	31½	1½	Warren R J Jr	LB 118	6.90	81-14	TrucePrevils118½Cstlemin1181It'sExciting1182	Rallied gamely	11
12Jan91- 4BM	fst	6f	:223	:452	1:112	ⓈMd 20000	6	8	42½	33	42½	61½	Loseth C	LB 118	10.10	77-15	Sam Shane118½ EL Gancho1181 Willie Kravesit118nk	No rally	12
24Dec90- 6BM	fst	6f	:223	:454	1:104	Md 32000	8	7	63	52½	43½	76½	Loseth C	B 118	13.20	79-13	KystonRunnr1164CrossThWirs1181MrktStudy116hd	Wide trip	8

Speed Index: Last Race: –5.0 3–Race Avg.: –7.0 3–Race Avg.: –7.0 Overall Avg.: –8.0
LATEST WORKOUTS Mar 2 GG 4f sly :554 H (d) Feb 22 GG 5f fst 1:012 B Feb 5 GG 4f my :53 H (d) Jan 19 BM 5f fst :592 H

24 Dec- Staring out in a Md32000 race, the youngster is beaten off by more than six lengths.

12 Jan- Dropped into a Md20000 sprint, the horse shows the required improvement.

27 Jan- The calendar says it's time to cross the Bay. Truce Prevails is entered in another Md20000 event, this time at Golden Gate Fields. Benedict calls on top reinsman, Ron Warren, to lead his colt to victory. The combo produces a top win price: $15.80.

No matter which track you call "home," trainers are always working their newcomers into position for an early win. It pays -- and, sometimes, it pays very well -- to recognize this pattern while you are searching for your key horse.

EXAMPLE: STANFORD LARK

Trainer Gregson elects to launch his runner's career at Del Mar.

Stanford Lark Dk. b. or br. g. 4, by Impressive—Contrast, by T V Lark
MCCARRON C J Br.—Dees Eleanor L (Cal)
Own.—Dees Eleanor L Tr.—Gregson Edwin
119
Lifetime 8 1 2 2 $37,500
1991 5 0 2 1 $20,825
1990 3 1 0 1 $16,675
Turf 1 0 0 0 $2,625

19Jly91- 3Hol	fm	1 1/16	①:472	1:113	1:421	3↑ⓢAlw 35000	3	3	31	21½	21½	41	McCarron C J	LB	118	*1.10	83-11	H'sOnAlrt117¾Notwithstndng114nkBlckBrk112hd	Always close	6
23Jun91- 3Hol	fst	1 1/16	:461	1:103	1:423	3↑Alw 35000	1	1	1½	1hd	2½	22½	McCarron C J	LB	119	2.60	85-17	CughtDeStr1132½StnfordLrk1192½PrfctlyProud1121	Held 2nd	6
1Jun91- 7Hol	fst	7½f	:221	:444	1:291	3↑ⓢAlw 32000	6	2	32	21	2hd	23	McCarron C J	LB	118	3.00	— —	Noble Valiant1183 StanfordLark1181½PowerFull121½	2nd best	8
5May91- 5Hol	fst	6f	:214	:443	1:094	3↑ⓢAlw 32000	6	3	53	52¾	54¾	66¾	McCarron C J	B	119	5.50	84-11	El Royale1195 Pappy Yokum119hd I WillReign115hd	Wide trip	8
16Mar91- 7SA	fst	6f	:214	:444	1:092	ⓢAlw 32000	1	3	31½	32	33	32½	Black C A	B	118	12.00	86-14	Edict1182½ Desert Waltz118nkStanfordLark1183	Always close	9
10Sep90- 6Dmr	fst	6f	:211	:442	1:10	3↑Md 50000	11	3	33½	31½	1hd	13½	Black C A	B	118	3.40	90-08	Stanford Lark1183½ Marfa's Boy1181½ Far Stool118¾	Driving	12
23Aug90- 6Dmr	fst	6f	:213	:443	1:084	3↑Md 50000	7	5	32	22½	34	36½	Black C A	B	117	*2.90	89-08	SpllVictorous1176Qun'sEmssry117¾StnfordLrk117½	Weakened	12
5Aug90- 2Dmr	fst	6½f	:222	:444	1:154	3↑Md 50000	7	10	63½	32	33½	59¾	Black C A		117	6.30	80-10	EmrldHill1172¾NorthrnTrty1154CordilStop1171½	Broke slowly	11

Speed Index: Last Race: +2.0 1-Race Avg.: +2.0 1-Race Avg.: +2.0 Overall Avg.: -3.4
LATEST WORKOUTS Aug 27 Dmr 3f fst :354 H Aug 22 Dmr 6f fst 1:124 H ●Aug 16 Dmr 5f fst :583 H Aug 11 Dmr 4f fst :53 H

5 Aug- The horse is well bet for a first-time starter. It is beaten by 8+ lengths.

23 Aug- The 3-year-old gelding is made a lukewarm favorite. This time it finishes third, beaten only 6+ lengths.

10 Sep- Put off by that third place finish, the public misses the pattern of improvement. Stanford Lark wins by 3 1/2 lengths for a payout of $8.80.

Always give a long, second look to these maidens, especially when they've shown us a dull debut. Should the horse's second race show a big improvement, you have a solid key horse candidate for today's contest!

"Play it Again, Sam"

When a newcomer fails to respond satisfactorily, the trainer will often reconsider his campaign. He may temporarily withdraw the animal from competition while he prepares it for its "second time around" or, maybe, if success still eludes him, a "third time around." Not every horse will work into condition at the same rate, but the cycles are usually pretty obvious.

Here are a few variations of our "improving horse" theme ...

EXAMPLE: VULCRESS

After two poorly-backed, indifferent races at Golden Gate, Trainer Hilling stables the non-maiden and plans a second coming at the Bay Meadows Fall meeting.

26 Aug-	Hilling starts his thoroughbred on the turf. She finishes sixth, beaten eight lengths.
9 Sep-	Her odds are higher but the 4-year-old lady turns in a much improved race: fourth, just 3 lengths short. This is our pattern.
8 Oct-	Many of the hep handicappers note the improvement and bet the horse down to 4 to 1. That "second time around" pays off to the tune of $10.00.

EXAMPLE: NILO

Play it again, Sam. The third time can be good, too. Trainer Mike Harrington withdraws his non-maiden newcomer twice before he turns it into a money machine, grinding out win tickets at delectable prices.

```
Nilo                              B. g. 3(May), by Tella Fib—Port a Belle, by Just the Time
                                  Br.—Doebler J F (Wash)            1990 11 4 1 1      $18,495
  BOULANGER G                115  Tr.—Harrington Mike               1989  0 M 0 0
Own.—Mellinger C                  Lifetime  11 4 1 1   $18,495

20Oct90-2SA   6½f :214 :45 1:16³ft  10  8 116   74½ 73½ 33½ 33    Boulanger G 2  25000  84-14 Distinctive Noble, Feint, Nilo     9
21Sep90-8Lga  1½ :46¹ 1:10⁴ 1:45 ft  5  8 120   26  23½ 2nd 1½   Schubert R 7 [S] 16000 79-21 Nilo, All Vibrant, Table For Six    7
14Sep90-7Lga  6f :21⁴ :44³ 1:09⁴ft  11  8 120   42½ 43  21½ 1½   Schubert R 3  20000  81-19 Nilo, Coaltar, Harbor Prince         7
6Sep90-9Lga   6½f :21⁴ :44³ 1:16 ft  11  8 117   5⁸  6⁵  6⁴  4¹² Schubert R 2  25000  79-20 Spnooch,ClssicInvestment,Arrozc 7
22Aug90-6Lga  6½f :23 :46⁴ 1:19¹m    5  8 120   2nd 2nd 1½  1²   Schubert R 3  12500  75-23 Nilo, Rich Lord, Indigo Warrior     6
   27Aug90- Lugged in late
4Aug90-9Lga   6f :22 :46⁴ 1:11¹ft   38  8 117   42½ 54½ 67½ 77½  Southwck WE 2 32000 76-20 Spnooch,ShrpEvnt,GnnrsMtMrt 10
26Jly90-8Lga  6f :21⁴ :45 1:10³ft   17  8 114   9¹⁸ 9¹⁰ 8¹⁴ 7⁶½ Southwck WE 1 25000 78-12 Lion'sBrew,ImCrfty,ShreTheDrm 9
   26Jly90—Broke slowly
15Apr90-5Lga  6f :22⁴ :46⁴ 1:12 gd  *2½   120   2nd 2½ 42½ 6⁷   Schubert R 7  32000 73-16 CrmonlSword,Grovr,BondToBGrt 7
4Apr90-8Lga   5½f :22³ :45⁴ 1:04 ft  8½   117   3½  3²  5⁴  6⁵⅜ Schubert R 6 Aw10600 88-09 Storm's Finale, Lion'sBrew,Parnu 7
10Feb90-9YM   6f :21⁴ :44 1:09¹ft   2½   121   2³  23  23  2¹   Schubert R 3 Aw4000  95-09 No Way Mister,Nilo,ClydeMyMan 7
   Speed Index: Last Race: (—)    3-Race Avg.: (—)    12-Race Avg.: (—)    Overall Avg.: -2.5
   Nov 2 Hol 4f ft :50⁴ H    Oct 14 Hol 6f ft 1:17¹ H    Oct 7 Hol 4f ft :49 H
```

Following two tries at Yakima Meadows, the 3-year-old gelding is rested for 53 days.

4 Apr & 15 Apr -	Two indifferent races at Longacres convinces Harrington his charge is still not quite ready. Nilo is held out of competition for more than three months.
26 Jul-	The horse runs seventh, but check the pre-stretch call. Nilo is 14 lengths behind.
4 Aug-	Raised a notch in class, the animal is still running seventh, but only 4+ lengths short at the second call.
22 Aug-	To the marked pattern of improvement, Harrington adds the ultimate *coup*: Nilo is dropped from 32,000 to 12,500. A steep slide. The public must be looking elsewhere. The gelding romps in and pays $12.00.
14 Sep-	Returning to the track in *eight days*, the horse is *dropped in class* and wins to reward its backers with $24.00 per ticket.
21 Sep-	Back in *seven days* and *dropped in class* once more, Nilo pays $12.00 to the faithful.

To repeat, Harrington has converted his thoroughbred into a veritable four-legged mint. Whenever you discover one of these, it's worth following, and sometimes it can be ridden all the way to the bank.

Here is an actual race example to illustrate the tenet of this "Improving Newcomers" section. This was a Maiden Special Weight for 3- and 4-year-olds at Calder Race Course on June 8.

 CALDER

7 FURLONGS. (1.23) MAIDEN SPECIAL WEIGHT. Purse $12,000 (Plus $1,300 FOA).
3-and-4-year-olds. Weight, 3-year-olds, 115 lbs. 4-year-olds, 122 lbs.

LASIX—Bay State Adjuster.

Bay State Adjuster
B. g. 3(Mar), by Baldski—Wayward Mistress, by Exclusive Ribot
Br.—Farnsworth Farm (Fla)
Own.—Sherman Michael H
Tr.—Sherman Lee A
Lifetime 1991 5 M 1 2 $5,240
5 0 1 2 1990 0 M 0 0
115 $5,240

12May91- 4Crc fst 7f	:223	:461 1:251	3♦ⒸMd Sp Wt	5 1 1hd 1hd 23 311	Rodriguez P A	b 114	*1.10	78-10 ClbrtyCrcl114½Nlwwstfddg1142¾BySttAdjstr114½	Used early 8
27Apr91- 7GP fst 6f	:214	:45 1:112	Md Sp Wt	4 5 12 12½ 12 42½	Fires E	b 120	3.00	85-10 Star Edition120² LordHardin120¾BagofMusic115nd	Weakened 11
12Apr91- 6GP fst 7f	:222	:453 1:242	Md 50000	7 5 11 1½ 2½ 3½	Fires E	b 120	*2.80	83-11 StrKlibur116noPyndPyndPy116½ByStteAdjuster120½	Game try 12
25Mar91- 3GP fst 6f	:222	:46 1:114	Md 40000	5 7 11½ 11½ 1½ 21½	Ramos W S	b 120	20.40	85-12 ChocoltTrt111½ByStteAdjstr120½StrEdition116no	Weakened 11
17Mar91- 6GP fst 6f	:22	:45 1:11	Md Sp Wt	6 4 63½ 65½ 710 88½	Ramos W S	b 120	50.10	81-13 Jaded Dancer120¹ Fight a Lee120½ Royal Rook120¹	Outrun 9

Speed Index: Last Race: -12.0 3-Race Avg.: -7.6 5-Race Avg.: -6.4 Overall Avg.: -6.4
LATEST WORKOUTS Jun 1 Crc 5f fst 1:01² B May 23 Crc 4f sly :48⁴ B ●Apr 22 Crc 3f fst :36¹ B

Warpath
Gr. c. 3(Apr), by Caro—Native Angel, by Exclusive Native
Br.—Appleton Arthur I (Fla)
Own.—Appleton Arthur I
Tr.—After Happy
Lifetime 1990 0 M 0 0
0 0 0 0
115

Speed Index: Last Race: (—) 3-Race Avg.: (—) 12-Race Avg.: (—) Overall Avg.: (—)
LATEST WORKOUTS May 28 Crc 4f fst :50² B May 21 Crc 6f gd 1:18³ Bg May 14 Crc 5f fst 1:03 Bg Apr 30 GP 7f fst 1:28 Bg

Yoga
Dk. b. or br. g. 3(May), by Topsider—Yolanda, by Exclusive Native
Br.—Hinkle Bros., Alan S. Kline, D. Par (Ky)
Own.—Tartan Stable
Tr.—Bracken James E
Lifetime 1991 2 M 0 0 $270
2 0 0 0 1990 0 M 0 0
108⁷ $270

27May91- 6Crc fst 6f	:22	:46 1:124	3♦ Md Sp Wt	1 10 96½ 68 57½ 68½	Castillo H Jr	114	3.80	78-10 HonstMstk114¾TopCnddt114½Rollo'sCht114³	Fractious gate 10
23Feb91- 4GP fst 6f	:221	:454 1:11	Md Sp Wt	10 4 31 34 46 59	Day P	120	9.40	81-11 NorthrnNoTrump120⁴ChosnRlr120¹PlyllNght120½	Weakened 10

Speed Index: Last Race: -10.0 2-Race Avg.: (—) 2-Race Avg.: -9.0 Overall Avg.: -9.0
LATEST WORKOUTS May 20 Crc 5f sly 1:04 B Apr 11 Kee 4f fst :49¹ B

Perfect Rex
B. g. 3(Feb), by Rexson's Hope—Perfect Party, by Banquet Table
Br.—Bar Lyn Farm (Fla)
Own.—Levatino R
Tr.—Warren Fred G
Lifetime 1991 10 M 1 0 $1,334
10 0 1 0 1990 0 M 0 0
115 $1,334

27May91- 6Crc fst 6f	:22	:46 1:124	3♦ Md Sp Wt	5 7 86½ 913 712 710	Hussey C	b 114	79.50	76-12 HonstMstk114¾TopCnddt114½Rolli'sCht114³	Broke outward 10
20Apr91- 8Tam fst 6f	:222	:462 1-13	Md Sp Wt	10 1 73 713102312293	Henry W T	b 118	6.40	51-23 MnFromthMoon118²½FortnFond118¹²FlowOnHim113¾	Outrun 12
3Mar91- FTam gc 6f	:231	:473 1:131	Md Sp Wt	9 1 2nd 1hd 22½ 513½	Henry W T	b 118	7.30	66-22 DiamondCoy118¹½KarateKick111ndStalwrrior118½	Gave way 12
16Mar91- 8Tam fst 6f	:224	:464 1:133	Md Sp Wt	3 2 11½ 1hd 22 44½	Henry W T	b 118	4.20	73-18 Where'sMyKeys118½DimondCoy118¾KrtKick1113½	Weakened 8
27Feb91- 5Tam fst 7f	:231	:471 1:271	Md 12500	9 6 57½ 69 826 825	Puckett H	b 118	6.10	54-18 Rabade118¹½ Coach's Ace112² Slew Jeans1125¾	Outrun 9
16Feb91- 1Tam fst 6f	:234	:473 1:131	Md Sp Wt	4 4 21½ 45 36½ 33½	Iorio S Jr⁷	b 111	9.50	76-19 ⒹHghrThrshld118²Mtch'sChrgr118¾PrfctR111no	No solid bid 7
16Feb91-Placed second through disqualification									
2Feb91- 1Tam gd 6f	:232	:48 1-14	Md Sp Wt	6 5 33 64 67½ 613¾	Adkins R M	b 118	16.40	62-22 DulExhust118hdHigherThrshold118⁴Chls'sChnc118¹	Fin early 8
25Jan91- 1GP fst 1⅛	:484 1:14 1:464	Clm 10500	2 4 41½ 71¹¹126¹¹213	Alferez J O	b 112	64.00	58-14 SuperStutz107½RunwyToo107½SureItsLeg1112no	Early factor 11
11Jan91- 1Crc fst 7f	:222	:462 1:271	Md 10500	9 10 94 86½1225¹226	Alferez J O	b 116	86.60	53-17 Sales Tip120½Sefaintent106½OhBrother116²½	Showed nothing 12
3Jan91- 5Crc gd 6f	:211	:463 1:132	Md 13000	1 10 911 89½ 712 913¾	Ramos W S	b 116	18.90	69-16 Falcon Mar120¹ R.C.Diamond120½ModCat120²	Showed little 10

Speed Index: Last Race: -12.0 3-Race Avg.: -16.6 9-Race Avg.: -17.0 Overall Avg.: -18.1
LATEST WORKOUTS Jun 4 Crc 5f fst 1:04² B May 25 Crc 5f fst 1:04 B May 17 Crc 4f fst :49¹ B

Nobiznesbreedin
B. c. 3(Apr), by All North—Matte Finish, by Stutz Blackhawk
Br.—Bento nPat (Fla)
Own.—Benton & Berry
Tr.—Zladie Ralph
Lifetime 1990 0 M 0 0
0 0 0 0
115

Speed Index: Last Race: (—) 3-Race Avg.: (—) 12-Race Avg.: (—) Overall Avg.: (—)
LATEST WORKOUTS May 29 Crc 3f fst :37² B May 16 Crc 5f fst 1:03⁴ Bg

Rosenose
Ro. c. 3(Feb), by Superbity—Budding Rose, by Nose for Money
Br.—Saumels Desiree & Jerry & Terry (Fla)
Own.—Samuels Desiree & T
Tr.—Saumels Jerry
Lifetime 1990 3 M 0 1 $1,30
3 0 0 1
115 $1,300

17Nov90- 2Crc fst 6f	:221	:454 1:12	Md Sp Wt	5 2 76¾ 711 611 510½	Green B	119	7.70	79-10 Kadiddy119¹ Scottish Ice119no Solid Sunny119³½	Outrun
30Sep90- 4Crc fst 6f	:222	:462 1:124	Md Sp Wt	10 1 67 59 46 35½	Green B	117	9.20	80-15 UnrelRgout117½Ensignio117½Rosenos117½	Improved position 1
16Sep90- 4Crc fst 6f	:223	:464 1:133	Md Sp Wt	6 6 63 75¾ 66 54½	Green B	117	27.30	78-15 SprnklsExprss117noMdnghtSnny117²Tomr'sDoctr112¹	Rallied 1

Speed Index: Last Race: -11.0 3-Race Avg.: -7.6 3-Race Avg.: -7.6 Overall Avg.: -7.6

```
Top Candidate          Dk. b. or br. c. 3(Mar), by Cherokee Fellow—Migdalia C, by Northern Bay        Lifetime        1991 4 M 2 0    $4,13
                              Br.—Parkhurst Farm Inc (Fla)                                             5 0 2 0         1990 1 M 0 0       $6
Own.—Parkhurst Farm Inc       Tr.—Azpurua Leo Jr                                                 115   $4,195
27May91- 6Crc fst 6f   :22   :46   1:12^4 3+Md Sp Wt   10 3 7^4¾ 5^7½ 4^4½ 2^3½ Lee M A      114  4.00  82-12 HonestMistk114^3½TopCndidt114^1½Rollo'sCht114^3  Closed well 1
8May91- 4Crc fst 6f    :22^2 :46^2 1:13   3+Md 25000    1 3 5^1½ 6^3½ 3^3 4^4¾  Bracho R A^5 109 10.00 80-16 SayDance114^3½OceanPro118^nkReunitedAgain114¾  No late bid 1
2May91- 1GP fst 6½f    :22^2 :45^3 1:17^3   Md 30000    4 7 5^3½ 5^8 5^8½ 5^7   Ramos W S    120  2.10  — — Dsrtr118^noPrt'sOutlook120^1½CutndPolshd118^2  Stumbled start 1
9Apr91- 6GP fst 7f     :22^1 :45^1 1:24^3   Md 20000    7 4 4^3½ 5^7 4^4½ 2^1¾  Ramos W S    116 19.20  81-15 MarinoMagic120^1¾TopCandidte116^1¾Mr.BonBon120¾  Gaining 1
8Jly90- 3Crc fst 5½f   :22^3 :47^1 1:07^2   Md 25000    1 7 9^12 9^14 9^16 6^14¾ Rydowski S R 116 11.20 75-12 Coastal Jim116^5 Brave Lord111¾ Dr. Fuisse116^7  Showed little
  Speed Index:  Last Race: -6.0       3-Race Avg.: -4.6        4-Race Avg.: -6.7          Overall Avg.: -6.7
LATEST WORKOUTS   ●May 26 Crc 5f fst 1:02 B    Apr 29 Crc 3f fst :37 B    Apr 25 Crc 3f fst :38 B    Apr 21 Crc 5f sly 1:04^2 B

The Wish Doctor        B. c. 3(Jan), by Lyphard's Wish—Relevant, by Hold Your Peace                    Lifetime        1991 2 M 0 0      $25
                              Br.—Wimborne Farm, Inc. & Diane L. Perk (Ky)                             2 0 0 0         1990 0 M 0 0
Own.—Tucker Paula J           Tr.—Root Richard R                                                 115   $250            Turf 1 0 0 0      $13
15May91- 4Crc fm *1 1/16 (T)      1:46^2 3+Md Sp Wt   8 5 4^4½ 4^3½ 4^5 5^5    Rydowski S R b 113 4.30 75-19 Dxtr'sExprss108^2½SuprRx113^hdBgofMusic113^1  Raced greenly
5May91- 6Crc fst 7f    :22^2 :45^3 1:26   3+Md Sp Wt   1 10 10^18 10^15 7^9¾ 5^12 .Velez J A Jr 114 11.10 73-13 PyndPyndPy114^6½BgofMusic114^4½ClbrtyCrcl114¾  Closed well '
  Speed Index:  Last Race: -14.0      1-Race Avg.: -14.0       1-Race Avg.: -14.0         Overall Avg.: -10.0
LATEST WORKOUTS   May 24 Crc 4f fst :49^3 B    May 13 Crc 3f fst :38 B    May 1 Crc 4f fst :50^1 Bg    ●Apr 23 Crc 6f fst 1:16^3 B

One Day Isle           Dk. b. or br. c. 3(Apr), by Stutz Blackhawk—Ammeal, by No No Billy              Lifetime        1990 0 M 0 0
                              Br.—Amlung Farm (Fla)                                                    0 0 0 0
Own.—B Glenmar Stable         Tr.—Triola Robert                                                  115
  Speed Index:  Last Race: (—)        3-Race Avg.: (—)         12-Race Avg.: (—)          Overall Avg.: (—)
LATEST WORKOUTS   Jun 6 Crc 3f fst :38^2 Bg    May 26 Crc 5f fst 1:05^3 B    ●May 21 Crc 6f gd 1:17^3 B    May 15 Crc 5f fst 1:03^2 B

Rollo's Chet           Ro. c. 3(Mar), by Spanish Drums—Willow Wisp, by Wardlaw                         Lifetime        1991 2 M 0 2    $2,6
                              Br.—Sunshine Bloodstock Group III (Fla)                                  3 0 0 2         1990 1 M 0 0      $1
Own.—Boudrias R               Tr.—Guerrera Robert J                                              115   $2,720
27May91- 6Crc fst 6f   :22   :46   1:12^4 3+Md Sp Wt   7 5 4¾ 2^hd 2^2 3^4¾    Acevedo D A  114  3.20  81-12 HonestMistke114^3½TopCndidt114^1½Rollo'sCht114^3  Weakened
1Jan91- 2Crc fst 6f    :22^1 :45^3 1:11^4   Md Sp Wt   4 4 3^1½ 3½ 3^2 3^2     Gaffalione S 120  4.30  89-06 Forest Ransom120¾ WildAcclaim120^1½Rollo'sChet120^3½  Hung
16Dec90- 4Crc fst 6f   :22   :46   1:13^2   Md Sp Wt   9 6 9^4 6^6½ 7^5½ 7^2¾  George D D   120 34.60  80-12 Scottish Ice120¾ Kid Shananie120^no SecretDance120¾  Outrun
  Speed Index:  Last Race: -7.0       3-Race Avg.: -6.6        3-Race Avg.: -6.6          Overall Avg.: -6.6
LATEST WORKOUTS   May 22 Crc 3f sly :39^2 B    Apr 21 Crc 4f sly :50 B
```

Here is the *Winning at the Track* P/M table as it appeared that day:

Calder Race Crse FL June 8
1st Race 7 f

PP	Horse	Notes	Odds	Ability Factor	Pure Speed	Early Speed	Late Speed	MF	P/M RATING
1	BayStateAdjstr	95/87	5:1	459	96	304	576	880	2620
2	Warpath	-st	10:1	0	0	0	0	0	0
3	Yoga	87/88	8:1	452	90	289	561	850	2522
4	PerfectRex	86/85	20:1	448	85	286	562	848	2487
5	Nobiznsbreedin	-st	10:1	0	0	0	0	0	0
6	Rosenose	80/89	8:1	458	90	276	572	848	2544
7	TopCandidate	87/92	3:1	463	92	288	573	861	2571
8	TheWishDoctor	83/77	8:1	455	82	249	547	796	2396
9	OneDayIsle	-st	10:1	0	0	0	0	0	0
10	Rollo'sChet	91/91	4:1	463	100	297	584	881	2665

The "Analyst" Screen of the *Pace Analyst* module appeared as follows:

Race: 1 CRC 7 f

PP	Horse		Morn. Line	Pole Speed
10	Rollo'sChet	91/91	4:1	91
1	BayStateAdjstr	95/87	5:1	90
7	TopCandidate	87/92	3:1	82
3	Yoga	87/88	8:1	82

1	BayStateAdjstr	95/87	5:1	92
7	TopCandidate	87/92	3:1	87
3	Yoga	87/88	8:1	87
10	Rollo'sChet	91/91	4:1	84

1	BayStateAdjstr	95/87	5:1	95
10	Rollo'sChet	91/91	4:1	90
4	PerfectRex	86/85	20:1	86
7	TopCandidate	87/92	3:1	84

* PACE ANALYST *

Expected Pole Speed.... 87 - 0:46.3

Pure Speed Estimate.... 88 - 1:27.1

Required Last Quarter..115 L/S 562

CAPABLE AT THIS PACE:			L/S
~~		Best	~~~
10-Rollo'sChet	91/91	91/123	584
1-BayStateAdjstr	95/87	90/119	576
7-TopCandidate	87/92	82/124	573
6-Rosenose	80/89	79/125	572
4-PerfectRex	86/85	77/122	562
		2nd	
7-TopCandidate	87/92	87/119	572
1-BayStateAdjstr	95/87	92/116	571
6-Rosenose	80/89	80/122	565
10-Rollo'sChet	91/91	84/120	565
		3rd	
1-BayStateAdjstr	95/87	95/114	571
7-TopCandidate	87/92	84/120	569
10-Rollo'sChet	91/91	90/115	564
6-Rosenose	80/89	80/123	563

RACE FILE: 6-8-91.crc

Pacesetters: # 1 # 10

The "Display" Screen of the *Pace Analyst* looked like this:

Race: 1 CRC 7 f

			Best Race			Second Best			
PP	Likely Pacesetters		Pole Speed	Last Qtr.	Late Speed	Pole Speed	Last Qtr.	Late Speed	P/M Rating
1	BayStateAdjstr	95/87	90	119	576	92	116	571	2620
10	Rollo'sChet	91/91	91	123	584	84	120	565	2665
PP	Best-4 P/M Horses								
10	Rollo'sChet	91/91	91	123	584	84	120	565	2665
1	BayStateAdjstr	95/87	90	119	576	92	116	571	2620
7	TopCandidate	87/92	82	124	573	87	119	572	2571
6	Rosenose	80/89	79	125	572	80	122	565	2544
PP	Selection - Display								
8	TheWishDoctor	83/77	77	119	547	83	113	545	2396
4	PerfectRex	86/85	77	122	562	77	122	555	2487

RACE FILE: 6-8-91.crc

Assuming a Pole Speed of 87 (a pace of 46 3/5 seconds) and a maximum of 3 lengths out at the half, this is what the *Graphics* module showed us:

```
Race:  1      CRC      7 f
                              WINNING AT THE TRACK - Graphics              BEST RACE
 ┌──────────────────────────┐ ┌──────────────────────────────────────┐ ┌───────────┐
 │PP│Horse        │Notes    │ │Pole Speed      │Last Quarter         │ │Pole/LS    │
 ├──┼─────────────┼─────────┤ ├────────────────┴─────────────────────┤ ├───────────┤
 │ 1│BayStateAdjstr│95/87   │ │==============»»»»»»»»»»»»»»»»»»»»»»»»»»│ │90 p 576   │
 │ 7│TopCandidate │87/92    │ │=============»»»»»»»»»»»»»»»»»»»»»»»»»» │ │87 / 572   │
 │10│Rollo'sChet  │91/91    │ │==============»»»»»»»»»»»»»»»»»»»»»»»»»»»│ │91 p 584   │
 │  │             │         │ │                                      │ │           │
 │  │             │         │ │                                      │ │           │
 ├──────────────────┬───────┤ ├────────┬───────┬───────┬─────────────┤ ├───────────┤
 │Pole Speed:    87 │ 87    │ │0:46.3 │Out: 3 │TV:17 │Min. L/S: 575 │ │  587      │
 └──────────────────┴───────┘ └────────┴───────┴───────┴─────────────┘ └───────────┘
                                                                      RACE FILE:
                                                                      6-8-91.crc
```

Based on the computer printouts, three contenders appeared to be key horse candidates: ROLLO'S CHET, BAY STATE ADJUSTER, and the public's favorite, TOP CANDIDATE.

Rollo's Chet was selected as the key horse in this race for the following reasons:

1.   The two pacesetters, Rollo's Chet and Bay State Adjuster, are not equal in talent. The ability of each horse to finish after contesting the early pace strongly favors Rollo's Chet (see the *Pace Analyst* Display Screen and the *Graphics* screen).

2.   Rollo's Chet can be expected to improve. The horse ran two races as a "green baby" six months ago, had been brought back in late May, pushed the pace, finished third, and now appears ready to take Top Candidate on again.

One other horse deserves attention: THE WISH DOCTOR. It's two initial races were considered unimpressive by the computer -- not an uncommon situation with races of this type. Why, then, should we consider this apparent "non-entity?" Two reasons: First, Richard Root is one of the better trainers at Calder; and second, the Improving Newcomers pattern. See it?

The results were as follows ...

Rollo's Chet and one of the first-time starters battled for the early pace. Unfortunately, Bay State Adjuster fell on the backstretch trying to keep up.

Rollo's Chet went on to win by almost 7 lengths. Top Candidate made a valiant effort to catch THE WISH DOCTOR in the stretch for second, but just failed. Rosenose finished fourth.

Times: 23 1/5   46 3/5   1:25 3/5

Rollo's Chet	$11.00	$6.00	$3.20
The Wish Doctor		8.00	3.60
Top Candidate			2.40

$2 Perfecta paid $79.40

Willie Who?

"A rose is a rose -- but not a Willie Shoemaker."

"What's the Shoe doing on this horse?"

That rhetorical question by a respected analyst in the *Daily Racing Form* taught us a lesson we will long remember. We, too, wondered what the great Willie Shoemaker was doing astride this specific horse. Off its past performances the animal appeared hard pressed to get out of the barn, much less the starting gate. Still, there it was, entered to run with one of the world's greatest jockeys on its back.

Later that afternoon we learned what this particular jockey was doing on the horse; just what he was paid to do -- win another race. For the first time in many months (years?) jockey Willie Shoemaker rode a winner which paid off in double digits. Most of the winning tickets were probably held by that small band of *aficionados* who bet their favorite jockey every time he or she rides. It's a guaranteed run to the poorhouse, but a top jockey can prolong the trip.

To repeat what has been said in earlier sections, shrewd trainers regularly turn to a top jockey when they believe they have a horse conditioned and properly placed for a winning effort. The services of that winning jockey are looked upon as "insurance," a further step to lock up that purse money.

Conversely, a trainer so foolish as to feed a dog or two to the likes of a Gary Stevens, LaFitte Pincay or a Chris McCarron will quickly become a Typhoid Mary ... a pariah to be shunned by the community of jockey's agents.

The importance of the jockey has been discussed (argued?) since the beginning of horse racing. Today, there are many qualified jockeys at most tracks, so most experienced handicappers believe that "jockeys don't WIN races, they LOSE them."

A long-time favorite among horsemen is a story told of Eddie Arcaro, "Old Banana Nose," the great jockey of the Golden Age of Sport.

Mounted for a stakes race, Arcaro listened quietly to the trainer's pre-race instructions.

"Lay back in the pack around the first turn. Get him to the outside, maybe fifth or sixth down the backstretch. Move him to fourth around the stretch turn, third by mid-stretch and then come right on in."

When the horse finished last, the trainer went berserk. He began screaming at Arcaro.

"You lousy cockroach! Why didn't you move right on in like I told you?"

"What?" Eddie responded laconically, "And leave the horse out there?"

Without getting into the middle of this, we believe the best rule, at least most of the time, is to bet the HORSE rather than the RIDER. However, there are *three* situations that justify immediate attention to the jockey assignment:

1.   The criteria to the key horse pattern outlined in this section: Whenever a trainer switches a horse from its regular rider(s) to one of the two or three leading jockeys, you have a key horse candidate. When the jockey switch is combined with any other of our winning patterns, you have a very strong indication of trainer intent.

2.   Whenever a capable jockey declines to ride our key horse candidate to ride another entry in the same race, beware! Why?

3.   Whenever an especially poor or totally-inept rider is assigned to the horse we handicapped as the key, re-examine the selection.

The public, especially the name freaks, often recognize these switches and overbet these particularly favored horses. At other times they let these same horses go postward at surprisingly profitable odds. Why? We suppose there are those still asking that rhetorical question: "What is (insert the name of a top jockey on your local racing circuit) doing on this horse?"

EXAMPLE: CHEROKEE RETURNS

At the time this horse was first claimed, it is returned right back to the same class soon after the mandated waiting period has elapsed.

26 May-   For that added insurance we mentioned, the trainer engages Gary Stevens to ride the horse. The public knows Stevens is a leading rider on their circuit, a Derby jockey and a big money winner, nationally. They make his mount the favorite, which pays $5.40 for the win.

EXAMPLE: PROUD GILLY

After winning its maiden race on March 1, the 3-year-old gelding runs a series of losing races under an assortment of jockeys.

Proud Gilly * — Ch. g. 3(Apr), by Proud Truth—Her B., by Time Tested — Lifetime 10 2 1 0 $28,475 — 1991 9 2 1 0 $28,475 — 1990 1 M 0 0 — Turf 2 0 0 0 $550

STEVENS G L — $16,000 — Br.—Darby Dan Fm-Knauss Brenda J (Ky) — 117

Own.—Dye G V Jr — Tr.—Harte Michael G

31Jly91- 1Dmr	my	1	:463	1:122	1:394	Clm 16000	9	3	3½	2hd	1½	12	Stevens G L	LBb	115	*2.70	67-33	Proud Gilly1152 Truly Royal1171½ Dr. Norman1152½	All out 6
24Jly91- 1Dmr	fst	1	:451	1:11	1:38	Clm 25000	4	4	42½	72½	75½	55¾	Nakatani C S	LBb	115	37.10	79-23	KeenLine116hdScreenTle1152DelwreDrive1151½	5-wide stretch 10
28Jun91- 1Hol	fst	1 1/16	:46	1:102	1:423	Clm 50000	2	4	46½	69½	717	722½	Baze R A	LBb	116	18.10	65-11	Renegotiable1173PicAPaster1162½TheCleners1164	No mishap 7
26May91-13TuP	fm	1⅜	①:53	3:004	3:132	3↑Hsta Vista H	1	5	613	1015	1024	1032½	Puglisi I L	Lb	105	13.00	47-20	CpelMeistr-Fr1202Glliri1156LordGrundy-Ir1166	Through early 10
13Apr91-10GG	fm	1 1/16	①:474	1:124	1:453 +	Alw 22000	1	2	24	1½	2½	52½	Nakatani C S	LBb	117	5.30	81-08	YouBlew117½CaptainRaj117hdRecentArrivl1171½	Bumped late 10
23Mar91- 1GG	gd	1	:461	1:103	1:364	Jkln Klgmn H	2	1	11	11	21	23	Nakatani C S	LBb	114	4.80	79-19	Nijinsky'sPrinc1183ProudGilly1143½BodyBubbls1151	Set pace 5
1Mar91- 2SA	sly	1⅛	:46	1:131	1:531	Md 32000	2	1	12	13½	18	15	Baze R A	LBb	117	3.00	64-31	ProudGilly1175SenorLonrd1172½ThClnrs1173½	Lugged out 7/8 6
31Jan91- 4SA	fst	1 1/16	:47	1:121	1:443	Md 32000	3	5	54	65½	55½	58¾	Baze R A	Bb	117	11.10	73-13	Mr. P.AndMax1151BigBarton1172¾Sharkster1171½	Lugged out 12
3Jan91- 2SA	sly	6½f	:214	:444	1:171	Md 32000	10	8	85¾	87½	72¾	55¾	Baze R A	Bb	118	10.90	79-13	ClstilGold118nkPltPtlr118hdCutOfRlity1181½	6-wide into lane 12
6Dec90- 6Hol	fst	7f	:22	:454	1:232	Md 40000	11	3	32	32	57	811½	Boulanger G	b	119	56.70	75-10	BurnAndTurn1177Undermn119½CtchTheExprss119½	Wide trip 12

Speed Index: Last Race: 0.0 — 3-Race Avg.: -10.3 — 6-Race Avg.: -8.8 — Overall Avg.: -12.0

LATEST WORKOUTS Aug 16 Dmr 4f fst :502 H — Jly 18 SA 5f fst 1:023 H — Jly 13 SA 7f fst 1:27 H — Jly 6 SA 5f fst 1:003 H

Trainer Harte finally goes for the brass ring at Del Mar. He brings the horse back in *seven days*. He *drops* the horse from Clm25000 to Clm16000. To virtually guarantee the win, he enlists the services of Gary Stevens.

31 Jul- The horse wins by two lengths. No surprise. With all those pluses the win still pays $7.40. A mild surprise.

Not all of the horses switched to Gary Stevens produce those low, low prices.

EXAMPLE: PRINCE WILD

Trainer Jack Van Berg watches his 2-year-old colt back off twice before taking decisive action.

Prince Wild — Dk. b. or br. c. 2(Mar), by Wild Again—Princess Girl, by Cornish Prince — Lifetime 5 2 1 0 $54,400 — 1991 5 2 1 0 $54,400

VALENZUELA P A — Br.—Durr R C & Calumet Farm (Ky) — 119

Own.—Bozak J & Joann — Tr.—Van Berg Jack C

22Jly91- 8Hol	fst	6f	:22	:441	1:093	Hol Juv Chp	7	3	2½	2hd	2hd	2½	Garcia J A	B	117	5.10	91-13	Scherndo117½PrinceWild1175BurnishedBronze120nk	Sharp try
22Jly91-Grade II																			
10Jly91- 3Hol	fst	5½f	:222	:454	1:04	Alw 32000	6	2	1hd	1hd	11	13	Stevens G L	B	118	*.50	93-12	PrincWild1183BordrCt1151½SingSingSky1154	As rider pleased
23Jun91- 4Hol	fst	5½f	:214	:452	1:041	Md Sp Wt	2	5	42½	51½	2hd	1½	Stevens G L	B	117	7.40	92-11	Prince Wild117½ Overstock117½ EnterThePlayer117¾	Driving
19May91- 6Hol	fst	5f	:214	:452	:574	Md Sp Wt	5	3	2½	11	31½	58½	Valenzuela P A	B	117	4.10	84-08	Stolen Script1172½ Jer Kei1173 Top Senator1171	Gave way
3May91- 6Hol	fst	4½f	:222	:452	:514	Md Sp Wt	8	2		21½	33	54¼	Lovato A J5	B	112	14.50	--	BurnishedBronz1171PrkLiutnnt1174TopSnator117no	Gave way

Speed Index: Last Race: +4.0 — 3-Race Avg.: +4.0 — 4-Race Avg.: +1.0 — Overall Avg.: +1.0

LATEST WORKOUTS Aug 16 Dmr 7f fst 1:272 H — Aug 8 Dmr 5f fst 1:014 H — Aug 1 Dmr 4f fst :484 H — Jly 10 Hol 5f fst 1:023 H

23 Jun- Presumably, the betting public felt even a great rider like Gary Stevens could not get a winning finish out of this youngster. They were wrong. He brought the runner home in a driving finish to pay an amazing $16.80.

EXAMPLE: NUITS ST. GEORGES

We are certain the grandstand bettors were asking that rhetorical question about his one: " What is Gary Stevens doing on this horse?"

Nuits St. Georges — Ch. b. or br. c. 4, by Play Fellow—Effinesse, by Raise a Bid
BAZE R A — Br.—Jaffe P (Ky) — 115
Own.—Jaffe P — Tr.—Peterson Douglas R
Lifetime 9 2 0 2 $88,160 — 1991 1 0 0 0 — 1990 6 2 0 2 $87,650

10Jan91- 6SA	fst	7f	$:22^4$	$:45^3$	1:22	Alw 42000	5	6	8^7	8^{11}	8^{13}	$8^{19\frac{3}{4}}$	Santos J A	LB	114	25.20	73-15	Dewdle'sDncer$116^{1\frac{3}{4}}$WyWild117^1Ptrolro-Ar$115\frac{3}{4}$	Broke slowly	8
21Apr90- 9OP	gd	1⅛	$:45^1$	1:10	1:48	Ark Dby	8	12	12^{14}	$11^{6\frac{3}{4}}$	9^{13}	$10^{16\frac{3}{4}}$	Bruin J E		122	17.40	74-09	SilvrEnding$122^{3\frac{3}{4}}$RlCsh122^5PowrLunch$118^{2\frac{3}{4}}$	6-wide into turn	13
21Apr90-Grade II																				
31Mar90- 9OP	fst	1 1/16	$:46^2$	1:12	1:46	Rebel	1	11	10^{13}	$10^{5\frac{1}{2}}$	2^{hd}	1^4	Bruin J E		114	30.90	72-27	NuitsStGorgs114^4MvrckMnr114^{hd}Trscon$122^{1\frac{1}{2}}$	Wide into lane	11
31Mar90-Grade III																				
17Mar90- 7SA	fst	1 1/16	$:47^4$	$1:12^2$	$1:43^3$	Alw 37000	4	3	$4^{1\frac{1}{2}}$	$4^{1\frac{1}{2}}$	3^2	3^3	Stevens G L		120	13.70	82-13	HwnPss$120\frac{3}{4}$FuturCrr$118^{2\frac{3}{4}}$NutsStGorgs120^4	Lacked room 1/4	8
4Mar90- 6SA	fst	1 1/16	$:47^1$	$1:12^3$	$1:45^2$	Md Sp Wt	8	10	$8^{6\frac{1}{2}}$	$6^{4\frac{1}{2}}$	$1\frac{1}{2}$	$1^{2\frac{1}{2}}$	Stevens G L		117	17.40	76-18	NuitsStGeorges$117^{2\frac{1}{2}}$Tbmn$117^{1\frac{1}{2}}$SpnishSteel$117\frac{3}{4}$	Steadied 3/8	12
17Feb90- 6SA	sly	1 1/16	$:46^3$	$1:11^2$	$1:43^3$	Md Sp Wt	8	3	4^2	$4^{2\frac{1}{2}}$	8^{15}	$8^{22\frac{3}{4}}$	Boulanger G		117	8.20	62-21	SirBeaufort117^8DesertRumor$117^{1\frac{1}{2}}$Forli'sLd117^{hd}	Brief speed	8
28Jan90- 6SA	fst	6f	$:21^4$	:45	$1:11^2$	Md Sp Wt	2	6	$7^{7\frac{1}{2}}$	6^8	5^5	3^2	Boulanger G		118	33.50	77-19	SqurCrk$118\frac{3}{4}$LilBitO'Lrcny$118^{1\frac{1}{2}}$NutsStGorgs$118\frac{3}{4}$	Closed well	9
14Oct89- 3AP	fst	7f	$:22^3$	$:45^3$	$1:22^4$	Md Sp Wt	3	10	$4^{1\frac{1}{2}}$	6^5	6^{13}	$6^{14\frac{3}{4}}$	Sellers S J		122	10.80	73-15	Bedeviled122^{nk} Boxing Lesson$122^{1\frac{1}{2}}$ Dury Lane$122\frac{3}{4}$		10
28Sep89- 5AP	fst	7f	$:22^3$	$:45^1$	$1:23^4$	Md Sp Wt	2	9	$4\frac{3}{4}$	$4^{3\frac{1}{2}}$	5^{10}	$5^{14\frac{1}{2}}$	Sellers S J		122	6.10	69-17	Lance$122^{1\frac{3}{4}}$ Boxing Lesson$122^{3\frac{1}{2}}$ Soul Train122^4		12

Speed Index: Last Race: –17.0 3–Race Avg.: –7.6 5–Race Avg.: -9.2 **Overall Avg.: –9.7**
LATEST WORKOUTS Apr 28 Hol 7f fst 1:27 H Apr 21 Hol 3f fst $:35^1$ H ●Apr 17 Hol 3f fst :35 H Apr 13 Hol 3f fst $:37^1$ H

Take a closer look and you will discover how trainer Peterson is preparing his thoroughbred for a winning race.

28 Jan- In his first race at Santa Anita the horse closes well.

17 Feb- In his second race the horse shows good early speed.

The colt now sports a pattern long cherished by old-time handicappers: Good speed from the gate in one race and a closing kick in another race. The horse is ready to put the two together. With a bit of luck, the colt will turn in a powerful run.

Peterson all but eliminates the luck factor when he sells the horse to Gary Steven's agent.

4 Mar- The horse wins and pays an unbelieveable $36.80. Now we know what Gary Stevens was doing on that horse.

EXAMPLE: MORNIN

This 5-year-old mare seems doomed to a career of perpetual maidenhood (seven consecutive losses) when trainer Henry Moreno turns to LaFitte Pincay. Pincay is a perennial top hand on the Hollywood/Santa Anita circuit.

```
Mornin                              Gr. m. 5, by Halo—Ilenia, by Navajo                        Lifetime      1991  2  0  0  0
  BAZE R A                                 Br.—Wichita Equine Inc (Ky)                   19  2  3  5     1989 12  2  3  4     $73,225
Own.—Kem Diane C                           Tr.—Moreno Henry                      115        $80,900      Turf  7  2  1  1     $45,025
14Feb91- 8SA  fm 1    ①:461 1:104 1:354    ⒻAlw 39000    9 5 66  87¾ 713 818¼ Baze R A     LBb 115 33.40  65-16 DH PrfrArts-Ir1151 DH VClr-Fr1141¾CIddMrs1142¾  No mishap 10
30Jan91- 5SA  fm 1⅛   ①:462 1:104 1:481    ⒻAlw 39000    5 6 68  912 914 919¾ Baze R A     LBb 115 15.80  63-17 FirsidFvorit114hdMySongForYou1161GrndAwrd1151¾  Faltered 9
7Aug89- 8Dmr fm 1⅛    ①:48  1:13  1:512 3↑ⒻAlw 38000  8 7 711 77  43  3nk Pincay L Jr      117  3.70  76-24 Edge Of Heaven117hd Bracorina117hd Mornin117¾  9
10Jly89- 9Hol fm 1 1/16 ①:464 1:104 1:421  ⒻAlw 31000    4 6 611 67¾ 53½ 1no Pincay L Jr      119  3.90  83-15 Mornin119no DH IvoryTowr119 DH StylshStr1192  Wide into lane 7
29Jun89- 9Hol fm 1    ①:454 1:111 1:362    ⒻAlw 31000    5 6 616 64½ 64½ 21½ Pincay L Jr      119  6.70  81-18 No Sales Tax1171½ Mornin119¾StylishStar119¾  Wide into lane 8
15Jun89- 8Hol fm 1 1/16 ①:461 1:103 1:413  ⒻAlw 31000    8 10 1011 76½ 77¾ 44½ Pincay L Jr     119  4.30  81-14 A Thrilling Moment1152¾ Paper Princess1171ToTheAltar119¾  10
2Jun89- 6Hol fm 1 1/16 ①:47  1:12  1:441 3↑ⒻMd Sp Wt  7 7 88½ 95¾ 63¾ 11  Pincay L Jr      117  5.10  73-21 Mornin1171NoblAndNc115noDlght'sTrbut1151¼  Wide into lane 12
6May89- 4Hol fst 1    :451 1:092 1:344 3↑ⒻMd Sp Wt    6 6 64¾ 56½ 56½ 48½ Garcia H J        114  4.80  81-09 Sticky Wile1098½ Delight's Tribute1151VoicesOfChildren114¾  8
23Apr89- 6SA  fst 1 1/16 :463 1:112 1:444   ⒻMd Sp Wt    9 2 2½  1hd 1hd 33½ Garcia H J5       112  9.00  74-17 Valdez Pride1172½ Delight's Tribute117¾ Mornin1122¼  12
9Apr89- 6SA  fst 1    :463 1:113 1:38      ⒻMd Sp Wt    10 7 74½ 52¾ 42¾ 32¾ Garcia H J5      112  7.80  75-14 Black Stockings1171 Valdez Pride1171¾ Mornin1121  10
    9Apr89-Wide 7/8 turn, into stretch
  Speed Index:  Last Race: -19.0      3-Race Avg.: -13.0       7-Race Avg.: -7.5          Overall Avg.: -8.3
 LATEST WORKOUTS  Mar 4 SA 6f gd 1:131 H     Feb 26 SA 5f fst 1:01 H     Feb 20 SA 4f fst :481 H     Feb 11 SA 4f fst :484 H
```

2 Jun- Even with a few good rides to her credit, Mornin showed just too many failures. The consistency crowd wasn't buying. The Pincay fans were lukewarm. Under the guidance of a master rider, the mare wins by one length and pays $12.20.

EXAMPLE: STICKY TABLE

Like Gary Stevens, Lafitte Pincay is sometimes allowed to go to the post at attractive odds.

```
Sticky Table *                      B. g. 4, by Never Tabled—Sticky Caper, by Gummo            Lifetime      1991  1  0  0  0
  HANSEN R D                        $8,000 Br.—Wygod M J (Cal)                           11  1  0  0     1990  8  1  0  0     $13,525
Own.—Wygod Mr-Mrs M J                      Tr.—Morey William J Jr                117        $14,000
19Apr91- 7GG  fst 6f    :222  :454 1:11      Clm 12500     2 10 106 86¾ 811 811¾ Hansen R D    LBb 119 14.10  71-16 Freezing Creek119¾ Play War1194 Whatasaros1192  No threat 12
     19Apr91-Lacked room far turn-to 1/8
19Dec90- 9Hol fst 1 1/16 :462 1:11 1:432     Clm 14000     9 2 3nk 53½ 911 917¼ Martinez F F5 LBb 109 65.10  66-17 Rflmkr115¾Md'sIntrc115nkCtOfArms1154¼  Broke out,bumped 11
8Nov90- 9Hol fst 1      :444 1:10  1:362     Clm 14000     6 7 72¾ 75½ 74½ 65¼ Desormeaux KJ LBb 113  5.20  76-17 GringoGreg115¾FreckleFaceBoi115¾He'sRaja1151  Bumped 1/4 11
27Oct90-14SA  fst 6f    :212  :442 1:102     Clm 13000     6 11 1110 85½ 86 64¾ Alvarado F T  LBb 115 44.70  79-15 CurraghView116¾FamousRod1181Fireliner113¾  4-wide stretch 12
15Jun90- 3Hol fst 1     :451 1:103 1:364     Clm 20000     2 6 64 44 44 48½  Desormeaux KJ  b 118  5.30  71-19 RondTwo1155DcMrry1151¾ExclIntprfrmr1171¾  Stumbled start 7
26May90- 1Hol fst 1 1/16 :462 1:11 1:441     Clm 32000     6 5 42½ 42 42½ 47¾ Pincay L Jr     b 119  7.30  71-16 CherokeeReturns1162¾ChifDr1161¾DistinctivNobl1163½  Evenly 8
11May90- 2Hol fst 1 1/16 :47 1:114 1:443  3↑Md 32000     9 2 1hd 1hd 1½ 13½  Pincay L Jr     b 117  8.70  77-15 Sticky Table1173½ Renegado I1131 Tuarn1181  Driving 12
20Apr90- 1SA  fst 6f    :214  :453 1:13      Md 28000      10 7 74¾ 84¾ 54½ 73 Kimes C5       b 111 30.90  68-20 Fast Roller118hd Dr. Hyde1181 Debette Glory118½  No factor 12
2Mar90- 4SA  fst 6f     :214  :453 1:113     ⓈMd 28000     5 6 65 44½ 36 510  Kimes C5       b 111  8.70  68-23 Hughly'sMoton1181¾WhskyJck1181¾Crcmstllr1185  No mishap 12
6Sep89- 4Dmr fst 1      :471 1:121 1:382     Md 32000      2 1 1hd 21½ 43½ 57½ Baze R A       b 117  9.70  66-15 Catebo112½ Gove1172½ Cub One1174  9
  Speed Index:  Last Race: -17.0      3-Race Avg.: -11.3       6-Race Avg.: -12.3         Overall Avg.: -11.4
 LATEST WORKOUTS  Apr 28 GG 4f fst :483 H     Apr 12 GG 6f fst 1:16 H     Apr 5 GG 5f fst 1:023 H     Mar 29 GG 4f fst :494 H
```

The 4-year-old gelding shows marked improvement in its first two March/April races at Santa Anita. This is a pattern we will discuss in detail elsewhere.

11 May- The horse is moved across town to the other pole of the Southern Cal Axis. Trainer Morey knows those two races have set his horse on edge. He enlists the services of the best jockey available - LaFitte Pincay. The public sees only two lackluster races and questions Pincay's appearance on a dog. The horse

leads at every call, wins by 3-1/2 lengths and pays a terrific $19.40!

EXAMPLE: COAT OF ARMS

The past performance lines of this gelding offer several commentaries on the winning patterns presented in this book.

Coat Of Arms Ch. g. 4, by Spend a Buck—A Status Symbol, by Exclusive Native
FAUL R J $12,500 Br.—Kilroy W S (Ky)
Own.—R&WCatalanoLtd&DoubleDown Tr.—Catalano Wayne M 117
Lifetime 9 2 1 3 $22,090 | 1991 1 0 0 0 | 1990 8 2 1 3 $22,090 | Turf 1 0 0 1 $990

13Jan91- 9SA	fst	$1\frac{1}{16}$	:47	$1{:}11^1$	$1{:}43^4$	Clm c-20000	10	6	$7^{3\frac{1}{2}}$	$7^{6\frac{1}{2}}$	10^{12}	11^{22}	McCarron C J	LBb	115	*2.60	62-20	Cesar Eduardo117^4Shearhope116^{hd}RadarAlert$115^{1\frac{1}{2}}$	Wide trip 11
28Dec90- 2SA	fst	1	$:46^3$	$1{:}11^3$	$1{:}37^2$	Clm 16000	4	7	8^8	$9^{5\frac{1}{2}}$	$7^{4\frac{1}{2}}$	$1^{1\frac{1}{2}}$	McCarron C J	LBb	115	*2.60	86-22	CotOfArms$115^{1\frac{1}{2}}$NoDblsMtch$113^{\frac{3}{4}}$Estrngd115^1	7-Wide stretch 10
19Dec90- 9Hol	fst	$1\frac{1}{16}$	$:46^2$	1:11	$1{:}43^2$	Clm 16000	8	1	2^{hd}	1^{hd}	3^{nk}	3^1	Santos J A	LBb	115	3.00	82-17	Riflemker$115^{\frac{3}{4}}$Medow'sInterco115^{nk}CotOfArms$115^{4\frac{1}{2}}$	3rd best 11
30Nov90- 3Hol	fst	$1\frac{1}{16}$	$:45^3$	$1{:}10^3$	$1{:}43^3$	Clm 25000	5	3	$3^{2\frac{1}{2}}$	$3^{2\frac{1}{2}}$	2^2	$2^{1\frac{1}{2}}$	Santos J A	LBb	115	2.90	80-19	RuleAll$115^{1\frac{1}{2}}$CotOfArms115^{no}QuitlyOrgnizd$115^{1\frac{1}{2}}$	Steadied 7/8 6
22Nov90- 5Hol	fst	1	$:45^1$	$1{:}10^2$	$1{:}36^2$	Clm 20000	1	3	3^{nk}	3^{nk}	3^{nk}	$3^{1\frac{1}{2}}$	Bellido A H5	LBb	110	16.70	81-12	Maxibob$115^{1\frac{1}{2}}$ RisingWine115^{hd}CoatOfArms110^{hd}	Lugged out 10
14Nov90- 5Hol	fst	6f	$:21^4$	$:45^1$	$1{:}10^3$	Clm c-16000	1	12	$5^{4\frac{1}{2}}$	6^5	$6^{4\frac{1}{2}}$	$6^{1\frac{1}{2}}$	Baze R A	B	115	31.00	86-16	Maxibob115^{nk} Kelly G.115^{hd}ColonelRumbo$115^{\frac{3}{4}}$	Saved ground 12
29Sep90-11Cby	fm	*$7\frac{1}{2}$f (T)	:23	$:46^3$	$1{:}29^3$	3↑Alw 9000	8	2	$4^{1\frac{1}{2}}$	3^1	2^{hd}	$3^{1\frac{1}{2}}$	Munoz O R	Bb	111	7.40	— —	Nice Cut111^{nk}Burloy$112^{1\frac{1}{2}}$CoatofArms111^{no}	Wide throughout 10
19Aug90- 1EIP	fst	$6\frac{1}{2}$f	$:22^3$	:47	$1{:}19^1$	3↑Md 16000	7	4	$4^{1\frac{1}{2}}$	$4^{1\frac{1}{2}}$	4^{nk}	$1^{1\frac{1}{2}}$	Troilo W D	Bb	115	9.70	88-15	Coat of Arms$115^{1\frac{1}{2}}$ [D]Sea Island120^2 Judd115^{no}	Rough trip 12
28Jly90- 8EIP	fst	1	$:47^1$	$1{:}12^3$	$1{:}39^2$	3↑Md Sp Wt	11	10	11^{15}	11^{18}	10^{24}	$9^{18\frac{1}{2}}$	McKnight J	Bb	112	13.00	57-20	VaguelyIrish121^{nk}MjorExhibition107^2JohnnyFst$112^{1\frac{1}{2}}$	Outrun 11

Speed Index: Last Race: −18.0 3–Race Avg.: −5.6 6–Race Avg.: −6.6 Overall Avg.: −5.3
LATEST WORKOUTS Feb 17 SA 5f fst $1{:}02^2$ H Feb 10 SA 5f fst 1:03 H

First, on August 19, the Ellis Park trainer drops his maiden runner into a claimer to snare a purse and a $21.40 mutuel. This move happens everywhere!

Second, twice at Hollywood Park, the horse is raced on *eight days rest.* Both efforts are good, but losers. Why? The animal is being raised in class both times. That's a no-no.

28 Dec- At last, the all-out effort. The horse is moved across town, entered in the *same class eight days* after its third place finish. The final insurance is afforded by jockey Chris McCarron, arguably the best jockey in North America. The public is ready, making Coat of Arms a moderate favorite. The winning payoff is $7.20.

EXAMPLE: SETI I.

This much-traveled gelding may eventually find a permanent home somewhere in the nation. It definitely is not a stakes runner.

Seti I. B. g. 4, by John's Gold—Run for Daylight, by Pass Catcher
DESORMEAUX K J Br.—Rabat K (NY) 114
Own.—Arnold D Tr.—Van Berg Jack C
Lifetime 22 3 2 8 $90,597 | 1990 18 3 2 7 $85,617 | 1989 4 M 0 1 $4,980 | Turf 10 2 1 4 $54,712
10Dec90- 7BM fm *1⅛ Ⓣ:472 1:123 1:484 B M Derby 4 10 119¾ 118¼ 53 65½ Doocy T T LBb 114 15.50 80-16 Sekondi-Fr114¾CourtesyTitle1153AppelingMissy1131 No rally 12
10Dec90-Grade III
11Nov90- 8Hol fm 1⅛ Ⓣ:464 1:101 1:463 Hol Dby 4 11 119½ 109¾ 78½ 77½ Garcia J A Lb 122 94.50 87-09 Itsllgreektome122hdSptimCil1222Anshn-GB1221¾ Steadied 7/8 12
11Nov90-Grade I
13Oct90- 8Haw gd 1⅛ Ⓣ:493 1:143 1:533 Haw Dby 10 5 53½ 76 43 3½ Miller S E Lb 115 8.90 66-37 Tutu Tobago113hdTakeThatStep122¾SetiI.1152 Wide into lane 11
23Sep90- 7LaD fm 1 1/16 Ⓣ:483 1:123 1:42 Tem Hill H 11 7 53 52½ 35½ 38½ McCarron C J Lb 115 8.40 88-07 In Excess-Ir1159 On theEdge116nkSetiI.1151 4-wide into lane 11
26Aug90- 7AP gd *1 Ⓣ:481 1:142 1:40 3↑Alw 17000 11 10 1013 96¾ 52½ 12 Sellers S J Lb 112 9.10 — — Seti I.1122 Imagine the Thrill122¾ Ala Dante1152¾ Driving 12
2Aug90- 8AP fm *1⅛ Ⓣ:49 1:134 1:512 3↑Alw 19500 5 7 99½ 98 78¾ 76½ Pettinger D R Lb 115 3.00 — — Mr. Relentless116½ Koko's Boy1221¼Kirgiz1151¾ Wide stretch 11
16Jly90- 6AP gd *1 Ⓣ:483 1:13 1:372 Alw 19500 3 5 75½ 53½ 32¾ 22½ Pettinger D R Lb 122 3.50 — — Forbidden Kiss1162½ Seti I.1222½PulltheLever1162½ Mild rally 10
28Jun90- 6CD fm 1 1/16 Ⓣ:481 1:132 1:442 Alw 31350 5 3 2hd 2hd 1hd 2nk Allen K K b 121 6.80 91-11 RvvthKng119hd DH SU.121 DH Gy'sBstB1183 Bore out stretch 7
28Jun90-Disqualified and placed third; Dead heat
13Jun90- 6CD fm *1 Ⓣ 1:37 Alw 27250 8 6 56½ 41½ 2hd 1hd Allen K K b 121 3.50 — — Seti I.121hd Lord of the Riff1095 Magic Field1122¾ Driving 10
3Jun90- 6CD fst 1 1/16 :474 1:133 1:47 Alw 26400 4 5 35 3nk 11 2½ Allen K K b 121 4.30 78-22 Power Lunch121½ Seti I.1217 Hays Dusty Pick112no 2d best 7
Speed Index: Last Race: -4.0 3-Race Avg.: -1.6 5-Race Avg.: -1.6 Overall Avg.: -1.3
LATEST WORKOUTS ●Feb 15 SA Ⓣ 5f fm 1:014 H (d) Feb 8 SA Ⓣ 6f fm 1:22 H (d) Feb 3 Hol 5f fst 1:024 H

Seti I. did pick up a purse during his brief stay in Chicago.

26 Aug- The trainer drops his runner out of the feature race and puts him in the hands of another great jockey, Johnny Sellers. A $20.20 mutuel is truly remarkable for a rider of this caliber.

EXAMPLE: SUPER FORT

This is another horse that was in danger of becoming a maiden forever. Always a bridesmaid but never a bride. Eight tries for a maiden win in its first year at the races.

Super Fort Dk. b. or br. g. 4, by Fort Calgary—Apple Plus, by Bold Joey
VALENZUELA F H $8,000 Br.—Dante T (Cal) 119
Own.—Boston Garden West Et al Tr.—Matos Gil
Lifetime 14 3 3 1 $22,663 | 1991 6 3 0 0 $12,775 | 1990 8 M 3 1 $9,888
16Mar91- 7GG fst 6f :214 :441 1:091 Clm 14000 9 6 53½ 52¾ 65¼ 73½ Valenzuela F H LB 116 27.80 89-08 LouisElQuarto117¾FamousRoad117¾Usurp112nk Steadied late 10
3Mar91- 9GG sly 6f :221 :453 1:113 Clm 14000 4 5 56 55 56½ 45¼ Valenzuela F H LB 116 12.80 74-27 Kyoed117¾LouisElQurto1174½PerfctPrnkstr117½ Showed little 6
24Feb91- 9GG fst 6f :22 :444 1:102 Clm 8000 7 4 2hd 2hd 1hd 1½ Valenzuela F H LB 117 9.50 86-13 Super Fort117½ Curragh View117noColoneoric117nk Held well 9
7Feb91- 4GG gd 1 :47 1:114 1:404 Clm 10000 2 6 68 59½ 58½ 57½ Sibille R LB 117 5.20 53-39 AskMToWin1171Impulsivnss1132½MistrJo1171 Crowded start 6
26Jan91- 9GG fst 6f :22 :444 1:102 Clm 6250 6 7 31½ 32 31 11 Hansen R D LB 117 *3.40 86-12 Super Fort1171 Chester B.117½LoverJuan1191 Rallied gamely 10
4Jan91- 3BM fst 6f :223 :453 1:113 Ⓢ Md 12500 1 2 1hd 1hd 12 11 Hansen R D LB 120 3.50 78-17 SuperFort1201AnExtrTwo1201½ThCrystlKid1202 Held gamely 9
16Dec90- 4BM gd 6f :224 :462 1:114 3↑Ⓢ Md 12500 7 5 2hd 2½ 34 46½ Valenzuela F H LB 119 3.60 74-18 DrmtcTrco1192LghtThLntrn1193Jos'sNghtOt1191½ Weakened 11
11Nov90- 2BM fst 6f :222 :451 1:093 3↑Ⓢ Md 18000 10 5 32 52½ 65 66 Frazier R L LB 117 6.00 86-09 Send Money Dad1192 Barry Versus1201½Raffar114hd Even try 12
26Oct90- 2BM fst 6f :221 :453 1:11 Ⓢ Md 14000 8 2 31½ 2½ 1hd 21 Martinez O A Jr LB 116 *2.60 84-12 PacMania'sBoy1181SuperFort1161½Mind'sRuler1181 Game try 12
5Oct90- 5BM fst 6f :221 :451 1:114 3↑Md 12500 5 3 2½ 31½ 3½ 32½ Martinez O A Jr LB 119 3.80 79-15 Burn Sun1192 Melanies Toy122nkSuperFort119½ Pressed pace 11
Speed Index: Last Race: -4.0 3-Race Avg.: -1.3 9-Race Avg.: -3.7 Overall Avg.: -4.2
LATEST WORKOUTS Feb 17 GG 4f fst :483 H

4 Jan- Trainer Matos starts the new year on a positive note. Ron Hansen, Northern California's winningest jockey, rides Super Fort to his first victory. The pay is $9.00.

EXAMPLE: PILES OF PLEASURE

Like all outstanding jockeys, Ron Hansen manages to get a bit of something extra from each of his mounts.

Piles Of Pleasure
Ro. m. 5, by Prince Card—Arlisa, by Pleasure Seeker
Br.—Moorhead G & Lynn (Wash)
Tr.—Hilling J M

SNYDER B D
Own.—Sabella L

Lifetime	1991	2	1	0	0	$7,150
	19	3	5	5	1990	3	0	0	0	$388
114	$39,140		Turf	7	1	2	2	$19,900

5Apr91-8CC fm 1½ ①:481 1:122 1:434 +	⑤Clm 32000	3 8 89 74½ 79½ 57½	Snyder B D	LB 116	25.50	85-07 Pichy Nany116¹ Half Cream116²½ Our Ole Lady116¼ No rally 9
6Jan91-7BM fst 1 :454 1:10¹ 1:36	⑥Clm 12500	7 8 85½ 85 51½ 1nd	Hansen R D	LB 116	6.90	90-15 PilesOfPlesure116nd Ctrto116¼GumboyGrl116½ Railled gamely 9
10Dec90-7BM fm *1⅛ ①:482 1:13³ 1:51	3↑⑥Hcp 12500s	1 5 64 75 61³ 66½	Schacht R	LB 114	4.00	65-21 FireseidFvorit118²½CopprSnd119¾LtstRcr113nd Bumped start 9
10Dec90-3BM fst 1½ :479 1:11½ 1:48½	3↑⑥Hcp 12500s	3 3 31 53½ 54½ 69½	Schacht R	114	3.90	51-16 Ms.DixieD117½ExcousFromRoum113¾PsDBourr116½ Gave Way 9
4Nov90-9Hol fst 1½ :462 1:11½ 1:44½	3↑⑥Clm 12500	6 12 94½ 99½ 99½ 99½	Baze R A	B 116	9.00	69-21 ComplAccord116¼Cribn-Mx116¾HollyDn116nd Broke poorly 12
11Dec90-9BM fst *1⅛ ①:474 1:124 1:504	⑥Hcp 12500s	3 3 33 22 32½ 31½	Gonzalez R M	116	6.90	75-19 Shady Speculation117¾ B' Gotcha112¼ Piles Of Pleasure116¼ 8
13Dec90-9BM fst 1¼ :454 1:364 2:031	3↑⑥Hcp 6250s	3 7 710 77³ 611 613	Chapman T M	118	3.10	85-14 Patinadee116³ Hight Light115³ Katy Jack113¼ 8
27Nov90-6BM fst 1⅛ :463 1:11³ 1:51	3↑⑥Hcp 6250s	7 11 1110 119½ 64¼ 31½	Frazier R L	119	2.70	84-21 Lady Kell116nk Sparkling Coleen113½ Piles Of Pleasure118¹ 11
16Oct90-4BM fm 1⅛ ①:472 1:41 2:212	3↑⑥Hcp 12500s	2 5 517 54½ 43½ 37½	Frazier R L	114	*1.70	69-23 Joys Of Love109¾ Katie Kould115nk Piles Of Pleasure114nk 9
7Oct90-10BM fm 1⅛ ①:472 1:13 1:46¹	⑥Alw 17000	10 9 94½ 52½ 1½ 1²	Frazier R L	116	5.70	72-17 Piles Of Pleasure116² Maroon Buck116nk Dusky Pine116¹ 11

Speed Index: Last Race: -8.0   3-Race Avg.: -9.3   5-Race Avg.: -9.4   Overall Avg.: -4.1
LATEST WORKOUTS   Mar 30 6G 6f fst 1:17⁴ H   Mar 23 6G 5f fst 1:02¹ H   Mar 16 6G 4f fst :50 H   Mar 19 6G 6f fst 1:14³ H

Consistency is a jewel. Consistency is a fetish of small minds. Whatever consistency is, Piles of Pleasure does not have it. The betting public figures not even Hansen can do much with this "one-win-in-ten-tries" dog. A handful of Hansen fans keep the odds from blowing a fuse in the tote board.

16 Jan-   Hansen does get that something extra from the mare. She rallies for the win, paying her backers $14.00 for each $2.00 ticket.

EXAMPLE: UNDAUNTED PIRATE

Rested for more than six months after breaking her maiden, the filly is (almost) ready when she runs at the Sonoma County Fair.

Undaunted Pirate
B. f. 3(May), by Pirate's Bounty—Daring Dann, by Twist the Axe
Br.—Wyyged M J (Cal)
Tr.—Bryner Ray

STANLEY M K
Own.—Thirlot B

Lifetime	1991	2	1	1	0	$12,750
	3	2	1	0	1990	1	1	0	0	$4,950
114	$17,700

7Aug91-11Bmf fst 6f :22 :443 1:10	⑥Alw 17000	6 4 32 1hd 1½ 1½	Warren R J Jr	Bb 116	3.00	90-15 UndntdPrt117⁴½FrntrNrsng116²⅓MstclMr116¼ Wide, held well 6
24Jly91-9SR fst 6f :213 :443 1:094	⑥Clm 25000	3 5 1¼ 2¹ 2½ 2¹	Stanley M K	Bb 114	12.20	90-14 LdnpRlkn116¹½UnduntdPrt114¹½ScrmnoLwr116¹ Ducked in 1/16 8
12Nov90-3Md 20000 fst 6f :223 :452 1:10¹	⑥Md 20000	9 5 3nk 2hd 2hd 1½	Stanley M K	Bb 117	13.00	89-12 UnduntedPirte117⅓MissPrking112⁴StrBolid112³ Held gamely 1

Speed Index: Last Race: +5.0   3-Race Avg.: +3.3   3-Race Avg.: +3.3   Overall Avg.: +3.3
LATEST WORKOUTS   Aug 17 Pln 4f fst :50⁴ H   Jly 17 Pln 4f fst :49¹ H   Jlv 10 Pln 6f fst 1:15⁴ H   Jly 3 Pln 6f fst 1:14¹ H

24 Jul-   The horse forces the pace all the way, finishing second by one length. A perfect pattern.

7 Aug-   The horse is then switched to Ron Warren for her race at the San Mateo County Fair (Bay Meadows Racetrack). Warren is second only to Ron Hansen on the Northern California circuit.

Possibly because of the jump in class, Undaunted Pirate pays
$9.60 for his victory.

EXAMPLE: ERRANTRY

After its quick trip to Santa Anita, the filly runs a disappointing third on
March 10. This despite the services of Roberto Gonzalez, no worse than the
third best rider in Northern California.

After running two indifferent races, the horse is rested, then pointed for
racing on the County Fair circuit.

9 Jul-   Rested for 74 days, Errantry comes back running. Entered in
            the feature race -- a handicap -- at the Solano County Fair, the
            horse pushes the pace, losing out deep in the stretch. Another
            perfect pattern.

25 Jul-   Trainer Larson leaves little to chance. He drop his entry from
            a handicap into an allowance sprint. Once more he turns the
            horse over to his favorite "money" rider, Roberto Gonzalez. The
            combination produces the anticipated win. The payoff is a nice
            $10.20.

The "hot" apprentice jockey is another switch to watch for, as discussed
earlier. New riders - apprentices - are always appearing on every race
program. The racegoer must quickly learn which are establishing themselves
as winners and attracting the attention of the successful trainers.

EXAMPLE: HILL TO CLIMB

Following a winless summer at Hollywood and Del Mar, Jim Benedict vans his filly north. She is rested for the winter and spring meets at Bay Meadows and Golden Gate Fields.

When three different riders fail to score a win, the trainer turns to a fourth, Bart Snyder, the leading apprentice rider on the Northern California circuit.

14 Mar— There is always plenty of money around to go on a "hot" apprentice. Still, that inconsistent "one-win-in-thirteen-tries" probably keeps the odds from sinking any lower. Snyder wins easily by 3 1/2 lengths to pay $11.00.

The "Capable" Jockey

Yes, it can be said: "jockeys don't win races, they lose them." Even world-class riders can blow a race that should be a snap for any apprentice. Pat Day's Breeders' Cup ride aboard Easy Goer was ghastly. More recently, Craig Perret, aboard Foreign Aid, singlehandedly lost a race that would have been won had he been a sack of flour. It happens. Even good riders put in a lousy race once in a while. Still, handicappers should be able to distinguish between the *capable* and the *inept*! Here are a few signs when looking for a "capable" rider:

1. A logical contender with good EARLY SPEED should never be allowed to duel with a "cheap speed" runner. In routes, the horse should be ridden to the first turn just fast enough to outrun all those nearer to the rail and, if possible, just ahead of the outside horses to force them wide. In sprints, the early speed horse should be urged to

the front and the jockey should never allow any closer to pull along side. A good jockey looks for the chance to get the horse "loose on the lead" (in front, alone) if it's possible.

2.   OFF-THE-PACE horses should be ridden within a reasonable distance of the leaders -- three or four lengths in sprints, and four or five lengths in routes. This, of course, depends on the pace and other factors that can't be judged here.

3.   A logical contender with good LATE SPEED should be ridden from the inside post fast enough to make the outside horses work for the lead, but not so fast to take the lead. An outside closer should be ridden fast enough to be behind the leaders on the turn but not so fast to be forced wide. In a field of eight or more, any jockey aboard a closer that starts a sprint from an inside post deserves a trophy if the horse finishes in the top two. That's the toughest of all spots.

4.   When a horse is running a turn, in most cases it must modify its stride to counterbalance the centrifugal force of the bend. Once it enters the straightaway, it usually needs to "change its lead" to return to its normal stride. A capable jockey will get the horse to complete this process quickly and then begin a fluid rider motion with his mount to make the stretch drive an efficient run to the wire. If an exhausted horse falls at the top of the stretch it is often due to its failure to accomplish this move.

Jockeys that win consistently by applying these riding basics can be called "capable." We only hope that those that don't will never be aboard our key horse candidates.

To repeat, we believe the best policy is to bet the horse, not the rider. However, one jockey switch that cannot be ignored occurs when the trainer suddenly changes from his regular rider -- or assortment of riders -- to one of the top two or three jockeys or the "hot" apprentice rider.

Should the trainer mix in one or more of our other key horse patterns an especially powerful contender frequently emerges.

The Last Mile

"The flat mile? It's the toughest distance in racing. The acid test for thoroughbreds."

The speaker is Farrell Jones, for many years a leading trainer on the rich tracks of Southern California. His listeners are a small group of racing writers gathered to watch the early morning workouts on Hollywood Park's training track.

"It's too long for a sprint and too short for a real route rating. The flat mile is always a dilemma for both trainers and jockeys."

Jones pauses to check his stopwatch. Surreptitiously, he is timing the workout of a rival trainer's horse.

"Old timers tell me the greatest miler of all was Equipoise, a front-running speedster who would savage any horse foolish enough to draw alongside. I'm told his world record for the mile stood for many years."

Jones glances at the horse galloping past and steals a peek at his timer.

"Every generation has its own favorites. I've always admired Native Diver, another blaze of lightning who would die before quitting."

Of course, Dr. Fager's world record of 1:32 1/5 set about twenty five years ago, is now regarded as the standard for the distance.

This was a particularly remarkable feat considering that the old Arlington Park surface was not considered to be as fast as many of the West Coast courses, and the Tartan Farm's blaze did it carrying 134 pounds!

Today, serious pace handicappers regard the mile to be the longest and, by far, toughest of the sprints. It is normally run around two turns, which explains why non-pace racing fans call it a route. But the mile is rarely won when a horse has to be rated as it is in a traditional distance race. Dr. Fager's second call point was clocked at 1:07 3/5, faster than most sprinters run an entire six panels all-out.

While Jones is long-gone from Hollywood Park, he sometimes used the mile race for his own esoteric purposes. And it is not unusual for present-day trainers to resort to the subterfuge to prepare an animal for a winning run -- and to protect the winner's odds at the same time.

Worked to perfection, the stratagem unfolds in a two-race sequence:

1.   The horse is entered in a race at a distance of one mile. It runs with the leaders throughout much of the race. Ultimately the runner tires, finishing near the back of the pack. The worse the beating, the more favorable for our betting purposes.

2.   The horse is entered in a 6 furlong race, or a 6 1/2 or 7 furlong sprint, and comes in a winner.

Many bettors tear up their tickets in disgust. "Nobody could have picked that horse to win." Not so! The signal was clearly flashed in the horse's running lines in the past performances.

For the purpose of this example, we show only the running times and the positions of the horse throughtout the race. Lengths ahead or behind have been omitted. However, the horses's time at the second call point is important and should not be ignored.

:45.1   <u>1:10.1</u>   1:37.3   2   <u>2</u>   6

In a mile race, the second running time (highlighted) is that of the leader at the second call point (six furlongs). A horse near the lead at that point will be a serious contender when running six furlongs, regardless of where it finishes the mile. In this example our horse finished sixth despite running second to a good six furlong time of 1:10.1.

Many race bettors see only that dismal finish and not the sparkling 6f Pole Speed effort hidden in the past performances. Rest assured the trainer has properly instructed his jockey and has carefully timed his animal to that all-important final quarter-pole. He now knows where to enter his horse for a highly probable winning run.

EXAMPLE: PHIL'S ILLUSION

The single win recorded by this 3-year-old filly provides a near-perfect illustration of the mile switch.

Phil's Illusion		B. f. 3(Mar), by Bates Motel—Hallucinate, by In Reality			
		Br.—Obrecht T (Md)	1990	9 1 1 0	$30,505
DESORMEAUX K J	118	Tr.—Bernstein David	1989	4 M 3 0	$17,525
Own.—Hersh P		Lifetime 13 1 4 0 $48,030	Turf	1 0 0 0	

13Oct90-9SA	6f :21³ :44¹ 1:09²ft	19	LB 117	5²½ 5²½ 8⁷½ 8¹¹½	VlnzlPA⁹	⑦Aw32000	77-16	CentenniTim,FrncSoir,MdiclMrvl 8
13Oct90—Wide trip								
17Sep90-11Fpx	6f :21³ :45 1:10³ft	5	LB 115	1½ 3¹ 2² 44¾	PdrzMA 2	⑦Aw34000	88-10	LttrsOfLov,RofMnd,TrrtorlWtrs 10
9Sep90-1Dmr	6f :21³ :44² 1:10¹ft	9	LB 118	2hd — 1½ 43¼	VlnzlPA³	⑦Aw33000	86-11	LeanPirte,Questioning,FrnceSoir 8
9Sep90—Running positions omitted because of weather conditions								
15Aug90 7Dmr	6f :21³ :44² 1:10 ft	12	LB117	2hd 1½ 11½ 2nk	VlnzlPA⁹	⑦Aw33000	90-14	SkyDrter,Phil'sIllusion,FrnceSoir 9
29Jly90-5Dmr	6½f :21⁴ :44² 1:15⁴ft	10	L 116	2hd 1hd10⁹½10¹³½	NktniCS 2	⑦Aw33000	76-07	Nordicn,TessOfHemt,TntPhyllis 10
30Mar90-7SA	6½f :22¹ :45⁴ 1:17²ft	14	119	1hd 2hd 3¹ 44	DihssyE 1	⑦Aw34000	79-19	Patches, TantePhyllis,LeanPirate 7
14Mar90-5SA	a6½f ⑦:20⁴ :43¹1:14 fm	10	114	4³ 43½10¹²10¹⁵	DsrmKJ3⑦La Habra		76-10	Smthngmrry,BrghtTMnd,FrstFt 11
14Mar90—Run in divisions								
10Feb90-4SA	6f :21⁴ :45 1:11³ft	3	117	2hd 2hd 11 13½	Stevens GL 12⑦Mdn		78-20	Phil's Illusion, Orianova, Cozzy 12
26Jan90-4SA	1 :46 1:11² 1:38²ft	4½	117	1hd 1hd 3½ 71½	ValenzuelPA 2⑦Mdn		64-19	PamperedStr,HilAtlntis,Conteuse 9
30Dec89-4SA	6f :21³ :44² 1:09⁴ft	2½	117	1½ 1¹ 11 21½	VlenzuelPA 19⑦Mdn		90-08	BYowBsl,Phl'sIllusion,LttlLuxrs 12
Speed Index: Last Race: -7.0		3-Race Avg.: -4.0		8-Race Avg.: -3.8				Overall Avg.: -6.2

30 Dec-   With a strong front running effort, Phil's Illusion finishes second in a fast six furlong race.

To both protect the horse's future odds and further prepare it for a winning run, trainer David Bernstein shrewdly avoids a repeat race at the sprint distance.

26 Jan-   Entered in a one mile race, the horse sets the pace to the three-quarter pole. She then drops out of contention, finishing seventh, badly beaten by nearly 12 lengths. Note the Pole Speed time -- 1:11.2.

10 Feb-   Running again at six furlongs, the filly romps in, paying $8.00. The winning time? 1:11.3.

There is no surprise here - provided one is reading the past performance lines correctly.

EXAMPLE: TIME FOR SHAMANS

Trainers at Hollywood Park frequently use the 6 1/2 furlong race in conjunction with the classic mile switch. This is also true for a few tracks on the East Coast ... especially Laurel and Belmont. Time For Shamans offers a fine illustration.

```
Time For Shamans *          Gr. g. 5, by Northern Jove—Sham's Princess, by Sham
                            Br.—Spendthrift Farm Inc (Ky)              1990 17 3 2 3   $27,125
 FLORES D R            115  Tr.—Sadler John W              $12,500    1989  7 0 0 1    $8,500
Own.—Sanger E or Fae        Lifetime 27 4 2 6  $58,175                 Turf  1 0 0 0
26Aug90-3Dmr 7f :221 :451 1:221ft  26 LB116 32 1hd 21½ 57¾ Lopez A D4 16000 83-12 Just Never Mind,Tonzatill,Geyser 9
    26Aug90—Bobbled start
12Aug90-1Dmr 6f :214 :444 1:09 ft  7½ LB115 75 52½ 53 55 DsormuxKJ9 c12500 90-09 Going Easy, Yobbo,Lyphard'sFan 9
    12Aug90—Wide trip
29Jly90-1Dmr 6½f :221 :444 1:161ft  5 L 115 31 31½ 2hd 23½ Davis R G7 12500 83-07 GStdLd,TmFrShmns,DRghtBDdl 12
21Jly90-2Hol 6f :214 :444 1:101ft 13 L 116 86¾ 76½ 65 42½ Flores D R6 12500 86-04 GoingEsy,PinepplJck,WildlyIrish 11
    21Jly90—Bumped start
8Jly90-1Hol 6f :22 :45 1:102ft  4½ L 121 77 65½ 44 44 Davis R G3 c10000 84-14 AudtNghtB,DmscsDrm,GongEsy 11
1Jly90-1Hol 6½f :22 :451 1:163ft  5½ L 118 2½ 2½ 11½ 11½ Davis R G12 10000 92-10 TmFrShmns,JtEch,DRghtByDdly 12
21Jun90-9Hol 1 :452 1:10 1:343ft  5½   115 1½ 1hd 24 611½ Davis R G9 10000 79-11 ThByChf,Gntlmn'sHnr,LckyStrt 12
9Jun90-1Hol 6f :22 :45 1:094ft  6½   121 42 42 34 35½ Davis R G11 10000 86-07 Tomocm,DmscsDrm,TmFrShmns 12
    9Jun90—Wide early
27May90-7GG 6f :214 :443 1:104sy 13   117 2½ 2hd 1½ 1no Frazier R L3 10000 84-19 TmForShmns,Bsngstok,Md'sMstk 8
20May90-2GG 6f :22 :453 1:12 sy  4½   117 33½ 32½ 32½ 46½ Warren RJJr7 c8000 71-23 Shmlssly,RunCougrRn,Don'sTryst 7
    20May90—Wide, weakened
  Speed Index: Last Race: -5.0   3-Race Avg.: -5.3   9-Race Avg.: -4.0   Overall Avg.: -4.6
```

9 Jun- The five-year-old gelding runs a good six furlong race, finishing third despite running wide early.

Like David Bernstein, the trainer opts to avoid a quick repeat of the sprint.

21 Jun- Entered at a flat mile, Time For Shamans is a powerful contender through the first six furlongs. It then drops back, finishing sixth, 11 1/2 lengths behind the winner.

Branded as a "quitter," this runner will be shunned in the future by numerous, unknowing race bettors: Those same bettors who failed to note the gelding's fast time of 1:10.0 for the first six panels.

1 Jul- Going 6 1/2 furlongs, Time For Shamans wins by 1 1/2 lengths and pays a nice $12.60. Again, no surprises. Just a welcome pari-mutuel payoff.

EXAMPLE: NO STORY

After a final all-out but losing try at Hollywood Park, the five-year-old
gelding is moved across town to Santa Anita.

[Racing form chart for No Story]

31 Dec-   Despite finishing three lengths short in his mile race, No Story
was forcing a strong pace through six furlongs.

26 Jan-   One more anomaly of race betting. After clearly signalling his
readiness, the horse is allowed to go postward in a six furlong
race at delectable odds of more than 12 to 1. Why? How can
this happen?

We can only hazard a few guesses.

The consistency crowd probably looked at that 12-race, no-win record for the
prior year and turned elsewhere. We'll never know what turned them off.
Collectively, we have a kaleidoscope of reasons why some horseplayers miss
the boat.

As we indicated early in the book, we watch the trainers. And this time the
trainer led us to the key horse candidate No Story right into the winners
circle. The payoff was a "money from home" $37.60.

One of those horseplayers doomed to die broke is personified by the nervous
little handicapper who surely must haunt every grandstand from Gulfstream
Park to Longacres.

This day he is hurrying for the subway after the last race at Aqueduct. He
is joined by a friend who asks the traditional question.

"How did you make out today, Mac?"

"It was in and out all day. I finally managed to break even and, man, I really need the money."

Not every horse meeting the criteria of this section will pay the juicy, boxcar price returned by No Story. The animal forcing the pace right to the wire will catch the attention of most speed handicappers and often run its next sixer at a very low price.

EXAMPLE: LATEST RACER

After winning its maiden race at Fairplex, Ted West tried his filly in a handicap race where it was defeated by eight lengths. He then moved his campaigner north to Bay Meadows.

14 Oct-   Contending at a flat mile, Latest Racer finishes second while running the six furlongs in a sharp 1:10.3. Any second place finish is guaranteed to draw the attention of every type of race bettor. This includes those bettors who proclaim that 40% of all winning horses ran second in their preceeding races.

8 Nov-   As expected, the filly is made the 4 to 5 favorite and wins its next race -- at six furlongs.

For betting purposes, we much prefer a horse finally beaten off in that mile race by several lengths or several horses, or both. Prion's past performance lines provide excellent examples of a race to bet and a race to avoid.

EXAMPLE: PRION

Trainer Bryan Webb has utilized the mile switch on at least two occasions.

Prion — B. g. 6, by Maheras—Filly Will Fly, by Flying Lark
MILLER D A JR — $6,250 — Br.—Ryncarz Dr-Mrs A J (Wash) — 119
Own.—Mt High Stable & Tolman — Tr.—Webb Bryan

Lifetime: 51 5 5 7 — $50,687
1991: 5 1 1 1 — $8,425
1990: 17 0 2 2 — $11,587

31Mar91-	5GG	fst	6f	$:22^{3}$	:45	$1:09^{4}$	Clm 6250	9	12	12^{13}	12^{14}	12^{17}	$12^{8¾}$	Miller D A Jr	LB	119	5.90	80-10	Arn'sDwn117^{nk}TrprsPrmr117^{2}LckyAdvnc119¾	Stumbled start	12
2Mar91-	4GG	sly	1	$:46^{2}$	$1:12^{2}$	$1:39^{4}$	Clm 10000	2	5	7^{10}	$5^{5½}$	4^{6}	$4^{6½}$	Miller D A Jr	LB	117	2.90	59-30	Hagley's Lion117^{nk} Interflip117^{3} SpanishHawk$117^{3½}$	Even try	8
21Feb91-	5GG	fst	6f	:22	$:45^{2}$	$1:10^{4}$	Clm 8000	5	6	$8^{8½}$	$7^{4½}$	$3^{3½}$	1^{2}	Espindola M A	LB	117	2.60	84-15	Prion117^{2} Geyser117^{nk} Maid's Mistake117^{3}	Drifted out 1/16	9
9Feb91-	9GG	fst	1	$:45^{4}$	$1:10^{1}$	$1:36^{2}$	Clm 10000	6	5	$5^{3½}$	4^{2}	3½	2½	Espindola M A	LB	117	3.80	82-13	Motel Affair117½ Prion117^{nk} Flint117^{1}	Game try	7
13Jan91-	1BM	fst	6f	$:22^{2}$	$:45^{1}$	$1:09^{3}$	Clm 8000	6	8	8^{11}	$7^{7½}$	$6^{4½}$	3^{1}	Hansen R D	LB	116	5.10	87-13	Oak Wine118½ Hot Metal113½ Prion116^{1}	Broke in tangle	8
27Dec90	3BM	fst	6f	$:22^{4}$	$:45^{1}$	$1:10^{1}$	3↑Clm 8000	3	4	$2^{1½}$	$4^{5½}$	5^{7}	$5^{3¾}$	Snyder B D^{5}	L	112	3.00	85-13	Hot Metal$117^{1½}$ Maid's Mistake117^{1} Town117^{1}	Weakened	8
5Dec90	10BM	fst	6f	$:21^{4}$	$:44^{2}$	$1:09^{1}$	3↑Clm 10000	9	3	$8^{9¾}$	8^{11}	$8^{8½}$	6^{4}	Warren R J Jr	LB	117	6.50	90-07	FlashyA.J.117^{2}DaytimeBargin117^{1}WellInTheAir117½	Wide trip	10
3Nov90-	3BM	fst	6f	$:22^{1}$	$:44^{4}$	$1:09^{2}$	3↑Clm c-10000	9	8	$10^{8¾}$	$10^{9¾}$	$8^{8½}$	$8^{5½}$	Judice J C	LB	117	4.80	88-10	NinjPrnc117^{1}Roy!lyDcortd$117^{1½}$Blogorsky117^{hd}	Showed little	12
12Oct90-	7BM	fst	6f	$:22^{3}$	$:45^{3}$	$1:10^{2}$	3↑Clm 16000	5	4	$9^{6¾}$	$10^{8½}$	7^{5}	$6^{2¾}$	Delgadillo C	LB	117	24.10	85-13	SftWtrGld112^{hd}StrtchItOt$119^{1½}$Wckdld117½	Ducked out start	10
23Sep90-	5Lga	fst	6½f	$:22^{1}$	$:44^{2}$	$1:15^{1}$	3↑Clm 12500	4	4	$5^{2¾}$	$4^{3½}$	3^{3}	$4^{1½}$	Delgadillo C	LB	116	3.40e	94-08	CrabSalad122^{1}FlshyA.J.119^{nk}SwiftWterGold122^{hd}	Closed well	12

Speed Index: Last Race: –10.0 — 3–Race Avg.: –3.6 — 8–Race Avg.: –2.2 — Overall Avg.: –2.6

LATEST WORKOUTS Mar 28 GG 5f fst $1:03^{3}$ B — Mar 21 GG 5f my $1:04^{2}$ H (d) — ●Mar 13 GG 5f my 1:01 H (d)

9 Feb- Entered in a race at one mile, the 6-year-old gelding is close to a required swift six furlong pace of 1:10.1. Prion hung on for a gamely second, beaten only one-half length. Not our ideal betting tool, but ....

21 Feb- To our pleasant surprise, Prion's second place finish did not completely destroy his odds. He wins the six furlong event, drawing away to pay a respectable $7.20. Another anomaly of race betting.

2 Mar- Again entered in a one mile race, the animal is far off a slow six furlong pace of 1:12.2. The track condition might account for the slow pace, but not for Prion's failure to stay near the front. This signal tells us the horse is not ready for a winning sprint.

21 Mar- Even though dropped in class, Prion runs the six furlong race just as our pattern predicted he would -- well out of the money.

Still, we will continue to search out and analyze Bryan Webb entries - expecially those dropping down in distance after running the flat mile.

Even when our Last Mile switch points typically to the winner, we have sometimes ended with tickets on a near-miss. As a tool for identifying the key horse, however, it is among the best.

EXAMPLE: DELIGHTFULL MOON

This filly from Longacres tagged us with a loss in her second race at Bay
Meadows.

14 Oct-　　Running second to Bargain Doll's blistering 1:09.1 for the first
　　　　　　six furlongs, Delightful Moon finishes the mile beaten by more
　　　　　　than 6 lengths.　Perfect.

14 Nov-　　The filly misses by 3/4 of a length in a six furlong sprint won
　　　　　　by a flyer in 1:09.3.　Not so perfect.

When we do lose, we hope we can always emulate Stanley the Stoic, another
of those apocryphal ghosts haunting the grandstands from Rockingham Park
to Del Mar.

Stan starts the day at Arlington Park (substitute the name of your local track)
with a $20.00 bet in the first race.　He wins.

Down to the fifth race and he has parlayed that first bet into $900.00.
Comes the final race of the day and Stan bets his entire bankroll, $2,000.00,
on a horse making the classic mile switch.　The animal runs second, beaten
by a nose in a photo finish.

Trudging to his car, he is joined by a friend.

"How was your day?"

Stan the Stoic shrugs.　"I dropped twenty bucks."

If you happen to live near a track where this trainer pattern is used regularly, you have, indeed, found yet one more great key horse tipoff.

In addition to the Last Mile maneuver, some trainers will mix in a jockey switch to further "insure" their potential victory or help boost their return at the window.

EXAMPLE: BRAZEN IRISH

After a winless summer on the Northern California County Fair racing circuit, the 6-year-old mare scored a near-miss at the Bay Meadows Fair. (The San Mateo County Fair races are run over the Bay Meadows track -- hence the designation Bmf).

Knowing that second place finish will severely depress the horse's future odds, trainer Howard Brewen wisely enters Brazen Irish in a mile race at the outset of the regular Bay Meadows fall meeting.

25 Aug-   After setting a six furlong pace of 1:11.3, the mare tires, finishing in sixth place -- just what we're looking for.

9 Sep-   The animal is entered in a six furlong race. To further "insure" the potential victory, trainer Brewen replaces apprentice Bart Snyder with veteran Ron Warren, Jr., a top rider at Bay Meadows and Golden Gate.

Even with all these signals flashing, Brazen Irish is allowed to go to the post at 3 to 1 odds. Her winning time is 1:11. The $8.00 return is akin to Pennies from Heaven.

Trainer Jim Benedict resorts to a more devious ploy to win a purse at handsome odds.

EXAMPLE: WINTER RESORT

Winter Resort Gr. g. 3(Mar), by Zamboni—Dade County, by Warm Front
SIBILLE R $12,500 Br.—Badlands Stable (Cal) **117** Lifetime 10 1 1 2 $7,537 | 1991 3 1 0 1 | 1990 7 M 1 1 $2,087
Own.—Harris Farms Inc Tr.—Benedict Jim

7Feb91- 5GG	gd	6f	$:22^2$	$:46^2$	$1:12^2$	Md 14000	3	2	$3^{2½}$	$2½$	1^{hd}	1^2	Belvoir V T^5	LBb	113	6.90	76-22	$WintrRsort113^2VsonryWondr118^{nk}HrToThr116^4$	Rallied inside	11
16Jan91- 4BM	fst	$1\frac{1}{16}$	$:46^4$	$1:11^4$	$1:44^1$	Md 12500	8	6	$6^{3½}$	$4^{3½}$	$6^{9½}$	$6^{11½}$	Caballero R	Bb	118	18.70	64-15	$AlskWntr118^{1½}Rym'sFol118^{¾}MlbKndGy118^{2½}$	Broke in tangle	9
5Jan91- 2BM	fst	1	$:46^3$	$1:11^2$	1:37	Md 12500	7	3	$2½$	2^{hd}	$3^{1½}$	$3^{6½}$	Caballero R	Lb	118	9.20	78-13	$YorCrr118^5SnstnlCmmndr118^{1½}WntrRsrt118^{nk}$	Weakened late	10
22Dec90- 2BM	fst	6f	$:22^2$	:46	$1:11^1$	(S)Md 12500	6	2	$9^{5½}$	$7^{4½}$	$6^{5½}$	$6^{7½}$	Caballero R	LBb	118	9.20	76-12	$BetABic118^2FlueOfOberwlln118^2JoyfulScor118^1$	Carried wide	12
22Nov90- 5BM	fst	6f	$:22^3$	$:45^1$	$1:09^4$	Md 12500	2	2	$4^{1½}$	3^3	$3^{4½}$	$5^{7¾}$	Caballero R	LBb	118	18.90	83-07	$SeaTheVerdict118^5RightConcept118^{nk}BoldTrojn118^{¾}$	No rally	12
12Oct90- 6Fno	fst	5½f	$:21^2$	$:44^3$	$1:03^2$	(S)Md 16000	4	4	$5^{4½}$	5^6	$4^{3½}$	3^2	McGurn C	LBb	118	2.70	93-05	$Pocket Pete118^1$ $Zanzibar118^1$ $Winter Resort118^{3½}$	Late rally	10
3Oct90- 6Fno	fst	5f	$:22^1$	$:45^3$	$:58^3$	Md 16000	7	2	3^{nk}	$3½$	$3^{1½}$	$4^{3½}$	McGurn C	Bb	118	6.60	84-09	$Exemplary118^2Dad'sMan118^{¾}RaiseNTime118^1$	Speed, no rally	10
7Aug90- 6LA	fst	4½f	$:21^3$	:45	$:51^2$	Md 32000	7	3		$5^{2½}$	$6^{4½}$	$6^{7½}$	Garrido O L	b	119	4.40	89-01	$ConstrctonMn119^{1½}StlnPrfrmnc119^{2½}OrSpy119^{no}$	No menace	8
1Aug90- 4LA	fst	4½f	:22	$:45^1$	$:51^1$	(S)Md 16000	6	6		$3^{1½}$	$3^{2½}$	$5^{8½}$	Sorenson D	b	118	5.80	91-03	$Reid's Gold118^{hd}$ $Starboard Port118^{2½}$ $Teddy Oso118^4$	Evenly	8
14Jly90- 1Boi	fst	5f	$:22^3$	$:45^3$	$:59^4$	Md Sp Wt	4	2	$3½$	3^1	2^2	2^2	Kiser G	b	120	*1.10	78-14	$BigCreekJulie121^2WinterResort120^1ImCptinToo115^4$	Kept on	10

Speed Index: Last Race: –2.0 3–Race Avg.: –8.0 8–Race Avg.: –7.1 Overall Avg.: –8.7
LATEST WORKOUTS Jan 31 GG 5f fst $1:01^2$ H Dec 31 BM 5f fst 1:02 H

Ignoring Boise, we begin tracking the gelding at Los Alamitos.

7 Aug- Returning in *six days*, the horse is *raised* in claiming price and is soundly beaten.

12 Oct- Running on *nine days* rest in the *same class*, the horse should win. It finishes third.

5 Jan- Following two respectable, middle-of-the-pack sprints, Winter Resort is entered in a mile race. The animal is pushing the pace at six furlongs before finishing six lengths out. This is our pattern. Now we wait for the horse to be returned to six furlongs.

16 Jan- Trainer Benedict confounds the savvy handicappers. He enters Winter Resort in a 1 1/16 mile route, a distance that he has never run and to which it is probably not suited. He runs a satisfactory pole speed, but is soundly defeated, as expected.

7 Feb- Payday! Winter Resort is entered in a six furlong race and a jockey switch to Vann Belvoir, a "hot" apprentice rider, makes the horse a key candidate. Winter Resort pushes the pace and draws off to win by two. The route insert probably helped the payoff, a healthy $15.80.

Note that Winter Resort demonstrated a continuing early speed pattern in the route. Also, the move to the slower Golden Gate surface promised to help him in the stretch. Otherwise, we would not have been as enthusiastic on February 7. Dropping from a route to a sprint is usually an unprofitable play.

EXAMPLE: WHAT A SPELL

Relying upon the Last Mile distance switch, trainer Craig Lewis has converted his 3-year-old colt into a galloping four-legged money machine.

23 Dec-   Entered in a Grade III stakes race, What A Spell finishes second in a flat mile race. The youngster was leading the field at six furlongs in 1:11.1.

7 Feb-   Racing in a 6 1/2 furlong sprint at crosstown Santa Anita, the horse wins to pay $8.40. This despite that second place finish and the drop in classification from a stakes race to an allowance race. Wish we had more of these to bet!

After failing to steal the Golden Bear Handicap at Golden Gate Fields, Lewis again enters his runner in a mile race at Santa Anita.

14 Mar-   On a track rated as "good," the horse posts a time of 1:10.3 for six panels. He is then outrun, finishing seven lengths behind the winner.

27 Mar-   What A Spell wins a 6 1/2 furlong handicap and pays another surprising $8.40.

Back in November, Lewis used a different distance switch to set up the maiden win for his colt. Going 1 1/16 miles, the horse forces a swift 1:09.4 pace for the six furlongs before running sixth, eight lengths short of the winner. Dropped down into a 6 furlong race for maidens, What A Spell leads all the way to a win payoff of $6.40.

It's an interesting maneuver, but not consistent enough for regular betting. We'll stay with The Last Mile:

1.   Running the flat mile, the horse must be on or near a credible pace for the first six furlongs. The animal must then drop out of contention, hopefully beaten by several lengths, or several horses.

2.   The horse must run its next race a 6, 6 1/2 or 7 furlongs.

One final note. Experienced handicappers, especially in the East, have discovered that "stretching out" from a 7 furlong sprint to a route is frequently a successful move ... moreso than stretching out from 6 furlongs. Dropping a horse back to a sprint from a route is less reliable. Of course, it is easier to ask the horse to run SLOWER than to ask it to run FASTER. For this reason, the Pole Speed (second call point) of the route, as well as workouts, are usually good means of judging whether the animal can stay in contention in the sprint.

A Big Drop

"I just don't know. Is the trainer buying a purse or unloading an unsound animal?"

This is the puzzled complaint frequently heard from handicappers confronted with a horse dropping steeply in claiming price. The more they puzzle, the better the odds are likely to be.

As we will show in our examples, horses dropping sharply in claiming price are seldom, if ever, claimed by other trainers. These professional conditioners of thoroughbreds are always looking for that potential stakes runner, that Derby winner. They will claim animals with obvious potential, horses running well in their current classes. Drop one of these sharp animals even slightly in claiming price and it will suddenly change ownership via the claiming route.

Aware of these facts of racing life, the knowledgeable trainer will deliberately drop a slow runner to a level where it has an excellent chance to win a purse. Occasionally that drop is a steep one. Neither the trainer nor his colleagues are interested in claiming stock which appears to have only a limited future.

With these facts in mind, we long ago developed our own criteria for horses dropping down in claiming price:

When the animal is entered for 60% or less of its previous claiming price (ie., a drop of 40% or more), we have a wager. Add in one more of our other key horse patterns and we have found a trainer determined to lock in a win.

EXAMPLE: FLYING BOUQUET

After claiming the 3-year-old filly, Trainer Greenman tries his acquisition at three levels; each time at a lower price.

11 Apr-   Dropped from Md20000 to Md12500, the lady is the leader at all calls, rewarding her backers with an $8.40 payoff.

EXAMPLE: AFRICAN ED

After one losing race on the Northern California County Fair circuit, trainer Art Sherman drops his gelding in price for its next run.

12 Jul-   That drop from Clm25000 to Clm16000 just isn't enough. The horse turns in a good third, but is a badly beaten seventh in its very next race at that same 16000 price.

14 Aug-   Sherman sees the light. This time he is going for the gold. The
           horse is dropped from Clm16000 to Clm6250. That is approxi-
           mately 40% of the previous asking price. African Ed is running
           where he belongs. His win tickets pay a pleasant $10.00.

EXAMPLE: QUICK THE TIGER

Sometimes it seems the rich really do get richer. A truly prosperous pair
teamed up to bring this gelding in a winner.

After showing well in a $40,000 sprint at Santa Anita, the horse is shipped
across town to Hollywood Park.

19 May-   Strangely, the animal with Delahoussye still riding turns in a
           dismal performance.

24 May-   *Five days later* the horse is dropped from its $40,000 bracket
           into a claimer for $16,000 animals. Eddie D. is still the rider.
           The public is quick to spot this one; the win price is $5.60.

Bobby Frankel tries Quick The Tiger once more on five days rest. A clever
move, but he pushes the horse up in class. A no-no. The horse loses. Even
Fast Eddie can't turn this trick.

Watching this prosperous pair work together brings to mind the story the
"have nots" like to tell of the "haves." It's not new, but it's a great tale.

We first heard the story shortly after Willie Shoemaker acquired an interest
in a racetrack in Kentucky. The world's winningest jockey was passing

through the holding barn when he encountered Charlie Whittingham, the trainer who regularly placed the Shoe on his best stakes runners.

When Shoemaker spotted his favorite trainer, he smiled and made his pitch.

"Hey Charlie, just the man I want to see. I'd like to talk to you about a loan."

Charlie replied: "Say, that's great, Shoe! How much can you loan me?"

Before we leave Quick The Tiger, consider that race on July 30. From a 12500 claimer at Hollywood Park the animal is dropped 50% into a 6250 race at Los Alamitos, a track with a much lower Purse Index. This unabashed bit of thievery nets another purse and a $10.00 mutuel.

To repeat, sometimes the rich really do get richer.

EXAMPLE: FAREWAY FORLI

Like Quick The Tiger, Hollendorfer's gelding is spotted by the public when it takes a steep plunge in class while being ridden by the best rider at Bay Meadows.

Fareway Forli — Ch. g. 3(Jan), by Forli—Miss Prompt, by Mr Randy
CHAPMAN T M — $10,000 — Br.—Atwood Richards Inc (Ky) — 117
Own.—Herrick & Rancho San Miguel — Tr.—Hollendorfer Jerry
Lifetime 9 1 0 2 $9,125 — 1991 3 0 0 0 $825 — 1990 6 1 0 2 $8,300

22Feb91- 7GG	fst	6f	:213	:444	1:103	Clm 12500	5	2	2½	2hd	1½	43	Chapman T M	LBb	117	7.40	82-11	Welcome Point1172½ Slowshoes117½ Concave117hd	Set pace	12
31Jan91- 3GG	fst	6f	:214	:45	1:103	Clm 20000	5	3	2hd	31	69½	616½	Hansen R D	Lb	117	*1.80	69-11	Exemplary116hd Mission Bear1171 Bold Trojan1178	Stopped	6
15Jan91- 8BM	fst	6f	:214	:443	1:10	Alw 20000	7	1	2hd	2hd	53½	65¾	Chapman T M	Bb	117	7.50	80-15	Magnificent Red117½ You Blew1172 Roughvus1171	Gave way	7
30Dec90- 2BM	fst	6f	:223	:453	1:094	Md 12500	3	3	11	12	15	15	Hansen R D	Lb	118	*2.10	91-12	Fareway Forli1185 Fleet Maxi1182 Irish Bairn1183	Drew off	12
15Nov90- 6Hol	fst	1 1/16	:454	1:112	1:453	Md 35000	3	1	23½	24	1013	1127¼	McCarron C J	LBb	117	7.00	45-23	LuLJdo119hdTrflorEght1171½SnorLonrd119½	Bumped at break	12
8Oct90- 1SA	fst	6f	:214	:453	1:122	Md 32000	9	5	2hd	1hd	1½	32	Pincay L Jr	LBb	118	3.50	72-17	Empty Floor118nk Underman1181½ Fareway Forli1182½	Tired	12
31Aug90- 4Dmr	fst	7f	:221	:452	1:234	Md 35000	4	1	1hd	1hd	42½	79¾	Valenzuela P A	Bb	116	5.10	72-13	SonnysRainbow1151Bozo'sFntsy1173½GoldBlly1151¼	Gave way	12
16Aug90- 4Dmr	fst	6f	:22	:452	1:104	Md 32000	7	3	2hd	3nk	4¾	34¾	Valenzuela P A	Bb	117b	29.80	81-10	ChifSssfrs1173GoldTrnd1171½DHFrwyForli117	Bumped at 1/16	11
16Aug90-Dead heat																				
6Aug90- 4Dmr	fst	6f	:22	:452	1:112	Md 32000	4	3	1hd	31	67½	912½	Desormeaux KJ	b	117	37.50	70-08	EldordoCount117½RedPottoes117½ChifSssfrs1171	Bumped 3/8	12

Speed Index: Last Race: -7.0 — 3-Race Avg.: -10.6 — 8-Race Avg.: -10.7 — Overall Avg.: -13.1
LATEST WORKOUTS Feb 28 GG 4f my :534 H (d) — Feb 18 GG 5f fst 1:023 H — Feb 11 GG 4f fst :471 H — Feb 5 GG 4f my :554 H (d)

Any horse previously ridden by McCarron and Pincay is certain to get a second, speculative look; from the name freaks, if no one else. Then, too, Bay Meadows has a much lower Purse Index than Southern California's major tracks.

30 Dec-   Ron Hansen satisfies the name players. That 60%+ discount in
the claiming price satisfies the class-happy bettors. Still, the
projected easy win pays a surprising $6.20.

If at first you don't succeed -- drop the horse still further. And further and
further.

EXAMPLE: CHERRY BLEND

Trainer Jude Feld did exactly that. He dropped the horse three times; steep
drops each time.

4 Apr-   From a lofty Clm80000 on February 8, the animal is finally
dropped from Clm25000 to Clm10000. The winning mutuel of
$12.80 is sufficient to cover the two previous losses and still
leave a substantial net profit.

Whenever a trainer drops a horse 50% in claiming price, the bettor is
near-certain to get a top run for his money.

EXAMPLE: CRYSTAL BLOOMER

After a promising debut at Stockton on June 12, the 4-year-old filly comes
a cropper at Pleasanton - the Alameda County Fair on June 27.

Crystal Bloomer — Gr. f. 4, by Crystal Water—Bloomer Miss, by Swaps
SIBILLE R — Br.—Cotton P & Eunice (Cal)
Own.—Cotton P & Eunice — Tr.—Cotton Perry — 114
Lifetime 21 2 3 1 $27,663 — 1991 4 1 1 0 $5,575 — 1990 10 0 1 1 $10,063

18Jly91- 9Sol	fst	1 1/16	:47^2	1:12	1:45^4	3+Hcp 10000s	5	1	1hd	1hd	1^1	2no	Rollins C J	Bb	113	7.70	88-20	Printsity122noCrystlBloomr113 1/2MissC.Courage116^3	Game effort	8
12Jly91- 7Sol	fst	6f	:22^4	:45^2	1:10^3	3+ⒻClm 6250	5	2	1 1/2	1^1	1^2	1^3 1/2	Rollins C J	Bb	116	8.60	88-10	CrystlBloomr116^3 1/2Sully'sPrincss111nkVgbondLc116^2	Handily	10
27Jun91-10Pln	fst	6f	:22^2	:44^3	1:10^4	3+ⒻClm 12500	7	4	6^3 1/2	9^12	9^17	9^15	Rollins C J	Bb	116	7.10	75-10	Sonesta116no Tosa Betty121no EasternCustom121 1/2	Far back	10
12Jun91-11Stk	fst	5 1/2f	:22^2	:45^1	1:04^4	3+ⒻClm 12500	5	1	3^1 1/2	4^2 1/2	3^1 1/2	5^3/4	Diaz I G		116	4.60	89-08	AnotherProspect116noSarosEros116noTosBetty121hd	Rail trip	7
30Nov90- 7BM	fst	6f	:22^2	:45	1:10^2	ⒻClm 12500	6	5	9^6 1/2	11^13	11^14	12^14 1/2	Warren R J Jr		121	8.60	73-13	Theregoesmry116^3NewBreeze121^1BridlWish116^1	Steadied 3/8	12
12Nov90- 9BM	fst	6f	:22^3	:45^3	1:11^1	ⒻClm 12500	2	2	2 1/2	3^1 1/2	4^3 1/2	6^8	Miranda V		122	12.60	78-12	Lurl'sPocktfl122^1NorthrnCross117^1PrtyPrncss122^1	Gave way	8
3Jly90-11Pln	fst	1 70	:48	1:12^1	1:41	ⒻClm 25000	6	2	3^2	6^5 1/2	7^12	7^16	Davis K M^5		109	4.90	76-10	Catlina114^3 Two Drums115hd Thanks Papa116^6	Wide early	7
28Jun90- 9Pln	fst	6f	:22^4	:45^4	1:10^4	ⒻAlw 20000	6	1	4^1	3^1 1/2	5^3 1/2	5^9 1/2	Steiner J J		114	7.70	82-12	Ali's Song114nk Princely Hug114^3 Andale116^3	Wide trip	9
31May90- 7GG	fst	1	:45	1:09^3	1:36	ⒻAlw 21000	3	3	5^4	4^5 1/2	3^4 1/2	2^3	Diaz I G^5		112	22.20	82-19	Tiffny'sGem117^3CrystlBloomr112hdFbulousMrk117hd	Late bid	9
25Apr90- 7GG	fst	6f	:21^3	:44^3	1:10	ⒻAlw 20000	2	6	8^5 1/2	10^9 1/2	10^15	9^12 1/2	Schvaneveldt C P		117	72.50	76-15	PowerBidder117^3 1/2GoForTresur117hdCountryInn117nk	Outrun	11

Speed Index: Last Race: 0.0 — 3-Race Avg.: -4.3 — 3-Race Avg.: -4.3 — Overall Avg.: -7.2
LATEST WORKOUTS — Aug 6 Pln 1 fst 1:41 H — Jly 16 Pln 3f fst :37^3 H — Jly 10 Pln 3f fst :35^4 H — Jly 5 Pln 4f fst :48^1 H

12 Jul- Staying with the same jockey, trainer Cotton drops his runner 50% into a 6250 claimer. The horse leads all the way, wins easily by 3 1/2 lengths. The payoff is a handsome $19.20.

EXAMPLE: JET BOOTS

Hollywood Park or Aqueduct, a trainer is a trainer; a purse is a purse. Gold is where you find it.

Jet Boots — B. f. 4, by Tri Jet—White Boots, by Bald Eagle
Br.—McGee Ray (Fla) — 1990 12 3 1 0 $52,200
Own.—Black Chip Stable — 112^5 — Tr.—Domino Carl J — $12,000 — 1989 9 1 1 1 $26,410
Lifetime 27 6 4 1 $110,410 — Turf 2 0 0 0

27Aug90-1Sar	1 1/8	:47^4	1:13^2	1:52 ft	5	109^5	1^2	4^2 1/2	5^27	5^48 3/4	ToscanoPR^3	Ⓕ 20000	28-23	Nofer,RisingSunflowr,IslofFlowrs	6
6Aug90-1Sar	1 1/8	:48	1:13	1:53^1 sy	5	108^5	2 1/2	1^1	2^1 1/2	5^4	ToscanoPR^6	Ⓕ 20000	67-18	Nofear, Mattazad, Olgiata	9
21Jly90-1Bel	7f	:22^3	:46^1	1:24^3 ft	7	117	2hd	2^3	7^12	7^26	Cruguet J^1	Ⓕ 25000	55-15	NorthrnWlly,DstyDonn,Alm'sLdy	7
23Jun90-1Bel	1 1/16	:47^1	1:12^3	1:46^3 ft	9	113	2^1	1hd	1 1/2	4^10 1/4	Cruguet J^8	Ⓕ 30000	58-26	TnyWhtL,UntndConqr,OrNwWrld	8
6May90-2Aqu	1 1/8	:47	1:13^1	1:52 gd	3	119^5	1hd	3^1	5^13	5^23 1/4	ToscnPR^1	ⒻAw34000	53-24	Brb'sSlew,Aspirtions,OneMorPss	5
22Apr90-9Aqu	1	:46^1	1:11	1:37 ft	11	116^3	1^1 1/2	1^2	1^2	1^3/4	ToscnPR^8	ⒻAw32000	77-24	Jet Boots,WonScent,Christiecat	10
10Apr90-4Aqu	1 1/8	:47^4	1:12^2	1:54^2 ft	4	109^5	2hd	1 1/2	1^2 1/2	1^2	ToscanoPR^3	Ⓕ 20000	64-38	JtBoots,ThitiTrty,KnightMinstrss	7
5Mar90-5Aqu	1 1/16 ⊡	:48^1	1:12^4	1:46^1 ft	15	113	4^3 1/2	5^7	7^18	7^22 3/4	Chavez J F^4	Ⓕ 45000	54-22	Cliffie, NoButter,GoldenT.Dancer	7

5Mar90—Stumbled st.
Speed Index: Last Race: -49.0 — 3-Race Avg.: -26.6 — 7-Race Avg.: -17.7 — Overall Avg.: -19.2
Sep 16 Aqu 5f gd 1:03^1 B — Aug 17 Sar 5f ft 1:04 B

5 Mar- Beaten so badly she nearly leads the next race, the filly has a win looming in her near future. Her jockey might be forgiven for paraphrasing that classic executive lament. "It really is lonely at the back of the pack."

10 Apr- Dropped more than 50% in claiming price and treated to rider upgrade, the lady breezes home to pay $10.00.

EXAMPLE: HELLEBORUS

Rested over the winter, the 9-year-old mare runs twice at Golden Gate before heading for the Alameda County Fair at Pleasanton.

Helleborus X — Dk. b. or br. m. 9, by Big Spruce—Dohn (Fra), by New Chapter
HANSEN R D — Br.—Hunt N B (Ky)
Own.—Arterburn-McVey-Olivier — Tr.—Arterburn Lonnie
118 — Lifetime 71 15 9 17 $171,757 — 1991 5 2 0 2 $11,312 — 1990 13 1 3 2 $25,750 — Turf 29 6 4 7 $96,400

13Aug91-13Bmf fst 1⅛ :47 1:121 1:514 3↑ⒻHcp 6250s 1 5 512 55½ 11½ 11½ Hansen R D Lb 116 2.40 81-25 Helleborus1161½MissC.Courg1165Honyngold1153 Rallied wide 5
23Jly91-6SR fst 1 :473 1:122 1:38 3↑ⒻClm 8000 7 6 69 58½ 46 35 Warren R J Jr Lb 116 *2.20 82-16 DelinExpress116½IfNotForYou1162½Hellborus1161½ No speed 7
3Jly91-13Pln fst 1 70 :472 1:124 1:433 ⒻClm 5000 8 8 812 54 12 15 Hansen R D Lb 116 2.70 84-11 Helleborus1165 Gin Mill116hd Gracious Hill1182 Rallied wide 8
21Jun91-9GG fm 1 1/16 Ⓣ:482 1:13 1:452 + ⒻClm 12500 3 9 99½ 86½ 64½ 67½ Castanon A L Lb 116 6.40 77-14 SissyMissy1162PilesOfPleasure115½PnicStricken1164 No rally 9
31May91-9GG fst 1 1/16 :461 1:103 1:431 ⒻClm 10000 6 10 1011 104½ 87½ 36½ Castanon A L Lb 1164 13.90 75-15 SissyMissy1164PnicStrickn1182½DH DlwrMdn116 Wide stretch 10
31May91-Dead heat
29Sep90-10BM fm 1 1/16 Ⓣ:482 1:13 1:454 3↑ⒻClm 10000 3— — — — — — Warren R J Jr LBb 114 6.20 — — LaBelleDame1132½Exclusividad-Ch1091LdyJon1163 Distanced 7
14Sep90-4BM fm 1 1/16 Ⓣ:482 1:133 1:461 3↑ⒻHcp 12500s 5 8 811 54 64¾ 63¾ Steiner J J Lb 117 3.80 70-26 SecretWedding117nkLCenrntol1141ChtingLight119¾ Wide trip 8
31Aug90-4BM fm 1 Ⓣ:464 1:111 1:373 3↑ⒻClm 22500 5 7 711 711 65¾ 58 Steiner J J Lb 114 2.80e 81-11 Bragora1164KatyJack114noCloisteredCutie1162¾ Broke slowly 7
22Jun90-7GG fm 1⅛ Ⓣ:49 1:132 1:522 + ⒻHcp 12500s 3— — — — — — Warren R J Jr b 119 2.40 — — T.R. Seven119hd Grand Award1131 Wings And Rings1141 9
22Jun90-Broke in tangle, lost rider
3Jun90-7GG fm 1⅛ Ⓣ:484 1:124 1:513 + ⒻClm 22500 3 9 917 812 68½ 31½ Warren R J Jr b 115 3.80 87-08 Al Capital1161 Goldarray117½ Helleborus115no Too late 9

Speed Index: Last Race: +6.0 3-Race Avg.: -0.3 4-Race Avg.: -2.7 Overall Avg.: -4.6
LATEST WORKOUTS Aug 22 BM 5f fst 1:032 H Aug 8 BM 5f fst 1:05 H Aug 1 BM 4f fst :52 H Jly 19 BM 4f fst :51 H

3 Jul- Lonnie Arterburn is after a purse. The mare is entered in a Clm5000 race. This is just 40% of her previous price tag. This is a horse in a free fall. To further lock up the purse, the trainer retains the services of Ron Hansen, Norcal's leading rider. This combination attracts the public and knocks down the odds. The horse wins by five lengths and pays $7.40.

We'll conclude this section with an example that illustrates several key horse patterns that have been mentioned earlier in the book.

EXAMPLE: MISSION BEAR

Mission Bear — B. g. 3(Jan), by Chivalry—Jena G, by Against the Snow
DOOCY T T — $8,000 Br.—Dempsey J (Cal)
Own.—Ardave Barbaccia &DeLaTorres — Tr.—Sanchez Adrian
117 — Lifetime 15 4 3 5 $41,950 — 1991 12 3 3 3 $36,775 — 1990 3 1 0 2 $5,175 — Turf 1 0 0 1 $4,500

10Aug91-3Bmf fst 6f :224 :461 1:111 Clm 8000 6 2 2½ 1hd 11 1hd Snyder B D LB 117 *1.40 84-14 MissionBear117hdQuietBlurr117noZnzibr1152 Held stubbornly 6
6Jly91-10Pln fst 6f :222 :442 1:102 Clm c-10000 8 1 31 2hd 2hd 2½ Kaenel J L LB 117 *1.10 91-08 Natural Prime115½ Mission Bear117hdObregon117½ Game 2nd 9
21Jun91-11Stk fst 5½f :22 :45 1:04 Clm 16000 5 4 52 55½ 55½ 34 Kaenel J L LB 117 *.80 90-08 FarChai1204DreamOfPirates120hdMissionBear117nk Late rally 8
31May91-7GG fst 1 1/16 :452 1:093 1:422 Hcp 12500s 6 4 43½ 21 2½ 46½ Schacht R LB 116 7.40 79-15 Manchurian1163 Pangbourne1143 Malagueta115½ Weakened 11
12May91-10GG fm 1 1/16 Ⓣ:47 1:121 1:443 + ⓇMnlghtDrH 9 2 26 2½ 3½ 32½ Chapman T M L 116 6.50 86-10 OtherIncom-Ir1151MritIncrs1171½MissionBr1161½ Lugged out 12
28Apr91-7GG fst 6f :212 :442 1:10 Clm 16000 5 3 47 35½ 33 21 Schacht R LB 119 6.60 87-15 ShmeOnTlly1171MissionBer119½RolGlimps1172 Rallied inside 10
6Apr91-5GG fst 6f :221 :454 1:112 Clm 12500 1 7 53½ 41 1hd 12½ Schacht R LB 119 *1.50 81-13 MissionBr1192½MityVicious1171½LgndryAppl117½ Rallied wide 12
28Mar91-7GG fst 6f :214 :443 1:093 Clm 25000 1 4 53½ 75½ 84½ 54½ Schacht R LB 115 3.30 86-13 FrmCountry1172PerfectHeist116½Exmplry115½ Drifted in late 9
6Mar91-8GG sl 6f :221 :453 1:113 Clm 20000 6 1 2hd 1hd 2hd 1hd Schacht R LB 117 4.00 80-26 MissionBear117hdTapTheWind1173½R.C.Dimond1172 Game try 7
13Feb91-8GG fst 1 :463 1:112 1:374 Clm 22500 5 1 1½ 2hd 31½ 54 Schacht R LB 115 4.50 72-24 FrmContry117½DmondbckDrgn1171½OnTmDy117no Weakened 7

Speed Index: Last Race: -2.0 3-Race Avg.: -1.6 7-Race Avg.: -0.5 Overall Avg.: -1.8
LATEST WORKOUTS Aug 21 BM 4f fst :493 H Aug 8 BM 3f fst :394 H Jly 31 GG 5f fst 1:053 H Jly 17 GG 4f fst :532 H

6 Mar- The classic mile switch is executed perfectly. Holders of winning tickets collect $10.00.

6 Apr-   Running on *9 days* rest, the gelding is dropped 50% in claiming price. The faithful collect $5.00.

6 Jul-   Dropping a bit less than our required 40%, Mission Bear runs second.

To repeat, we will continue to seek out those horses taking that steep drop in claiming price.

The Invaders

Crime does not pay. Well, in most walks of life, this old adage may be true. Not so in this sport, if you move your horses between major and minor racetracks. The term used in this industry is "stealing purses," which describes exactly what some trainers do very well. It's not really illegal, of course, but handicappers should recognize this pattern used by some trainers.

This trackside opportunist is more interested in picking up easy purses than in winning at high odds. The quickest way to that easy money is a trip to a track rated below the one where the horse is a regular runner. A Purse Index, described in the back of this book, will make the major/minor differences clearer. Most veteran handicappers probably already know a handicap race at Hollywood Park, Santa Anita or Del Mar is a few (several?) notches better than a similar race at Bay Meadows, Golden Gate Fields, Los Alamitos or the other lesser tracks throughout California. In the East, the differences between Penn National, Delaware Park, and Charles Town vs. the higher-quality Pimlico and Laurel tracks, just an hour or so away, can be striking. Yet, horses are rotated between them regularly.

These same track differentials exist throughout all of North America, East to West, there are always major and minor tracks. The movement of horses between these facilities provides the criteria for this chapter:

> Whenever a regular runner from a major track suddenly appears on the card at a lesser track, beware of the purse snatcher. We will bet with the trainer even though the public may recognize the ploy and overbet the "Hollywood" horse.

We have our own rule against betting horses that are almost always underlays; that is, betting horses to win with odds of less than 5 to 2.   But we find many good bets even among the cagey.   Sometimes we are pleasantly surprised when the public is seemingly deceived by patently obvious patterns.

EXAMPLE: GROWLER SANDUE

Bettors see only the horse's poor finishes at Hollywood Park and Santa Anita. His consistent early speed is lost in the shuffle.

8 Aug-   Rested for *eight days*, the gelding is then entered in a race at Los Alamitos.   It is entered for only 40% of its previous claiming price.   The horse leads all the way, paying $12.20 to its knowledgeable backers.

Note: Apparently assuming Growler Sandue is fond of Los Alamitos, trainer Chavez runs him again on *eight days rest*. Good. However, he is moved up from Clm4000 to Clm7000. Bad. A no-no. The animal runs second.

Even as they flash their larcenous signals, many of these sly fellows snare a purse while rewarding their backers with respectable payouts.

EXAMPLE: APASIONADO

Following a third place finish at Fairplex, the 3-year-old colt shows little in races at Santa Anita and Hollywood Park.

Apasionado — B. c. 3(May), by Wolf Power (SAf)—Rhonda F, by Vested Power — Lifetime 8 1 0 1 $12,560 — 1991 4 1 0 0 $9,950 — 1990 4 M 0 1 $2,610

SOLIS A — $20,000 — Br.—Warner Josephine P (Ohio) — 115

Own.—Alpert D & H — Tr.—Stute Melvin F

18Apr91- 7SA	fst	1	:46^3 1:12 1:38^1	Clm 25000	3 1 1^1 1^{hd} 1^{hd} 4$^{7\frac{1}{2}}$	Delahoussaye E	LBb	116	17.20	68-25	DelawareDrive115^{nk}Californian115^{nk}TheCleners115^7	Gave way	9
15Mar91- 5SA	fst	6½f	:20^4 :43^4 1:17	Clm 40000	3 6 6^8 9^{13} 11^{17} 11^{14}	Nakatani C S	Bb	115	56.00	71-16	Dark Ice116^{nk} LicoriceBreeze116^{3}FarBest115^1	8-wide stretch	11
18Feb91- 3GG	fst	6f	:21^3 :44^3 1:10	Md 32000	3 2 1^{hd} 2^{hd} 1^{hd} 1^{nk}	Hansen R D	Bb	118	*3.00	88-08	Apsiondo118^{nk}Myysrbrown118^{4}Grndoso116$^{1\frac{1}{2}}$	Ducked in start	7
21Jan91- 4SA	fst	6½f	:21^3 :45^1 1:18^4	Md 40000	4 3 2$^{\frac{1}{2}}$ 2$^{1\frac{1}{2}}$ 1$^{\frac{1}{2}}$ 5$^{3\frac{3}{4}}$	Solis A	Bb	118	6.00	72-18	Cliforin118^{no}CobCnyon118^{2}Tnk'sRulr118^{hd}	Broke in, bumped	11
6Dec90- 6Hol	fst	7f	:22 :45^4 1:23^2	Md 40000	10 5 5$^{4\frac{1}{2}}$ 6$^{4\frac{1}{2}}$ 6^8 6$^{8\frac{1}{2}}$	Solis A	B	119	45.00	80-10	BurnAndTurn117^{7}Undermn119$^{\frac{1}{2}}$CtchTheExprss119$^{\frac{1}{2}}$	Wide trip	12
15Nov90- 6Hol	fst	1$\frac{1}{16}$	:45^4 1:11^2 1:45^3	Md 40000	5 3 3$^{6\frac{1}{2}}$ 5^6 8$^{8\frac{1}{2}}$ 8$^{13\frac{1}{2}}$	Berrio O A^5	B	114	10.30	59-23	LittleJudge119^{hd}TraflgrEight117$^{1\frac{1}{2}}$SenorLeonrd119$^{\frac{1}{2}}$	Faltered	12
24Oct90- 1SA	fst	6½f	:21^3 :44^4 1:16^4	Md 32000	9 6 6$^{4\frac{1}{2}}$ 5^5 5$^{5\frac{1}{2}}$ 5$^{10\frac{1}{2}}$	Stevens G L	B	118	7.30	76-14	PrinceOfHony118^{0}RlntlssRod118^{2}HrprMdow118^{nk}	No mishap	12
17Sep90- 6Fpx	fst	6f	:22^1 :46 1:12^2	Md 32000	7 5 4^2 4$^{1\frac{1}{2}}$ 4$^{1\frac{1}{2}}$ 3$^{3\frac{1}{2}}$	Lopez A D	B	118	10.90	80-10	Skylaunch118$^{1\frac{1}{2}}$ First West118$^{1\frac{1}{2}}$ Apasionado118^2	Evenly	10

Speed Index: Last Race: -13.0 — 3-Race Avg.: -9.0 — 6-Race Avg.: -9.5 — Overall Avg.: -10.2

LATEST WORKOUTS — Apr 30 Hol 4f fst :48 H — Apr 25 Hol 4f fst :47^2 H — Apr 9 SA 4f fst :47^3 H — Apr 3 SA 5f fst 1:00^2 H

Convinced by those four fruitless efforts, trainer Stute ships his horse north to Bay Meadows: The major/minor shift.

18 Feb- Dropped 20% in claiming price and ridden by Ron Hansen, number one rider in the north, Apasionado wins as a mild favorite, paying $8.00.

EXAMPLE: MERIT INCREASE

The young gelding runs two poor races at Santa Anita. This is enough for trainer O'Neill. The horse is vanned north for easier pickings at Golden Gate.

Merit Increase — B. g. 3(Feb), by Relaunch—Beauty Hint, by Gallant Romeo — Lifetime 4 1 1 0 $7,075 — 1991 4 1 1 0 $7,075 — 1990 0 M 0 0

WARREN R J JR — Br.—Glen Hill Farm (Fla) — 114

Own.—Dallas P — Tr.—O'Neill Brad

3Apr91- 7GG	fst	1$\frac{1}{16}$	:46^4 1:12 1:45^4	Clm c-12500	2 5 4^4 3^3 2^3 2^1	Warren R J Jr	B	117	3.00	68-32	SpecilProof117^{1}MeritIncrese117$^{\frac{1}{2}}$Intermmbr117^2	Raced wide	8
5Mar91- 2GG	fst	1$\frac{1}{16}$	:46^3 1:11^3 1:45^1	Md 16000	9 7 5^6 3$^{1\frac{1}{2}}$ 1^1 1^2	Warren R J Jr	B	118	3.30	72-12	Merit Increase118^{2}Varney118$^{\frac{1}{2}}$PapaOscar118^5	Very rough trip	9
7Feb91- 2SA	fst	6f	:21^2 :44^3 1:10^4	Md 28000	7 7 8^{10} 9^{13} 10^{10} 9$^{11\frac{1}{4}}$	Goldberg S F^5	B	112	40.30	70-17	NrthrnEmpr118$^{2\frac{1}{2}}$Krring-GB118$^{2\frac{1}{2}}$LpYrBy118^1	6-wide stretch	12
10Jan91- 2SA	fst	6f	:21^3 :44^3 1:10^2	Md 32000	11 6 4$^{2\frac{1}{2}}$ 5^5 6^{11} 7^{16}	Santos J A		118	16.10	68-15	ShameOnTally118$^{1\frac{1}{2}}$WildTech118^{4}WildPhoneCll118$^{\frac{1}{2}}$	Wide trip	12

Speed Index: Last Race: 0.0 — 2-Race Avg.: -8.0 — 2-Race Avg.: -8.0 — Overall Avg.: -11.5

LATEST WORKOUTS — Mar 29 GG 5f fst 1:01^4 H — Mar 2 SA tr.t 5f my 1:05 H — Feb 21 SA 3f fst :39^3 H

5 Mar- Dropped nearly 60% in claiming price, the horse is assigned to Ron Warren, no worse than the second best rider in Northern California. With all of these signals flashing "go," the animal still returns a winning mutuel of $8.60.

As illustrated in the above examples, even with the major/ minor switch and a drop in class, the purse snatcher likes the added reassurance provided by a top jockey.

It is this obsession with "great" jockeys which explains the perpetual demand for the services of Bill Hartack despite his irascibility. It was long rumored he was even sought out by trainers who kept pin-studded Hartack dolls hanging in their stables.

Another apocryphal tale tells of the trainer instructing Hartack prior to the running of a stakes race.

"Look, Bill, you're comin' outta the ten hole. Get him over to the rail, dead last if need be. Make it a slow first quarter, maybe twenty-three. Second quarter maybe forty-five plus. Push him into the front pack around the stretch turn, ready for action at the eighth pole."

Hartack listened in silence, nodding absently at the the lengthy instructions. When the tainer finished, the jockey mounted the horse for the post parade.

The trainer watched happily as Hartack ran the race much like he had been instructed. Suddenly he screamed in disbelief. Reaching the eighth pole, the jocky eased his horse, pulled it to the outside rail.

The horse and rider trotted across the finish line long after the race was over. The trainer was waiting, cussing out the jockey, demanding an explanation.

"Look, you clown, I told you exactly how to ride that race. What happened?"

"When I reached the eighth pole I ran out of instructions. I didn't know what to do, so I pulled up the horse."

Many of the purses stolen through the major/minor switch are done so at low, low odds. As one astute handicapper laughingly explains, "it takes a thief to catch a thief." The betting public is often quick to catch a thief with his hand in the cookie jar.

EXAMPLE: BALLA COVE-IR

The 4-year-old colt shows early speed in several handicap races before shipping north.

Balla Cove–Ir — B. c. 4, by Ballad Rock—Coven, by Sassafras
NAKATANI C S — Br.—McCalmont Mrs V (Ire)
Own.—KingBrothersStb&RoyalTSt — Tr.—McAnally Ronald
119 — Lifetime 20 4 2 2 $255,466 — 1991 2 0 1 0 $12,000 — 1990 11 2 0 1 $97,462 — Turf 13 3 1 2 $207,879

13Feb91- 7SA	fst 1	:452 1:092 1:342	Alw 55000	5 5 63 811 89 77	Nakatani C S	LB	120	3.20	80-15	TnkrPort117no ExmplryLdr116½DrpTrcolr1151½	4-wide stretch	9
18Jan91- 8SA	fst 1 1/16	:462 1:101 1:413	Royal Owl H	9 3 3½ 21½ 21½ 2½	Nakatani C S	LB	114	31.60	94-15	StylishStud115½BallaCove-Ir1142½ElegntBrgin1141½	Sharp try	9
8Dec90- 8Hol	fst 1	:442 1:081 1:332	Affirmed H	6 2 2½ 32½ 32½ 54½	Solis A	LB	114	13.30	93-12	Greydar116nk Lee'sTanthem117½DefensivePly1231½	Weakened	7
8Dec90-Grade III												
21Oct90- 8SA	fm 1 1/8	Ⓣ:464 1:102 1:463	Volante H	6 4 42½ 31 42 44	Meza R Q	LB	115	22.50	89-08	InExcess-Ir1172½Wrcrft118½BrtonDene-Ir1131½	Bumped early	8
21Oct90-Grade III												
22Sep90- 8BM	fm 1 1/16	Ⓣ:48 1:114 1:431	Ascot H	6 5 52½ 52½ 78 54½	Chapman T M	LB	117	5.20	84-14	Itsallgreektome1221 NobleDr.112½ProForSure117hd	Wide trip	7
22Sep90-Grade III												
1Sep90- 8BM	fm 1	Ⓣ:462 1:104 1:354	Round Tble H	6 5 43 42½ 2hd 12	Chapman T M	LB	117	*1.50	90-07	Balla Cove1172 Native Wood111½OfficerHawk116½	Drew clear	6
25Jly90- 8Dmr	fm 1	Ⓣ:49 1:122 1:36	[R]Oceanside	3 3 32½ 33½ 89½ 812	Desormeaux K J	L	116	4.20	82-05	ForstGlow116no ProForSur1173BlAirPstr115½	Very wide drive	9
25Jly90-Run in divisions												
22Jun90- 7Hol	fm 1 1/16	Ⓣ:472 1:112 1:413	[R]Str Dst	6 4 33 31½ 31½ 42	Desormeaux K J		117	*2.30	85-15	TightSpot1172Predecessor114hd KeptHisCool112no	Wide drive	7
26May90- 8Hol	fm 1 1/16	Ⓣ:461 1:093 1:401	W Rogers H	8 4 45 43½ 42 32½	Desormeaux K J		116	13.60	92-06	Itsallgreektome1141½Warcraft120½BllCove116nk	Troubled trip	9
26May90-Grade III												
5May90- 6Hol	fm 1	Ⓣ:454 1:092 1:343	Splt Br Cp H	7 2 21½ 21½ 41½ 73½	Flores D R		118	5.60	87-08	Itsallgreektome112no Wrcrft120nk RobynDncer115½	Weakened	9

Speed Index: Last Race: –4.0 — 3–Race Avg.: –0.3 — 7–Race Avg.: –3.0 — Overall Avg.: –0.4
LATEST WORKOUTS Mar 21 SA 4f fst :464 H — Mar 16 SA 6f fst 1:133 H — ●Mar 9 SA 6f fst 1:114 H — Mar 4 SA 6f gd 1:132 H

Bay Meadows bettors are not naive. They well know the difference between handicap racing at Hollywood Park and Del Mar and handicap racing at their local track.

1 Sep- With "old pro" Tommy Chapman riding, the horse runs with the leaders, finally drawing off by two lengths. The payoff is a low $5.00.

EXAMPLE: INTERNIGHT

This 4-year-old filly won three races at Southern California's two major tracks before she was claimed for $20,000.

Internight * — B. f. 4, by Interco—Midnight Clear, by Damascus
DOOCY T T — $50,000 Br.—Creaser & Warwick (Cal)
Own.—Poyer & Steinmann — Tr.—Vince James J
116 — Lifetime 18 5 2 3 $86,775 — 1991 6 3 1 1 $51,350 — 1990 7 2 1 1 $31,650 — Turf 1 0 0 0

4Apr91- 8GG	fm 1 1/8	Ⓣ:484 1:132 1:513	ⒻAlw 26000	3 7 712 67 88 75½	Doocy T T	LB	121	4.60	84-11	Aloha Corrine116nk Let Fly118nk Pasquinade116½	Wide trip	8
17Mar91- 3GG	sly 1 1/16	:462 1:111 1:433	ⒻBrown BessH	5 6 512 45 34½ 37½	Doocy T T	LB	117	*1.70	72-27	Catlina1152½ Pixie Place1155 Internight1175	Evenly late	6
2Mar91- 8GG	sly 1 1/16	:474 1:12 1:454	3↑ⒻⓈCmpnllnvH	5 7 79½ 68 42 2hd	Doocy T T	LB	114	6.50	69-38	Art College115hd Internight1142 Azusa116no	Just missed	8
6Feb91- 8GG	gd 1 1/16	:473 1:132 1:48	ⒻAlw 24000	7 5 611 55½ 11½ 11	Doocy T T	LB	121	2.50	58-44	Internight1211CvrBrsAll1211¼VgulyChrming1184	Rallied wide	7
21Jan91- 10BM	fst 1	:463 1:11 1:363	ⒻAlw 21000	4 5 53 31½ 2hd 11	Doocy T T	LB	115	*2.10	87-11	Internight1151MesquiteMiss111½SellCluse1162	Rallied gamely	9
3Jan91- 5SA	sly 1 1/8	:47 1:113 1:51	ⒻClm c-20000	6 5 66½ 54½ 31 1½	Pincay L Jr	LB	117	*1.50	75-18	Internight117½DynmicAtNight115½Cvern1157¼	Lugged in late	6
5Dec90- 9Hol	fst 1 1/16	:461 1:111 1:441	ⒻClm 16000	5 7 74½ 75½ 31½ 1½	Dettori L F	LB	115	8.10	79-20	Internight115½Valueval115½FrannyFrizzle115nk	4-wide stretch	11
21Apr90- 9SA	fst 7f	:223 :452 1:24	ⒻClm c-25000	6 7 53½ 55½ 45½ 46½	Sorenson D		117	12.80	76-17	LuckDunIt1134½FstDiscovery1151½RshDcision112nk	No threat	10
21Mar90- 3SA	fst 1	:472 1:121 1:382	ⒻClm 25000	4 6 52½ 47 47 47	McCarron C J		118	2.80	68-24	Proclmton1187MyPtsyL111noBlSont116hd	Broke out,bumped	7
21Feb90- 2SA	fst 1	:47 1:124 1:394	ⒻMd 35000	4 8 65½ 52½ 41 1hd	McCarron C J		115	3.30	68-28	Internight115hd Valueval1105½RashDecision115nk	Checked 1/8	10

Speed Index: Last Race: –5.0 — 1–Race Avg.: –5.0 — 1–Race Avg.: –5.0 — Overall Avg.: –2.6
LATEST WORKOUTS Apr 30 BM 4f fst :52 H — Apr 24 BM 4f fst :582 H — Apr 17 BM tr.t 3f fst :382 H — Mar 28 BM 4f fst :49 H

Trainer Vince ships his newly acquired horse to Bay Meadows where she is immediately entered in an allowance race. She should be the odds-on favorite but the bettors are apparently a bit leery of that seeming jump in class. They see those rides under McCarron, Pincay, et al, but ignore the Purse Value Index.

21 Jan- Internight runs with the leaders, drives ahead at the wire to return $6.20 to the win bettors.

Vince likes the setting, snatches another quick purse (not our bet) and settles in for the spring campaign at Golden Gate.

There are times when a cagey trainer can follow a low payoff with a pleasant reward for his backers. Meanwhile, he has claimed two purses.

EXAMPLE: ROLANDTHEMONARCH

Running fairly close under Pincay and Stevens, the gelding is shipped to Golden Gate for his maiden win.

Rolandthemonarch B. g. 4, by Wavering Monarch—Mary Roland, by Relaunch — Lifetime 5 2 0 1 $28,750 — 1991 4 2 0 0 $25,900 — 1990 1 M 0 1 $2,850 — Turf 1 1 0 0 $13,750
FAUL R J — Br.—Glencrest-Tasher-Weinstein (Ky) — 120
Own.—High Desert Stable — Tr.—Wingfield Robert

31Mar91-10GG	fm	1 1/16 (T)	:494	1:142	1:45	+	Clm 50000	2	1	1hd	1hd	1hd	1½	Patterson A	B	117	10.30	87-13	Rolndthmonrch117½FtdForFrtn117½CnnnBr1161½	Held gamely	9
23Mar91- 7SA	fst	7f	:222	:45	1:23		Alw 32000	7	11	63	65½	811	79½	Velasquez J	B	121	25.90	78-11	Mxbob119no PonyYokum1194½GoldnVoygr1211	Stumbled start	11
1Feb91- 6GG	fst	1	:47	1:111	1:354		Md Sp Wt	3	2	31½	2hd	2hd	1½	Patterson A	B	119	*1.40	86-17	Rolandthemonarch119¾Crtgo119¾SplendidGold1193	Game try	7
17Jan91- 6SA	fst	6f	:213	:442	1:09		Md Sp Wt	8	3	63½	54	54¼	43½	Stevens G L		119	17.10	88-12	Barron Ribot119hd Catskill119hd Habastar1193	No mishap	10
12Dec90- 6Hol	fst	6f	:22	:452	1:10	3↑	Md 50000	7	5	41½	43	33½	33½	Pincay L Jr	B	119	10.00	87-10	High Purpose119¾ Udino1192½Rolandthemonarch119no	Evenly	12

Speed Index: Last Race: 0.0 1--Race Avg.: 0.0 1-Race Avg.: 0.0 Overall Avg.: -2.2
LATEST WORKOUTS May 1 Hol 3f fst :38 H Apr 25 Hol 7f fst 1:303 H Apr 14 Hol 5f fst 1:012 H Mar 21 Hol 3f fst :362 H

1 Feb- Local bettors know the difference between north and south. The win is worth a low $4.80.

31 Mar- Trainer Wingfield is soon back for more. Golden Gate bettors are ignoring the Purse Value Index. That Alw32000 race at Santa Anita is not for Kal Kan candidates. Rolandthemonarch leads all the way and pays an amazing $22.60.

EXAMPLE: THE MEDIC

Following three fine efforts in Southern California, Gary Jones ships his 7-year-old horse north for the San Francisco Handicap.

The Medic — B. h. 7, by Sweet Candy (Ven)—Mel Has Flipped, by Flip Sal

MEZA R Q — Br.—Sexton H (Ky) — **121**

Own.—Giammarino Dr E — Tr.—Jones Gary

Lifetime							
42 9 11 10	1991	2	0	0	1	$33,750
$870,280	1990	8	2	1	3	$156,875
	Turf	33	8	10	7	$817,855

9Mar91- 8SA	fm	1	Ⓣ:45	1:081	1:331	Arcadia H	10	8	77	75½	64½	4½	Meza R Q	LBb	116	20.70	95-10	Mdjristn115noTrebizond116nkMjorMoment114nk	Bumped 3/16	13
9Mar91-Grade III																				
21Jan91- 8SA	fm	1¼	Ⓣ:462	1:344	1:583	Sn Marcos H	3	5	43½	41½	42½	33	Meza R Q	LBb	115	17.60	92-07	FlyTillDwn120nkVguelyHidden1152¾ThMdic1151	Even in drive	8
21Jan91-Grade III																				
31Dec90- 8SA	fm	1⅛	Ⓣ:473	1:111	1:471	3↑Sn Gbrl H	2	6	96¾	85	94¾	83½	Warren R J Jr	LBb	116	10.40	85-13	InExcss-Ir117hdRouvgnc-Fr1131½Kntyr-Ir115nk	Blocked drive	11
31Dec90-Grade III																				
18Nov90- 8Hol	fm	1⅛	Ⓣ:491	1:124	1:474	3↑Citation H	3	4	43½	44	33½	33½	McCarron C J	LBb	116	3.10	85-10	ColwyRlly-En1141½ExclusivePrtner1172ThMdic1163½	3rd best	5
18Nov90-Grade II																				
20Oct90- 8BM	fm	*1⅛	Ⓣ:472	1:122	1:482	3↑Tanforan H	2	4	33½	43	4¾	1no	Warren R J Jr	LBb	117	1.60	89-11	TheMedic117noPlsntVrity1191½EskrIslnd114hd	Wide into lane	5
20Oct90-Grade III																				
5Oct90- 8SA	fm	1⅛	Ⓣ:452	1:084	1:444	3↑Alw 60000	7	3	2½	2hd	2hd	3¾	Meza R Q	LBb	119	3.00	100 —	ExclusivePrtner121¾Ultrsonido-Ar117nkTheMedic1192½	Hung	7
3Sep90- 8BM	fm	1 1/16	Ⓣ:473	1:113	1:42	3↑Sn Frn H	5	4	41¾	3½	11½	12	Warren R J Jr	LBb	113	5.00	95-05	TheMedic1132MisterSicy1152ShiningStel116hd	Wide into lane	6
17Aug90- 8Dmr	fm	1	Ⓣ:471	1:104	1:352	3↑Clm 200000	4	6	63½	42½	33	2hd	Valenzuela P A	LBb	120	3.80	97-07	YoungHl114hdTheMdic1201½MjorCurrnt1126	Bumped at start	7
29Jun90- 7Hol	fm	1 1/16	Ⓣ:471	1:111	1:413	Ⓢ Fiesta H	1	6	1011	106¾	87½	55¾	Desormeaux KJ	b	114	12.60	81-13	LvThDrm116nkFlyTllDn1152¾EclsvPrtnr1161½	Wide into drive	12
3Jun90- 8Hol	fm	1 1/16	Ⓣ:462	1:102	1:40	Alw 60000	3	3	33½	43½	43½	33½	Delahoussaye E	b	116	4.20	91-07	Bosphorus116hd Just As Lucky1183½ The Medic1161¾	3rd best	7

Speed Index: Last Race: +6.0 3–Race Avg.: +1.0 10–Race Avg.: –0.6 Overall Avg.: –0.6

LATEST WORKOUTS Mar 22 Hol 4f fst :484 H Mar 16 Hol 3f fst :364 H Mar 5 Hol 3f gd :373 B Mar 1 Hol 4f sly :472 H

Maybe the local bettors are put off by those claiming races in The Medic's past performances. Possibly they discount the impending ride by Ron Warren. Warren is a much-sought-after, highly successful jockey on the Bay Meadows/Golden Gate axis. Whatever their reasons, the bettors let the horse go postward at 5 to 1 odds.

3 Sep- The Medic draws off by two lengths and returns a surprising $12.00 mutuel.

20 Oct- You can fool some of the people some of the time. The public is ready for this one. Warren is up, but the odds are down. Jones snatches another purse, but the win price is a meager $5.20.

The Hollywood Park/Los Alamitos switch is a favorite with Southern California's purse snatchers. The purses are small but the win prices are often high.

EXAMPLE: SUMMERTIME LUCK

Summertime Luck B. g. 3(Mar), by Hagley—Cinematique (Fra), by Silent Screen
Br.—Green Willow Fms&PepineSt (Md) 1990 8 1 0 1 $7,070
SORENSON D 117 Tr.—Dollase Wallace $5,000 1989 1 M 0 0
Own.—Summertime Stables Lifetime 9 1 0 1 $7,070

13Sep90-7Fpx 6f :22¹ :45⁴ 1:11 ft 32 L 114 96½ 75½ 78¼ 79½ Sorenson D 10 10000 81-10 SergentJyTe,DonutKid,SuchDrg 10
13Sep90—Broke slowly
30Aug90-9Dmr 6½f :22 :45 1:16³ft 65 LB114 11⁸ 118¾ 55 56¼ Sorenson D 8 14000 78-14 Hghty'sNotn,VldRmrk,BgBdWlf 12
10Aug90-3LA 6½f :22 :46⁴ 1:18¹ft 7¾ L 119 8⁶ 63¼ 4³ 11¼ Sorenson D 9 M12500 84-08 SmmrtmLck,EldordoBy,TrchTm 10
6Jly90-1Hol 1⅛ :47 1:12² 1:45⁴ft 26 L 116 1¹ 2½ 9¹⁴ 12²⁶ NakataniCS 6 M32000 45-22 Warrior, Circumstellar, Bassman 12
30May90-4Hol 1⅛ :47¹ 1:12¹ 1:52¹ft 9¼ 115 31½ 32½ 89¾ 11¹⁷ Solis A 3 M32000 56-23 Md'sIntrc,PcktflOfKs,ShrThCrn 12
13May90-2Hol 1 :45³ 1:10⁴ 1:36⁴ft 54 115 118½ 6⁸ 4⁴ 3⁶ Solis A 3 M32000 74-17 Cllm,PocktflOfKys,SmmrtmLck 12
13May90—4-wide stretch
5Apr90-2SA 6½f :22¹ :46¹ 1:18²ft 8 113⁵ 2hd 42 8¹¹ 9¹⁹ NakataniCS 5 M32000 59-18 BeeLineBen,Zmies,CordilSteppe 11
23Feb90-4SA 6f :22 :46 1:12²ft 7¾ 118 3¹ 52¼ 10¹² 10¹⁶¾ Solis A 5 M32000 57-26 RstlssHlo,RunRunRdolph,GoB.C. 11
23Feb90—Bumped start
28Aug89-6Dmr 6½f :22⁴ :45¹ 1:17¹ft 8¼ 116 85¾ 87¾ 7⁸ 813¾ DlhoussyE 12 M45000 68-14 Z. Trump, Ash Hab, Hesmybaby 12
28Aug89—Wide 3/8 turn
Speed Index: Last Race: -9.0 3-Race Avg.: -8.3 6-Race Avg.: -13.8 Overall Avg.: -16.2
Sep 22 Hol 3f ft :36³ H Aug 26 Dmr 5f ft 1:01³ H Aug 20 Dmr 3f ft :36 H Jly 29 Dmr 4f ft :49² H

One third place finish and four dismal performances on the "big time" carousel are enough to discourage most bettors.

10 Aug- The horse is switched to Los Alamitos, definitely a minor track. From M32000 at Hollywood Park, the gelding is now entered for M12500. That's approximately 40% of its previous claiming price. The crowd is still not convinced. The horse's win price is $17.60.

The next time you spot a trainer setting up this maneuver, don't cry, "stop thief!" Just grab his coattails and consider it a key horse candidate. It can be a profitable indicator.

One final, important note to this section: It is often said there are "horses for courses." Handicappers should not ignore this phenomenon. For example, in Maryland, some horses win easily at Pimlico, but are never successful at Laurel, and vice versa. Whenever you see this money-making variation to the "invader pattern" described in this chapter, you can take it to the bank!

The Monster

In the majority of contests when eight, ten, or twelve horses compete for the purse money, only four or five can be regarded as solid contenders for the win and place slots. And once the gate opens, it can be said that in most races as many as two or three horses have a legitimate chance to win. From this moment on, pace, or sometimes just plain luck, will determine which among these few will emerge as the victor.

Once in a while, not very often really, ONE horse stands out, head and shoulders above the others. So dominant is this one single competitor that it makes little difference what the pace is or how it unfolds. This "Monster," as we call it, is so superior that only the worst racing luck will prevent it from winning the contest.

Users of the *Winning at the Track* Software turn to their *Pace Analyst* and *Graphics* Modules to help them identify this unique betting opportunity. The Monster represents about the only time in racing when odds of less than 5 to 2 can be considered an overlay! Of course, handicappers not using a computer can also see the Great One, but it just requires a little more work.

"Depth of Talent"

Probably the best way to measure the extent by which one horse stands above the rest is to judge how many others in the contest have run as well as our Monster's BEST and SECOND BEST efforts. This is what we call "Depth of Talent" and it can be measured any number of ways, depending upon the tools available.

The Monster is identified by ranking: 1) the best and second-best races of each horse; and 2) the best and second-best Pole Speed figures in those races. The Pole Speed is defined as the time that it takes the horse to run to the second call point in that contest. Our Monster ranks at the top of all four categories.

Racegoers without a computer can refer to second call point times and pre-calculated Speed Ratings (from the *Daily Racing Form*, Andy Beyers, or some other source) to make the necessary comparisons. Although these figures would be crude by our standards, they do, nonetheless, offer a means to this end.

EXAMPLE: THE CONSERVATOR

The following example was a MSW mile race at Calder Race Course on September 22. In this case, our Monster was a 2-year-old colt named THE CONSERVATOR. A win ticket on this horse paid a mere $3.40 and he topped a modest $101 trifecta. But the likelihood of The Conservator not winning this race was very small.

4 CALDER 1 MILE CALDER START FINISH

1 MILE. (1.37^3) MAIDEN SPECIAL WEIGHT. Purse $17,000. (Plus $2,200 FOA) 2-year-olds. Weight, 116 lbs.

LASIX—David's Prospect.

Hogan's Doctor — Gr. c. 2(Apr), by Family Doctor—Sister Hogan, by Father Hogan — Lifetime 5 0 0 1 $2,850 — 1991 5 M 0 1 $2,850
Br.—DiPietro Salvatore J (Fla)
Tr.—Richards Robert J Jr — **116**
Own.—DiPietro Salvatore J
24Aug91- 4Crc fst 7f :22^4 :46^3 1:26^4 Md Sp Wt 11 2 6^{5¾} 8^{3½} 7^6 5^{6¾} Martin C W 116 9.30 74-15 Bronze Spruce116^2 Hi Wheels116^{3}Shahpour116^{no} No menace 12
21Jly91- 4Crc fst 6f :22^2 :46^1 1:13^2 Md Sp Wt 12 1 5^{3½} 4^6 5^8 5^{5¾} Toribio A R 116 26.80 77-13 Earplug116^1 Harry's Dougie116^{1½} Tahiti Boy116^{1¾} Outrun 12
4Jly91- 3Crc fst 5½f :22^4 :46^2 1:06 Md Sp Wt 1 6 4^{2½} 4^5 5^9 4^6 Velez J A Jr 116 19.50 90-11 Oh My BlueBoy116^{no}Earplug116^{4½}Poulaind'Or116^{1½} Mild gain 12
8Jun91- 5Crc fst 5f :22^3 :47^2 1:00^4 Md Sp Wt 5 5 2^{1½} 2^{2½} 3^{4½} 4^4 Estevez R 116 5.00 88-10 Tank Buster116^{2}Boots'nBuck116^{2}SpeedyKris116^{hd} Weakened 8
27May91- 5Crc fst 5f :22^4 :48^1 1:02 Md Sp Wt 2 8 6^2 5^{2½} 4^3 3^{2½} Penna D 116 26.40 84-12 ByondThrpy116^{2½}Boots'nBck116^{hd}Hogn'sDctr116^2 Slow gain 9
Speed Index: Last Race: (—) 3-Race Avg.: (—) 12-Race Avg.: (—) Overall Avg.: -5.2
LATEST WORKOUTS Sep 14 Crc 7f fst 1:29 B Aug 17 Crc 6f fst 1:16 B Aug 4 Crc 6f fst 1:16 B

Niceanlight — B. c. 2(Apr), by Majestic Light—Nice Tradition, by Search Tradition — Lifetime 2 0 0 2 $3,450 — 1991 2 M 0 2 $3,450
Br.—Kirk Ronald K (Ky)
Tr.—Root Richard R — **116**
Own.—Sessa John C
2Sep91- 4Crc fst 6f :22^1 :45^4 1:12^2 Md Sp Wt 6 9 8^{7¾} 8^{8½} 6^9 3^4 Velez J A Jr 117 2.80 84-12 RideandDrive112^{4}AlwaysSilver117^{hd}Nicenlight117^2 Late rally 10
18Aug91- 4Crc fst 6f :22^3 :47 1:13^1 Md Sp Wt 7 6 5^{2½} 3^{1½} 3^1 3^{4½} Velez J A Jr 116 2.80 79-13 Ultimtenticmnt116^{hd}Silvrlinr116^{4½}Nicnlight116^{1½} Lacked rally 8
Speed Index: Last Race: (—) 3-Race Avg.: (—) 12-Race Avg.: (—) Overall Avg.: -6.0
LATEST WORKOUTS Sep 19 Crc 4f fst :50^2 B Sep 12 Crc 1 fst 1:44^3 B Aug 13 Crc 6f fst 1:16^3 Bg Aug 7 Crc 6f sly 1:17^1 B

Fantasy Five — B. c. 2(Apr), by Huckster—Caterea, by Catullus — Lifetime 2 0 0 1 $1,085 — 1991 2 M 0 1 $1,085
Br.—Murphy W F & Annabel (Fla)
Tr.—Estevez Manuel A — **116**
Own.—Mijal Stables
8Sep91- 4Crc sly 7f :22^3 :46 1:25 Md Sp Wt 7 8 9^{11} 8^{12} 6^{11} 5^{10} Castillo H Jr 117 35.00 80-12 Shahpour117^{no}TheConservator117^{4}CheapShdes117^5 Mild bid 11
17Aug91- 2Crc fst 7f :23^2 :47^3 1:27^3 Md 25000 9 2 8^{4½} 6^{5½} 4^{6½} 3^3 Castillo H Jr 116 4.70e 74-16 Diplojet116^{2½} Show Style116^{½} Fantasy Five116^{1½} Late rally 10
Speed Index: Last Race: (—) 3-Race Avg.: (—) 12-Race Avg.: (—) Overall Avg.: -9.0
LATEST WORKOUTS Sep 3 Crc 6f fst 1:17^3 B Aug 27 Crc 5f fst 1:03 H Aug 8 Crc 5f sly 1:04 B Aug 1 Crc 5f fst 1:03 B

Ensign Perfect — Gr. c. 2(Mar), by Blue Ensign—Faultless Tee, by Tuder Grey — Br.—Nick P. Cutlich (Fla) — Tr.—Gomez Frank — 116 — Lifetime 6 0 0 1 $1,740 — 1991 6 M 0 1 $1,740
Own.—Robinson J Mack

1Sep91- 4Crc fst 6f :22^2 :47^1 1:13^2 Md 40000 11 6 52½ 51½ 34½ 34¾ Velez J A Jr b 117 25.40 79-13 HiWheels117nkChepShdes1174EnsignPerfect117nk Tght qrtrs 12
18Aug91- 4Crc fst 6f :22^3 :47 1:13^1 Md Sp Wt 3 7 72¾ 74½ 74¼ 56¼ Rodriguez P A b 116 27.60 77-13 Ultimtenticement116hdSilvrlinr1164½Nicnlight1161½ No threat 8
4Jly91- 3Crc fst 5½f :22^4 :46^2 1:06 Md Sp Wt 6 3 1110 1214 1017 1111¼ Nied D b 116 87.60 84-11 Oh My Blue Boy116no Earplug1164½ Poulaind'Or1161½ Outrun 12
8Jun91- 5Crc fst 5f :22^3 :47^2 1:00^4 Md Sp Wt 7 7 64½ 56 67 67½ Nied D b 116 13.80 84-10 Tank Buster1162 Boots 'n Buck1162SpeedyKris116hd No rally 8
27May91- 5Crc fst 5f :22^4 :48^1 1:02 Md Sp Wt 9 9 93½ 87 76½ 64¾ Nied D b 116 32.10 81-12 ByondThrpy1162½Boots'nBck116hdHogn'sDctr1162 Wide turn 9
12May91- 5Crc fst 4½f :23 :47^3 :54 Md Sp Wt 8 7 812 813 813½ Nied D 116 13.00 80-10 MjcFontn1164½OhMyBlBy1112¾ByndThrpy1161½ Showed little 8

Speed Index: Last Race: (—) 3-Race Avg.: (—) 12-Race Avg.: (—) Overall Avg.: -7.6
LATEST WORKOUTS Sep 17 Crc 6f sly 1:17^3 B Sep 10 Crc 5f sly 1:05^2 B Aug 25 Crc 5f fst 1:02^1 H Aug 17 Crc 3f fst :36^3 H

Two Ton — Dk. b. or br. c. 2(Feb), by Honest Pleasure—Skiddoo U, by Stutz Blackhawk — Br.—Wold Keith (Fla) — Tr.—Brittain Jacqueline — 116 — Lifetime 3 0 1 0 $1,975 — 1991 3 M 1 0 $1,975
Own.—Wold Elaine J

11Sep91- 3Crc fst 6f :22 :46 1:13^4 [S]Md 35000 1 9 97¾ 87½ 53½ 2no Lester R N 117 18.80 81-16 Jeblar's Power117no Two Ton117nkSenorBo113hd Just missed 10
30Aug91- 6Crc fst 6f :22 :45^3 1:13^4 Md 25000 6 5 1016 915 77 52¾ Lester R N 116 98.80 78-18 FortunateJet1161½FreebieOne116½BoldBlackhwk109¾ Gaining 11
21Aug91- 6Crc fst 6f :22^3 :46^4 1:13^3 Md 30000 12 12 1211 1111 108½ 1011½ Velez J A Jr 116 38.40 70-18 Randy116½ Mighty Bet1162½NanookOThSouth1141½ No factor 12

Speed Index: Last Race: (—) 3-Race Avg.: (—) 12-Race Avg.: (—) Overall Avg.: -6.3
LATEST WORKOUTS Sep 6 Crc 4f gd :51 B Aug 17 Crc 5f fst 1:02^4 B Aug 11 Crc 5f fst 1:03^2 B Aug 4 Crc 5f fst 1:03^2 Bg

The Conservator — Dk. b. or br. c. 2(Apr), by Irish Tower—Mystique Traveller, by Pretense — Br.—Farnsworth Farms (Fla) — Tr.—Sherman Lee A — 116 — Lifetime 3 0 2 1 $7,050 — 1991 3 M 2 1 $7,050
Own.—Sherman Michael H

8Sep91- 4Crc sly 7f :22^3 :46 1:25 Md Sp Wt 3 7 1hd 11 12½ 2no Rodriguez P A 117 *1.40 90-12 Shhpour117noTheConservtor1174ChepShdes1175 Just missed 11
18Aug91- 2Crc fst 6f :22^4 :46^4 1:12^1 Md Sp Wt 4 6 53 43 23½ 21½ Toribio A R 116 3.50 87-13 CrflGstr1161½ThConsrvtr1164KndrgrdnChmp116½ Closed well 8
4Aug91- 4Crc fst 6f :22^4 :47 1:13^3 Md Sp Wt 6 5 74½ 65½ 57 33½ Toribio A R 116 5.60e 79-16 TahitiBoy116¾Harry'sDougie1162½TheConservtor116½ Gaining 11

Speed Index: Last Race: (—) 3-Race Avg.: (—) 12-Race Avg.: (—) Overall Avg.: -1.0
LATEST WORKOUTS Sep 18 Crc 4f gd :48 H Sep 1 Crc 5f sly 1:01 H Aug 25 Crc 4f fst :48^2 H Aug 14 Crc 5f fst 1:02 B

David's Prospect — B. c. 2(Apr), by Fortunate Prospect—Cadence, by Greton — Br.—Farnsworth Farm (Fla) — Tr.—Edwards Oliver S — 116 — Lifetime 3 0 0 0 $450 — 1991 3 M 0 0 $450
Own.—Melin D & Olga

2Sep91- 4Crc fst 6f :22^1 :45^4 1:12^2 Md Sp Wt 8 2 31½ 42½ 712 89¼ Lee M A Lb 117 12.30 78-12 Ride andDrive1124AlwaysSilver117hdNiceanlight1172 Faltered 10
4Aug91- 4Crc fst 6f :22^4 :47 1:13^3 Md Sp Wt 10 1 21 32½ 79 98¼ Valles E S b 116 40.50 74-16 ThitiBoy116¾Hrry'sDougie1162½ThConsrvtor116½ Early speed 11
27Jly91- 4Crc sly 5½f :22^4 :47 1:06^1 Md Sp Wt 2 4 53 912 813 810½ Martinez W 116 20.20 84-13 D.J.Cat1163¾BronzeSpruce1161CarefulGesture1162½ No threat 11

Speed Index: Last Race: (—) 3-Race Avg.: (—) 12-Race Avg.: (—) Overall Avg.: -7.6
LATEST WORKOUTS Sep 13 Crc 1 fst 1:45^3 B Aug 27 Crc 6f fst 1:16^4 Bg Aug 14 Crc 4f fst :48^4 H

Test His Heart — Dk. b. or br. c. 2(Mar), by Surreal—Stethescope, by Whitesburg — Br.—Robert Bakerman (Fla) — Tr.—Edwards Oliver S — 116 — Lifetime 3 0 1 1 $1,850 — 1991 3 M 1 1 $1,850
Own.—Bakerman Robert

12Sep91- 3Crc fst 6f :22^2 :46^3 1:13^2 Md 16000 5 10 129 119 79½ 24 Castillo H Jr b 113 23.60 79-16 DshingDoc1174TstHisHrt1132½LognofthMist1172½ Closed well 12
29Aug91- 4Crc fst 6f :22^4 :47 1:14^2 Md 16000 4 8 115½ 119½ 87½ 88 Castillo H Jr b 116 3.90 70-17 CopCollr116½BoldBoBob1161½MrnngAngls1161½ Showed little 12
11Jly91- 3Crc fst 5½f :23^2 :48^1 1:06^4 Md 18000 7 6 62¾ 56 48 35½ Castillo H Jr b 116 15.80 86-14 ARealMiracle1163½FleetGry1122½TestHisHert116hd Bore in str 12

Speed Index: Last Race: (—) 3-Race Avg.: (—) 12-Race Avg.: (—) Overall Avg.: -6.0
LATEST WORKOUTS Sep 8 Crc 3f sly :38^2 B Aug 27 Crc 3f fst :38^3 B Aug 20 Crc 3f sly :36^4 B Aug 13 Crc 4f fst :50 B

Wonmorerabbit — B. g. 2(Apr), by Compliance—Bunnys Wedding, by Crash Course — Br.—Richard Bomze (N.Y.) — Tr.—Musgrave Shawn — 116 — Lifetime 2 0 0 0 $250 — 1991 2 M 0 0 $250
Own.—Solomon H

11Sep91- 6Crc fst 6f :22^3 :46^4 1:14 Md 35000 3 2 34½ 43¾ 54½ 54 Azeff Y7 111 20.10 76-16 Show Style117½ Skyway117hd Scream Machine1172½ Faltered 12
18Aug91- 4Crc fst 6f :22^3 :47 1:13^1 Md Sp Wt 4 3 31 41¾ 51½ 77½ Azeff Y7 109 34.60 76-13 Ultimtenticement116hdSilverlinr1164½Nicnlight1161½ Faltered 8

Speed Index: Last Race: (—) 3-Race Avg.: (—) 12-Race Avg.: (—) Overall Avg.: -9.5
LATEST WORKOUTS Sep 4 Crc 5f sly 1:05^2 B Aug 15 Crc 3f fst :37 B Aug 7 Crc 5f sly 1:03^2 Bg Aug 1 Crc 4f fst :50^1 B

Oh My Joey Pie — B. c. 2(Mar), by Major Moran—Jenny's Nandy, by Great Above — Br.—Bush John (Fla) — Tr.—Tortora Emanuel — 116 — Lifetime 2 0 0 0 $950 — 1991 2 M 0 0 $950
Own.—Bee Bee Stables Inc

15Sep91- 4Crc sly 6f :22 :45^2 1:12^2 Md Sp Wt 4 7 64½ 56½ 46 46¾ Ramos W S b 117 10.60 81-11 AlysSlvr117nkBrc'sFlly1173½KndrgrdnChmp1173 Lacked rally 8
25Apr91- 5GP fst 4½f :22^3 :46^1 :52^3 Md Sp Wt 10 10 89¾ 914 910½ Lee M A 116 3.90e — — GvThmThGt116¾Boots'nBck1111½PntVndr1111½ Showed little 10

Speed Index: Last Race: (—) 3-Race Avg.: (—) 12-Race Avg.: (—) Overall Avg.: -8.0
LATEST WORKOUTS Sep 13 Crc 3f fst :37^3 B Sep 8 Crc 4f sly :48^3 Hg Sep 4 Crc 5f sly 1:02^2 H Aug 30 Crc 5f fst 1:02^3 H

Grand Gate — B. c. 2(Jan), by Gate Dancer—Inthethickefit, by Irish Ruler — Br.—J. Robert Harris, Jr. (Fla) — Tr.—Tucker Mark S — 116 — Lifetime 1 0 0 0 $160 — 1991 1 M 0 0 $160
Own.—Harris J Robert Jr

15Sep91- 4Crc sly 6f :22 :45^2 1:12^2 Md Sp Wt 2 8 812 815 813 712¾ Vasquez J 117 20.40 76-11 AlwysSlvr117nkBrc'sFolly1173½KndrgrdnChmp1173 No factor 8

Speed Index: Last Race: (—) 3-Race Avg.: (—) 12-Race Avg.: (—) Overall Avg.: -13.0
LATEST WORKOUTS Sep 11 Crc 3f fst :39^2 Bg Sep 6 Crc 5f gd 1:02^2 H Aug 30 Crc 5f fst 1:03 B Aug 24 Crc 5f gd 1:04 B

Feisty Slew — B. c. 2(Jan), by Slew the Coup—Correnda, by Run the Gantlet — Br.—Judie Kaplan (Fla) — Tr.—Novaton Juan I — 116 — Lifetime 4 0 0 0 $236 — 1991 4 M 0 0 $236
Own.—Perkins A M

31Aug91- 1Crc fst 6f :22^2 :46^4 1:13^4 Md 16000 11 2 84 79 810 912¾ Daigle E T7 109 112.60 68-20 RelScore116noToclosetothfir116noDshingDoc1161 Never close 12
15Aug91- 3Crc fst 6f :22^4 :46^4 1:13 Md 16000 2 5 77 912 816 717 Daigle E T5 111 113.30 68-16 Blazing Cat1168½ Cold Novel1091½ BirdiesSun1162½ No factor 12
31Jly91- 2Crc gd 5½f :22^4 :47^4 1:08^3 Md 16000 10 2 24 36 512 911½ Beitia A O 116 12.30 72-15 JohnnyBsh1162½PgMrty'sDr.1161¾ColdNovl1161½ Early factor 10
17Jly91- 3Crc fst 5½f :23 :48^1 1:07^4 Md 16000 10 5 77¾ 913 814 712¾ Rodriguez P A 116 25.70 74-16 Scudbuster116¾ Air Exchanger1168½ Oslan1161½ No factor 11

Speed Index: Last Race: (—) 3-Race Avg.: (—) 12-Race Avg.: (—) Overall Avg.: -12.7

The Conservator's best race (8 Sep) had a second call point time of 46 seconds flat (a Pole Speed of 76 in a mile race). In it's second-best race (18 Aug) the horse ran 47 2/5 seconds at the second call point (an adjusted Pole Speed of 65). The computer uses a parallel speed table to adjust these internal fractions. No other horse in the race ran faster at the second call point in their respective races and finished as well as did our Monster. The following table shows that The Conservator is ranked first on each of the four top columns.

Race: 4   CRC   1 Mile

PP	Horse		Morn. Line	Pole Speed
6	TheConservator	76/86	2:1	76
7	DavidsProspect	74/71	20:1	74
10	OhMyJoeyPie	71/75	15:1	71
2	Niceanlight	65/79	4:1	65

6	TheConservator	76/86	2:1	65
2	Niceanlight	65/79	4:1	65
1	HogansDoctor	67/66	15:1	65
9	Wonmorerabbit	65/68	20:1	65

1	HogansDoctor	67/66	15:1	67
6	TheConservator	76/86	2:1	62
5	TwoTon	65/75	6:1	59
8	TestHisHeart	61/73	10:1	59

```
* PACE ANALYST *
Expected Pole Speed.... 66 - 1:13.4
Pure Speed Estimate.... 68 - 1:43.3
Required Last Quarter..169   L/S   676

CAPABLE AT THIS PACE:                      L/S
~~~~~~~~~~~~~~~~~~~~~~~ Best               ~~~
 6-TheConservator  76/86    76/179    724
 2-Niceanlight     65/79    65/181    705
 5-TwoTon          65/75    65/177    697
 8-TestHisHeart    61/73    61/178    690
10-OhMyJoeyPie     71/75    71/172    690
                            2nd
 6-TheConservator  76/86    65/186    721
 2-Niceanlight     65/79    65/175    688
 5-TwoTon          65/75    60/177    687
 1-HogansDoctor    67/66    65/172    679
                            3rd
 6-TheConservator  76/86    62/177    690
00-                         00/000    0000
00-                         00/000    0000
00-                         00/000    0000
           Pacesetters: #  6  #    7
```

The two pacesetters in the contest were expected to be #6, The Conservator, and #7, David's Prospect. The computer indicated that we could expect the Pole Speed (the time at the second call point) for #6 to be about two lengths faster (76 vs. 74) than for #7. Judging by the comparative ability of each, and if the race unfolds as it should, David's Prospect will give up the chase by the time they reach the top of the stretch. This is the display screen of the *Pace Analyst* Module. It shows how the two pacesetters' best and second-best efforts compare:

Race: 4   CRC   1 Mile

		Best Race			Second Best			
PP	Likely Pacesetters	Pole Speed	Last Qtr.	Late Speed	Pole Speed	Last Qtr.	Late Speed	P/M Rating
6	TheConservator 76/86	76	179	724	65	186	721	2936
7	DavidsProspect 74/71	74	166	680	64	169	670	2691
PP	Best-4 P/M Horses							
6	TheConservator 76/86	76	179	724	65	186	721	2936
2	Niceanlight 65/79	65	181	705	65	175	688	2822
5	TwoTon 65/75	65	177	697	60	177	687	2760
10	OhMyJoeyPie 71/75	71	172	690	59	163	640	2740
PP	Selection - Display							
8	TestHisHeart 61/73	61	178	690	58	175	672	2722
1	HogansDoctor 67/66	65	176	689	65	172	679	2734

RACE FILE: 9-22-91.crc

Since today's race will be at a tough distance of 1 mile, the youngsters will probably be asked to run a relatively slower pace -- perhaps a Pole Speed of 65 (1:14) to 67 (1:13 3/5). Given this possibility, Niceanlight could be more competitive. Niceanlight has run a 65 Pole Speed in his best and second-best races and managed a respectable late speed effort in each case. Also, these Last Quarter figures (closing abilities) in both contests were much better than those of David's Prospect.

The Conservator's dominance appeared just as dramatic when the horses were compared using the *Graphics* Module:

Here is a comparison of each horse's best race ...

Race: 4   CRC   1 Mile

WINNING AT THE TRACK - Graphics   BEST RACE

PP	Horse	Notes	Pole Speed	Last Quarter	Pole/LS
1	HogansDoctor	67/66	≡≡≡≡≡》》》》》》》》》》》》》》》》》》》》》》》		65 / 689
2	Niceanlight	65/79	≡≡≡≡≡》》》》》》》》》》》》》》》》》》》》》》》》》》》		65 / 705
3	FantasyFive	61/73	≡》》》》》》》》》》》》》》》》》》》》》》》》		61 / 686
4	EnsignPerfect	64/73	≡≡≡≡》》》》》》》》》》》》》》》》》》》》》》		64 / 688
5	TwoTon	65/75	≡≡≡≡≡》》》》》》》》》》》》》》》》》》》》》		65 / 697
6	TheConservator	76/86	≡≡≡≡≡≡≡≡≡≡≡≡≡≡≡》》》》》》》》》》》》》》》》》》》》》》》》》		76 p 724
7	DavidsProspect	74/71	≡≡≡≡≡≡≡≡≡≡≡≡≡≡≡》》》》》》》》》		74 p 680
8	TestHisHeart	61/73	≡》》》》》》》》》》》》》》》》》》》》》》》》		61 / 690
9	Wonmorerabbit	65/68	≡≡≡≡》》》》》》》》》》》》》》》》》》		64 / 676
10	OhMyJoeyPie	71/75	≡≡≡≡≡≡≡≡≡≡≡》》》》》》》》》》》》》》》》		71 / 690
11	GrandGate	61/68	≡》》》》》》》》》》》》》》》》》》		61 / 670
12	FeistyStew	60/58	》》》》》》》》》》》》		60 / 650

	Pole Speed: 73	0	0:00.0	Out: 0	TV:17	Min. L/S:	0	n/a

This is a comparison of each horse's second-best race ...

Race: 4   CRC   1 Mile
.... 2nd BEST RACE

PP	Horse	Notes	Pole Speed	Last Quarter	Pole/LS
1	HogansDoctor	67/66	================》》》》》》》》		65 / 679
2	Niceanlight	65/79	================》》》》》》》》》》》		65 / 688
3	FantasyFive	61/73	============》》》》》》》》》》		59 / 671
4	EnsignPerfect	64/73	==============》》》》》》》》》》		62 / 678
5	TwoTon	65/75	============》》》》》》》》》》》》		60 / 687
6	TheConservator	76/86	================》》》》》》》》》》》》》》》》》》》》》》》		65 p 721
7	DavidsProspect	74/71	================》》》》》》		64 p 670
8	TestHisHeart	61/73	=========》》》》》》》》》》》		58 / 672
9	Wonmorerabbit	65/68	==================》》》》》》		65 / 673
10	OhMyJoeyPie	71/75	=========		59 / 640
12	FeistyStew	60/58	=========》》		58 / 647

2nd Best

Pole Speed: 65	0	0:00.0	Out: 0	TV:17	Min. L/S: 0	n/a

Each horse's best and second-best P/M Ratings (overall ability) also shows
how The Conservator towers above the others ...

Race: 4   CRC   1 Mile
Best/Second Best P/M Ratings

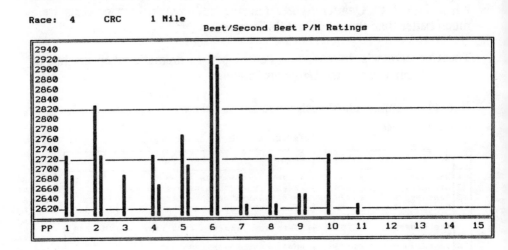

The rule for sensible trifecta betting is really quite simple: NEVER BET A TRIFECTA UNLESS YOU HAVE CONFIDENCE IN THE SELECTION OF THE FIRST TWO HORSES. In this case, our confidence cup was overflowing!

FOURTH—$17,000; 2 yo; 1 mile; won driving; winner-dk.b., or br.c., 1992, by Irish Tower-Mystique Traveller; owner M H Sherman; trainer Lee A Sherman; time 23 4/5 48, 1:14 1:41.

Horse, Weight	P	¾		Str		Fin		Equv
The C'nsrvtor, 116	6	1	hd	1	hd	1	3	0.70
N'cnlight, 116	2	3	hd	2	4	2	2	4.30
Test 'Heart, 116	8	F		7	2½	6	2	25.10
Two Ton, 116	5	6	½	5	hd	4	3½	8.80
Ensign P'rfct, 116	4	4	½	3	½	5	1	13.10
Fantasy Five, 116	3	9	1½	8	5	6	·1	31.20
David's Pr'spct, 116	7	2	1½	4	1½	7	1	49.60
Hogan's D'ctor, 116	1	5	4	7	hd	8	9½	15.30
Grand Gate, 116	11	12		11	hd	9	no	98.70
Oh' Joey Pie, b116	10	10	2	9	hd	10	1	9.40
W'nmr erbbit, 116	9	8	1½	10	1½	11	1	75.90
Feisty Slew, 116	12	11	2½	12		12		155.90

6-The C'nsrvtor (Rodriguez)	3.40	2.60	2.20
2-Niceanlight (Velez)		3.40	3.00
8-Test His Heart (Nunez)			5.00

PERFECTA (6-2) PAID $9.80

TRIFECTA (6-2-8) PAID $101.00

EXAMPLE: SPECTACULAR SUE

The next illustration is a similar maiden contest to again show how one horse can stand out above the others. Our Monster, Spectacular Sue, was easy to see with or without a computer.

Here is how the *DRF* appeared on November 10:

5 HIALEAH 7 FURLONGS HIALEAH START FINISH

7 FURLONGS. (1.20³) MAIDEN SPECIAL WEIGHT. Purse $13,000. (Plus $2,600 FOA). Fillies, 2-year-olds. Weights, 119 lbs.

LASIX—Spectacular Sue, Link to Pleasure, Spilled Beans.

Spectacular Sue — Gr. f. 2(Jan), by Spectacular Bid—In Concert, by Riverman — Lifetime 3 0 2 0 $5,900 — 1991 3 M 2 0 $5,900
Own.—Gilardi F D — Br.—Sarant E & G & Winick (Fla) — Tr.—Mendez Jose A — 119
23Oct91- 7Crc fst 6f :22 :454 1:122 ⓕMd Sp Wt 8 1 51½ 3½ 22 24 Alferez J O L 118 1.80 84-17 AllOurBest1184SpectculrSue1181WestSideSecret1183 Gamely 8
21Sep91- 5Crc fst 6f :214 :46 1:13 ⓕMd Sp Wt 7 2 31 33 43 54½ Toribio A R 117 2.10 81-12 Run for Baby117½ Smokey Gray117hd LoriGail1171½ Faltered 10
7Sep91- 3Crc sly 6f :214 :453 1:132 ⓕMd Sp Wt 9 2 34 36 22½ 22½ Toribio A R 117 24.60 80-14 Ravensmoor1172½SpectacularSue1173½Sam'sSylvi1171 Rallied 12
Speed Index: Last Race: +1.0 3-Race Avg.: -4.0 3-Race Avg.: -4.0 Overall Avg.: -4.0
LATEST WORKOUTS Nov 4 Crc 5f fst 1:01 H Oct 18 Crc 4f fst :48 H Oct 11 Crc 5f sly 1:022 B Oct 4 Crc 5f sly 1:024 B

Joyce D. — Ch. f. 2(May), by Huckster—Wilint, by Nostrum — Lifetime 0 0 0 0 — 1991 0 M 0 0
Own.—DeLoach Alvin — Br.—Alvin DeLoach (Ohio) — Tr.—Miralles Hipolito — 119
Speed Index: Last Race: (—) 3-Race Avg.: (—) 12-Race Avg.: (—) Overall Avg.: (—)
LATEST WORKOUTS Nov 1 Crc 6f fst 1:183 B Oct 26 Crc 5f sly 1:051 B Oct 19 Crc 5f fst 1:042 B Oct 12 Crc 5f fst 1:042 B

Link to Pleasure — Dk. b. or br. f. 2(Feb), by English Pleasure—Sequence, by Graustark — Lifetime 3 0 0 1 $2,450 — 1991 3 M 0 1 $2,450
Own.—Bakerman Robert — Br.—Folsom Robert S (Ky) — Tr.—Estevez Manuel A — 119
3Nov91- 3Crc fst 6f :221 :454 1:131 ⓕMd Sp Wt 3 6 42 55¾ 43½ 34¾ Moore B G Lb 119 16.30 79-14 Sm'sSylvi1191½Smbcrioc1193½LinktoPlesure1191 Lacked rally 11
23Oct91- 7Crc fst 6f :22 :454 1:122 ⓕMd Sp Wt 4 8 85¾ 75¾ 47 48 Moore B G Lb 118 24.90 80-17 AllOurBest1184SpectculrSue1181WstSidScrt1183 Lacked rally 8
31Aug91- 3Crc fst 7f :223 :461 1:271 ⓕMd Sp Wt 7 5 42 42½ 95½ 78¼ Castillo H Jr Lb 116 7.50 71-20 BlncheBeMin1111½SkippityDoD1161½SmoothndBlu1161 Faded 11
Speed Index: Last Race: -7.0 3-Race Avg.: -6.3 3-Race Avg.: -6.3 Overall Avg.: -6.3
LATEST WORKOUTS Oct 13 Crc 5f fst 1:02 B Oct 6 Crc 4f fst :492 H Sep 22 Crc 3f fst :37 B

Alex and Sam — Ch. f. 2(Apr), by Fight Over—Island Maid, by Coastal — Lifetime 3 0 0 0 $1,110 — 1991 3 M 0 0 $1,110
Own.—Niblet Pauline — Br.—Niblet Tom (Fla) — Tr.—Plesa Edward Jr — 119
27Oct91- 6Crc fst 7f :222 :453 1:263 ⓕMd Sp Wt 6 3 31 56 1225 1224 Velez J A Jr L 118 11.60 58-16 SmokeyGray1181½Sambcrioc1182PrincesseMdge118 Stopped 12
12Oct91- 4Crc fst 7f :223 :463 1:281 ⓕMd Sp Wt hd 21 31½ 42 Lester R N L 118 14.70 72-14 Interjection118no Lori Gail118hdHucksterRose1182 Weakened 10
7Sep91- 3Crc sly 6f :214 :453 1:132 ⓕMd Sp Wt 7 5 45½ 410 1118 1014 Castillo H Jr 117 10.90 69-14 Ravensmoor1172½SpectacularSue1173½Sm'sSylvi1171 Faltered 12
Speed Index: Last Race: -26.0 3-Race Avg.: -19.0 3-Race Avg.: -19.0 Overall Avg.: -19.0
LATEST WORKOUTS Nov 6 Crc 5f fst 1:02 H Oct 21 Crc 1 sly 1:463 B Oct 5 Crc 6f fst 1:16 B Sep 21 Crc 5f fst 1:031 B

Spilled Beans — B. f. 2(Jan), by Secretariat—Endurable Heights, by Graustark — Lifetime 2 0 0 1 $2,880 — 1991 2 M 0 1 $2,880
Own.—Drazin Dennis — Br.—Overbrook Farm (Ky) — Tr.—Croll Warren A Jr — 119
23Oct91- 3Kee fst 6½f :232 :472 1:193 ⓕMd Sp Wt 6 3 52½ 43 32½ 34½ Black C A B 120 4.00 78-12 SmrtDuck120nkSecrtritLss1204SpilldBns1206 Bid, flatten out 7
~~13Oct91- 3Kee fst *7f 1:293 ⓕMd Sp Wt~~ 8 7 815 818 9½ 46½ Black C A 118 5.80 76-10 GrlOnMssn1182WstrnFlr1182½SUrFlds1182 Improved position 9
Speed Index: Last Race: -10.0 2-Race Avg.: -12.0 2-Race Avg.: -12.0 Overall Avg.: -12.0
LATEST WORKOUTS Oct 8 Kee 5f fst 1:032 B Sep 24 Mth 3f fst :37 B Sep 11 Mth 5f fst 1:034 B

Our Late Decision — B. f. 2(Apr), by Explosive Bid—Angel Love, by Foreign Power — Lifetime 5 0 1 0 $7,570 — 1991 5 M 1 0 $7,570 — Turf 1 0 1 0 $7,000
Own.—Aljure David — Br.—Vintage Acres Farm (Fla) — Tr.—Romero Jorge E — 119
~~4Oct91- 8Medfm 5f ⓣ:212 :444 :571 ⓕProm 4 4 31 42 43½ 33 Santagata N b 113 29.80 88-07~~ LtestScndl1203OurLteDcision113nkMissLglity120½ Gained 2nd 7
20Sep91- 4Medfst 6f :223 :464 1:131 ⓕMd Sp Wt 10 3 11 1hd 21 85¾ Santagata N b 117 13.70 70-13 In View117½ Meaghan's Toy1171½StalwartPleasure117nk Tired 12
4Sep91- 3Medfst 6f :223 :461 1:12 Md 30000 1 8 33 33½ 34 44½ Mojica R Jr5 b 108 19.50 77-10 GoodtmSnny118noRockyMrcn1182½CrrLck1142 Lacked fin bid 8
21Jly91- 1Mth fst 6f :221 :46 1:123 ⓕMd 28000 5 3 2hd 25 310 617½ Douglas R R 113 23.80 61-13 PointSpred1175½PremierProspct1175JnMcWrd1171 Gave way 10
12Jly91- 3Mth fst 5½f :22 :453 1:044 ⓕMd Sp Wt 2 5 54½ 58 813 823 Pezua J M 117 62.40 72-17 SuperDoer1175CptureTheCrown117noMrilyn'sMgic1171½ Faded 9
Speed Index: Last Race: -17.0 3-Race Avg.: -18.6 4-Race Avg.: -16.7 Overall Avg.: -14.4
LATEST WORKOUTS Nov 8 Hia 3f sly :37 B Nov 4 Hia 3f fst :36 H Oct 3 Med 3f fst :352 H Sep 28 Med 3f fst :351 H

Panacakes — Dk. b. or br. f. 2(May), by Seattle Song—Sparkling Spear, by Raise a Native — Lifetime 1 0 0 0 $170 — 1991 1 M 0 0 $170
Own.—Piser D H — Br.—North Ridge Farm (Ky) — Tr.—Gulick James G — 119
5Oct91- 4Crc fst 1⅛ :481 1:142 1:50 ⓕMd Sp Wt 8 10 109¾ 811 811 811¾ Lee M A 117 31.70 60-16 MarketPlz1172SmoothndBlue117½SmokeyGry117nk No threat 10
Speed Index: Last Race: (—) 3-Race Avg.: (—) 12-Race Avg.: (—) Overall Avg.: -24.0
LATEST WORKOUTS Nov 5 Hia 4f fst :504 B Oct 2 Crc 3f fst :372 Bg

Sunflower Fields — Ch. f. 2(Jan), by Fit To Fight—Tender Camilla, by Prince Tenderfoot — Lifetime 3 0 0 1 $2,820 — 1991 3 M 0 1 $2,820
Own.—Humphrey G Watts Jr — Br.—Humphrey G Watts Jr (Ky) — Tr.—Pierce Joseph H Jr — 119
~~25Oct91- 4Kee fst *7f~~ 1:302 ⓕMd Sp Wt 5 12 95½ 76 79½ 914¾ Black C A 118 5.30 63-16 Persian Affair1183 Mt.Sequoia1182½FashionRidge1185 Outrun 12
~~13Oct91- 3Kee fst *7f~~ 1:293 ⓕMd Sp Wt 1 1 58½ 512 37½ 34½ Bailey J D 118 1.90 78-10 GrlOnMsson1182WstrnFlowr1182½SunflowrFlds1182 Mild gain 9
20Sep91- 4Medfst 6f :223 :464 1:131 ⓕMd Sp Wt 4 5 108½ 73½ 72½ 42½ Marquez C H Jr 117 5.20 74-13 InView117½Meaghan'sToy1171½StalwrtPlesure117nk Mild gain 12
Speed Index: Last Race: -21.0 3-Race Avg.: -15.3 3-Race Avg.: -15.3 Overall Avg.: -15.3
LATEST WORKOUTS Oct 22 Kee 4f fst :482 B ●Oct 6 Kee 5f my 1:02 B ●Sep 16 Mth 3f fst :353 Hg

Jean's Force — B. f. 2(Mar), by Rajab—Jean Gerard, by Sun Helmet — Lifetime 0 0 0 0 — 1991 0 M 0 0
Own.—Rolling Oaks Farm — Br.—Veneri Al Delli Jr (Fla) — Tr.—Hyland Angel — 119
Speed Index: Last Race: (—) 3-Race Avg.: (—) 12-Race Avg.: (—) Overall Avg.: (—)
LATEST WORKOUTS Oct 31 Hia 4f fst :52 Bg

Tropical Bue Bue — Ch. f. 2(Jan), by Runaway Groom—Sheila's Girl, by Victorian Era — Lifetime 1 0 0 0 — 1991 1 M 0 0
Own.—Rutherford Mike — Br.—Miller J Fred III (Fla) — Tr.—Brothers Frank L — 119
7Aug91- 7AP gd 5½f :221 :454 1:052 ⓕMd Sp Wt 1 10 108½ 1010 714 613½ Sellers S J 118 4.50 77-16 CdillcWomn1187½Lil'MissAtttud1183TngoChrl1181½ Late rally 12
Speed Index: Last Race: -7.0 1-Race Avg.: -7.0 1-Race Avg.: -7.0 Overall Avg.: -7.0
LATEST WORKOUTS Oct 21 Kee 4f fst :51 B

Unlike the prior example, Spectacular Sue had a commanding Pole Speed advantage of at least four lengths over every other competitor when the best race of each was compared. When each horse's second-best race was compared, a Pole Speed advantage was still evident. The unknown talents of the three first-time starters really represented the only major handicapping uncertainty.

This is how the first *Pace Analyst* screen ranked the best, the second-best, and third-best races of all the contestants. Spectacular Sue's second-best and third-best Late Speed figures (both 566) were better than every other horse's BEST Late Speed figure except for Link to Pleasure's 569. THAT is depth of talent!

Race: 5   HIA   7 f

PP	Horse		Morn. Line	Pole Speed
1	SpectcularSue	90/93	4:1	90
3	LinkToPleasure	86/89	8:1	86
4	Alex&Sam	86/67	12:1	86
6	OurLateDecsion	86/78	5:1	85

PP	Horse		Morn. Line	Pole Speed
1	SpectcularSue	90/93	4:1	87
6	OurLateDecsion	86/78	5:1	86
3	LinkToPleasure	86/89	8:1	85
4	Alex&Sam	86/67	12:1	82

PP	Horse		Morn. Line	Pole Speed
1	SpectcularSue	90/93	4:1	86
3	LinkToPleasure	86/89	8:1	86
4	Alex&Sam	86/67	12:1	86
6	OurLateDecsion	86/78	5:1	85

```
* PACE ANALYST *
Expected Pole Speed.... 87 - 0:46.3
Pure Speed Estimate.... 76 - 1:27.3
Required Last Quarter..104   L/S  529

CAPABLE AT THIS PACE:                    L/S
~~~~~~~~~~~~~~~~~~~~~~ Best              ~~~
1-SpectcularSue  90/93      90/117      575
3-LinkToPleasure 86/89      86/118      569
6-OurLateDecsion 86/78      85/112      542
5-SpilledBeans   80/80      80/115      541
8-SunflwrFields  s83/82     83/112      540
                        2nd
1-SpectcularSue  90/93      87/118      566
3-LinkToPleasure 86/89      85/118      564
4-Alex&Sam       86/67      82/110      533
00-                         00/000      0000
                        3rd
1-SpectcularSue  90/93      86/118      566
3-LinkToPleasure 86/89      86/108      542
00-                         00/000      0000
00-                         00/000      0000

            RACE FILE: 11-10-91.hia
            Pacesetters: # 1 # 6
```

The *Graphics* Module pointed to the same outcome ...

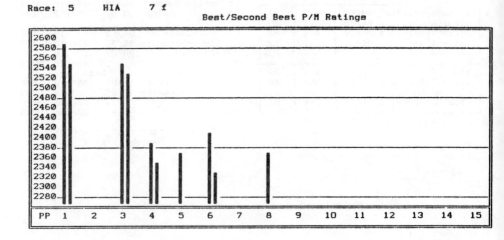

Pace handicappers expecting to cash a trifecta ticket in the same manner as before would have been disappointed. The jockey of the expected place horse, Link to Pleasure, allowed her to get caught up in the pace rather than rating the horse to attain a more favorable outcome. Perhaps the jockey was afraid that our Monster would end up "stealing the race." So, between these two, Spectacular Sue proved much superior -- not to our surprise, of course. And, as it usually happens, the defeated animal folded for most of the remaining field.

Was trainer Manny Estevez responsible for this costly mistake? We'll never know. In the meantime, Spectacular Sue paid a very generous $5.20 for an easy 8-length victory.

FIFTH — $13,000; 7 fur.; f., 2yos., mdn., spcl. wght., cl.$10,400; winner, $10,400; time, 23 1/5, 46 3/5, 1:11 4/5, 1:24 3/5; winner gr f 1989 by Spectacular Bid—In Concert; trainer, Jose Mendez; owner, F.D. Gilardi.

PP-Horse, Weight	St	½	Str	Fin	Eqv
1-SpectaclrSue,119	4	1-h	1-4	1-8½	1.60
4-AlexAndSam,119	6	3-1	2-2½	2-1½	32.60
8-SnflwrFields,119	8	8-½	4-1½	3-1	7.40
5-SpilledBeans,119	9	9-5	5-3½	4-2	2.60
3-LinkToPlsure,119	5	2-2	3-½	5-3	9.60
2-Joyce D.,119	7	5-h	6-2	6-2	52.20
10-TrpclBueBue,119	2	6-1	7-h	7-½	5.10
9-Jean'sForce,119	3	7-1	8-5	8-7	52.80
6-OurLateDcsn,119	1	4-1	9-1	9-no	8.30
7-Pancakes,119	10	10	10	10	42.50

1-Spectacular Sue(Rdrgz)	6.20	3.80	3.40
4-Alex And Sam (St. Leon)		20.60	8.60
8-Sunflower Fields (Velez)			5.20

PERFECTA (1-4) paid $125.20
QUINELLA (1-4) paid $75.80
TRIFECTA (1-4-8) paid $884.80

EXAMPLE: MEDIEVAL FLYER

In this 6f contest at Hialeah Park on November 29, Medieval Flyer was almost, but not quite, a Monster. However, the distinction of being our Key Horse was awarded to him once the handicap process was complete. The post position of his principal competitor (and the public's favorite in the race), In A Flurry, was a major consideration. Also, it should be noted that Medieval Flyer made it into the race from the *Also Eligible* list and is returning in *seven days*. Both are further confirmation that this horse deserves to be our Key Horse selection.

2 **HIALEAH**

6 FURLONGS. (1.08) MAIDEN CLAIMING. Purse $6,500. Fillies. 2-year-olds. Weight, 119 lbs. Claiming price $16,000; for each $1,000 to $14,000, allowed 2 lbs.

LASIX—Phoenix Square.

In a Flurry — B. f. 2(Feb), by Baldski—Save a Minute, by Bold Hour — Lifetime 1991 12 M 2 2 $5,890
Own.—Three G Stable — $16,000 Br.—Farnsworth Farm (Fla) Tr.—Olivares Luis — 119 — 12 0 2 2 $5,890

12Nov91- 4Hia fst 6f :23 :474 1:143 ⒻMd 16000 6 9 74½ 73¾ 31 3hd Sweeney K H b 119 4.50 69-20 Real Bad Wind115hd ⒹWagons West115no In a Flurry1193 11
12Nov91-Steadied, checked deep stretch; Placed second through disqualification
30Oct91- 1Crc fst 7f :23 :464 1:271 ⒻMd 13000 3 6 75 86½ 44½ 35½ Rodriguez P A b 114 9.90 73-15 Onlymymothrknows1184½PhonxSqr1141InFlrry1143 Late rally 9
17Oct91- 2Crc fst 7f :231 :464 1:262 ⒻMd 15000 5 9 71½ 43½ 66¾ 69 Rodriguez P A b 118 7.30 74-15 OriginlFshion1145DisyBrown118hdLdyJennF.1181 Bumped str 12
4Oct91- 2Crc fst 7f :23 :464 1:264 ⒻMd 15000 7 7 62¾ 42½ 68 610 Rodriguez P A b 118 7.30 71-18 Footsie Cat1132½ GradeA.Egg1184½J.C.'sMiss111no Weakened 12
1Sep91- 1Crc fst 6f :222 :463 1:133 ⒻMd 25000 6 8 95½ 109½ 815 813½ Valles E S b 117 4.10 69-13 Copln'sCcht1172½SovrignLn1173TunInToThCt1172½ No threat 10
17Aug91- 5Crc fst 7f :233 :48 1:271 ⒻMd Sp Wt 4 6 42 42 58 47½ Lee M A b 116 3.50 71-16 Sendbrod1163½PrincesseMdg116hdSmoothndBlu1164 Faltered 8
4Aug91- 3Crc fst 6f :221 :463 1:143 ⒻMd 25000 12 1 55 35½ 31½ 2no Gonzalez M A b 116 10.50 77-16 Unreal Impulse108noInaFlurry1162LividLass116nk Just missed 12
7Jly91- 3Crc fst 5½f :224 :471 1:073 ⒻMd 25000 8 7 87 87½ 69½ 67¾ Lee M A b 116 5.90 80-13 Appeal ToGlory1162Doc'sAnswer1162½PrettyMiss1163 Outrun 9
26Jun91- 4Crc fst 5f :231 :473 1:004 ⒻMd 30000 5 9 95¾ 810 58 46 Lee M A b 116 16.10 86-13 OnSwtGl1091½ⒹApplTGlry1161½OhMySllyBrns1163 Impr. pos. 11
26Jun91-chmced third through disqualification
Speed Index: Last Race: -11.0 3-Race Avg.: -11.3 9-Race Avg.: -10.1 Overall Avg.: -10.1

Tic Tocker — B. f. 2(Feb), by Pass the Line—Wendi's Turn Now, by The Axe II — Lifetime 1991 2 M 0 0 $120
Own.—Appleton Arthur I — $14,000 Br.—Appleton Arthur I (Fla) Tr.—Alter Happy — 115 — 2 0 0 0 $120

30Oct91- 1Crc fst 7f :23 :464 1:271 ⒻMd 13000 7 1 2hd 22 54¾ 511 Sipus E J Jr 114 11.50 68-15 Onlymymothrknows1184½PhonxSqur1141InFlrry1143 Faltered 9
5Oct91- 1Crc fst 7f :224 :464 1:272 ⒻMd 13000 3 7 4¾ 31 89½ 79½ Lee M A 114 10.50 68-17 EskimoSong1183LaPocha1091½BluingTea118nk Stead 3/8 pole 12
Speed Index: Last Race: -17.0 2-Race Avg.: -16.0 2-Race Avg.: -16.0 Overall Avg.: -16.0
LATEST WORKOUTS Nov 27 GP 5f fst 1:024 B Nov 19 GP 5f fst 1:023 B Nov 9 Crc 1 fst 1:48 B Oct 24 Crc 5f fst 1:031 B

Lark's Casting — Dk. b. or br. f. 2(Mar), by Never Lark—Top Casting, by Forever Casting — Lifetime 1991 2 M 0 0 $140
Own.—Barnes Jack W Jr — $14,000 Br.—Barnes Jack W Jr (Ohio) Tr.—Kelley Bill P — 115 — 2 0 0 0 $140

12Nov91- 4Hia fst 6f :23 :474 1:143 ⒻMd 16000 3 2 31 3½ 118½1112 Yang C C b 119 79.70 57-20 RealBadWind115hdⒹWagonsWest115noInFlurry1193 Stopped 11
5Nov91- 3Crc gd 6f :22 :461 1:134 ⒻMd 18000 5 8 108¾1111111311113 Suckie M C b 115 39.00 68-13 RaditionLdy1151½ClssyPistol119½TresFinesse1191 Never close 12
Speed Index: Last Race: -23.0 2-Race Avg.: -21.0 2-Race Avg.: -21.0 Overall Avg.: -21.0
LATEST WORKOUTS Nov 1 Crc 3f fst :361 H Oct 26 Crc 4f sly :503 B Oct 19 Crc 4f fst :502 B Oct 6 Crc 3f fst :363 Bg

Phoenix Square — Dk. b. or br. f. 2(Apr), by Silver Buck—Hurry Phoenix, by L'Aiglon — Lifetime 1991 8 M 1 1 $2,080
Own.—Thomas Becky — $14,000 Br.—Schwartz David (Fla) Tr.—Plesa Edward Jr — 110^5 — 8 0 1 1 $2,080

5Nov91- 1Crc gd 1 70 :494 1:15 1:482 ⒻMd 15000 7 5 117¾1212109 1010 DeCarlo C P L 118 12.90 61-24 EmrldEvnng114½LdyJnnF.118noGldInMyDrms109nk Thru early 12
30Oct91- 1Crc fst 7f :23 :464 1:271 ⒻMd 13000 6 4 41¾ 54¾ 31½ 24½ DeCarlo C P L 114 44.90 74-15 Onlymymothrknows1184½PhonixSqur1141InFlurry1143 Rallied 9
11Oct91- 1Crc fst 1 1/16 :494 1:161 1:51 ⒻMd 15000 7 2 3nk 87¾1015 921 Lester R N 117 98.30 46-23 Hoocheegirl1172LadyJeannaF.1171CulturalWve1103½ Stopped 10
26Aug91- 3Del fst 5f :223 :472 1:001 ⒻMd 16000 2 6 98¾1011 1015 816¾ Delguidice R Jr 118 28.70 63-14 MrchingStr1185½BrelyBeutiful1122ShootthStrs118¾ No factor 10
11Aug91- 7Lrl fst 6f :222 :463 1:141 ⒻMd 16000 1 8 77½ 813 915 915½ Henry W T b 119 52.70 55-22 DessGirl1191Hoochiecoochiemm119noBoldClient1191¾ Outrun 10
27Jly91- 3Lrl fst 5½f :233 :49 1:071 ⒻMd 25000 4 8 99¾ 910 88¼ 812¾ Vasquez J b 119 18.90 70-20 SweetDessa119noToughDolly1195½Bebopaloobop119nk Outrun 9
19Jly91- 5Pha fst 5f :223 :464 :593 ⒻMd 25000 2 4 42½ 48½ 36½ 37 Molina V H b 119 16.80 77-12 U First1191¼ SuperDonkey1125½PhoenixSquare1190 No threat 5
4Jly91- 1Pha fst 5f :223 :472 1:012 ⒻMd 25000 9 5 43¼ 59 816 815½ Bush W V 119 18.50 60-20 Jetta Zetta1172¾ Trey Femme117no Goluska1122¾ Tired 9
Speed Index: Last Race: -11.0 3-Race Avg.: -19.0 6-Race Avg.: -16.3 Overall Avg.: -18.0
LATEST WORKOUTS Nov 22 Hia 5f fst 1:031 B ●Nov 20 Hia 1 fst 1:46 B Nov 15 Hia 6f fst 1:174 B Oct 22 Crc 6f gd 1:182 B

Silent Wizard O/T — Ro. f. 2(Jun), by Westheimer—Reel Sterling, by Silent Screen — Lifetime 1991 2 M 0 1 $725
Own.—King Julie A — $14,000 Br.—Wisniewski Mary F (Mo) Tr.—King Julie A — 115 — 2 0 0 1 $725

5Nov91- 3Crc gd 6f :22 :461 1:134 ⒻMd 18000 12 2 87½ 77¾ 911 911½ Rodriquez H Q 115 10.60 69-13 RditionLdy1151½ClssyPistol119½TresFiness1191 Showed little 12
24Oct91- 1Crc fst 6f :222 :464 1:141 ⒻMd 16000 3 8 62¾ 75½ 57 36½ Rodriquez H Q 114 15.70 72-14 Priceless Rosemary1183Delson1093½SilentWizard114no Rallied 12
Speed Index: Last Race: -18.0 2-Race Avg.: -16.0 2-Race Avg.: -16.0 Overall Avg.: -16.0
LATEST WORKOUTS Nov 23 Hia 3f fst :353 H Nov 15 Hia 4f fst :493 B Oct 22 Crc 3f gd :363 Hg ●Oct 12 OTC tr.t 5f fst 1:023 B

Spinnin Cannon X — Ch. f. 2(Feb), by Loose Cannon—Hidden Glance, by Gentle Smoke — Lifetime 1991 2 M 0 0 $125
Own.—Pace H — $14,000 Br.—Bronzione & Jones (Fla) Tr.—Herrera Humberto — 115 — 2 0 0 0 $125

24Nov91- 2Hia fst 6f :224 :464 1:131 ⒻMd 14000 6 5 86½ 89½ 59 58 St Leon G 117 67.30 70-19 DressdtoGo1191½ToCosttoCost1151½NowClbrity1191 Mild bid 12
8Nov91- 1Crc fst 6f :222 :47 1:142 ⒻMd 15000 12 4 56 67 11181118½ St Leon G 119 11.30 61-16 LoveIsAll1151½TimelessReward1152½MascarLshes119hd Faded 12
Speed Index: Last Race: -11.0 2-Race Avg.: -17.0 2-Race Avg.: -17.0 Overall Avg.: -17.0
LATEST WORKOUTS Nov 7 Crc 3f fst :383 Bg Nov 5 Crc 3f sly :362 Bg Nov 1 Crc 3f fst :373 Bg

Sun Valley Spirit — Br. f. 2(Mar), by Family Doctor—Hippy Associate, by L'Aiglon — Lifetime 1991 0 M 0 0
Own.—Pruitt J Crayton — $14,000 Br.—Pruitt J Crayton (Fla) Tr.—Jolley T Wynn — 115 — 0 0 0 0
Speed Index: Last Race: (—) 3-Race Avg.: (—) 12-Race Avg.: (—) Overall Avg.: (—)
LATEST WORKOUTS Nov 21 Hia 5f fst 1:033 Bg Oct 25 Kee 4f my :512 Bg Oct 17 Kee 4f fst :51 Bg

Smart and Pretty — B. f. 2(Apr), by Wise Times—Granny Smith, by Stonewalk — Lifetime 1991 3 M 0 0 $324
Own.—Somers & Waumsch — $14,000 Br.—Justice Paul Gregory (Ky) Tr.—Waumsch Joseph J — 115 — 3 0 0 0 $324
28Sep91- 4Del fst 5f :22 :461 :583 ⒻMd Sp Wt 10 4 87 814 821 821¼ Luzzi J B Jr b 120 9.50 67-16 AlrishCross1205CandyWood1201½StleStepper120no No threat 11
14Sep91- 4Del sly 5f :222 :472 1:001 ⒻMd 16000 9 6 62¾ 53½ 44½ 44¾ Hilburn K D b 120 7.90 75-19 ShootlheStrs1172¾Gbril'sLight1141¾PloPlo117nk Needed rally 11
1Sep91- 2Del fst 5½f :231 :49 1:08 Md 20000 8 9 89¾ 87¾ 75¾ 67 Pham V D b 117 35.20 60-20 Ace Eyes1201 Gayquare1142TrustyBuckaroo116¾ No menace 9
Speed Index: Last Race: -17.0 3-Race Avg.: -11.6 3-Race Avg.: -11.6 Overall Avg.: -11.6
LATEST WORKOUTS Nov 24 Hia 5f fst 1:034 B Nov 19 Hia 4f fst :50 B

P. M.'s Hope — Dk. b. or br. f. 2(Mar), by Rexson's Hope—Pia Mia, by Pia Star — Lifetime 1991 6 M 0 0 $368
Own.—Elsie A Rose Stable Inc — $14,000 Br.—Rose Harold (Fla) Tr.—Rose Harold J — 115 — 6 0 0 0 $368
22Nov91- 4Hia fst 6f :221 :462 1:13 ⒻMd 13000 10 11 1110 89½ 69½ 512½ Nunez E O 115 72.80 64-16 FightingTune1196½UnrelRose115½MedievlFlyr1193½ Mild rally 12
2Aug91- 4Crc fst 6f :222 :464 1:133 ⒻMd 16000 5 7 78½ 712 815 811½ Martin C W 113 84.70 70-18 NoMecourtney1165½KeyChnce112noBeutifulBrth116nk Outrun 11
25Jly91- 3Crc fst 6f :223 :472 1:152 ⒻMd 16000 5 5 62¾ 1220 1229 1225½ Green B 116 240.00 40-15 LcThndr111hdThrlmsthld1162½Onlthrns1161½ Showed nothing 12
12Jly91- 5Crc fst 5½f :231 :48 1:082 ⒻMd 16000 2 10 108¾ 917 914 1011½ Alferez J O 112 85.80 72-15 FstFlti1121SpnishBombshll1121½LuckyThundr1162¾ No factor 12
5Jly91- 3Crc fst 5f :23 :473 1:01 ⒻMd 16000 2 5 78½ 613 614 613½ Alferez J O 116 24.30 77-11 Sgt. Wendy1166 Carol's Tune1162¾ Tic Tac Dac114hd Outrun 10
28Jun91- 2Crc fst 5½f :23 :474 1:081 Md 18000 8 12 99½ 819 816 715½ Alferez J O 116 21.90 70-10 TwinkInMyEy1131Concord'sSolo1093¾LtRunnr116½ Off slowly 12
Speed Index: Last Race: -20.0 3-Race Avg.: -23.0 6-Race Avg.: -19.0 Overall Avg.: -19.0
LATEST WORKOUTS Nov 1 Crc 6f fst 1:181 B Oct 25 Crc 5f sly 1:041 B Oct 19 Crc 4f fst :49 H

Distinctively Blue — Dk. b. or br. f. 2(Mar), by Distinctive—Blue Time, by Targowice — Lifetime 1991 0 M 0 0
Own.—Long B — $16,000 Br.—Delzone & Long (Fla) Tr.—Posada Laura — 119 — 0 0 0 0
Entered 28Nov91- 7 HIA
Speed Index: Last Race: (—) 3-Race Avg.: (—) 12-Race Avg.: (—) Overall Avg.: (—)
LATEST WORKOUTS Nov 19 Hia 5f fst 1:03 B Oct 18 Crc 5f fst 1:051 B Oct 5 Crc 5f fst 1:033 Bg Sep 29 Crc 5f fst 1:04 Bg

Imperial Lure — Dk. b. or br. f. 2(Feb), by Imperial Dilemma—Lure the Lady, by L'Enjoleur — Lifetime 1991 7 M 0 0 $430
Own.—Izquierdo J C — $14,000 Br.—Agusti Wilfredo A Jr (Fla) Tr.—Azpurua Manuel J — 115 — 7 0 0 0 $430
24Nov91- 2Hia fst 6f :224 :464 1:131 ⒻMd 13000 8 7 74¾ 66 68½ 66 Verenzuela J L 115 37.60 70-19 DrssdtoGo1191½ToCosttoCst1151½NwClbrty1191 Showed little 12
12Nov91- 2Hia fst 6f :224 :464 1:112 ⒻMd 15000 8 4 42 55 612 618½ Martinez R R7 110 6.90 66-20 TresFiness1198MoodyRdhd1175ChosnConfssion1192 Faltered 9
8Nov91- 3Crc fst 6f :222 :464 1:14 ⒻMd 13000 2 12 96 75¾ 68½ 68½ Ramos W S 115 11.40 71-16 ⒹSstSun1192FrstCortshp119noOnforDorothy1152 No menace 12
1Nov91- 3Crc fst 6f :223 :473 1:151 ⒻMd 15000 5 3 41¾ 31 41¾ 54 Martinez R R7 112 4.90 70-21 TunerupCptin112½CstlebytheS1151½RlBdWind115½ Weakened 9
22Oct91- 3Crc fst 6f :223 :471 1:144 ⒻMd 13000 11 2 74½ 84¾ 41 31½ Bracho J A7 107 13.60Ⓓ 74-17 GrdA.Egg118noOnlmmthrkns1181½ⒹImprlLr1072 Bore inward 12
22Oct91-Disqualified and placed twelfth
10Oct91- 1Crc gd 6f :23 :473 1:141 ⒻMd 15000 3 4 21 31½ 54½ 79½ Nunez E O 118 15.70 69-19 Talaento1144½ Twirling Judi1141 Delson1112½ Faded 12
27Sep91- 3Crc fst 6f :23 :474 1:144 ⒻMd 13000 10 2 72½ 63¾ 77½ 76½ Nunez E O 113 29.20 69-21 TonTonMacoute1172½HutHut1132½DisyBrown1171 No menace 11
Speed Index: Last Race: -11.0 3-Race Avg.: -12.6 7-Race Avg.: -11.1 Overall Avg.: -11.1
LATEST WORKOUTS Oct 19 Crc 3f fst :38 B

Also Eligible (Not in Post Position Order):

Medieval Flyer — Ch. f. 2(May), by Medieval Man—Peace Movement, by Admiral's Voyage — Lifetime 1991 6 M 0 1 $1,400
Own.—Mekamy Oaks Inc — $15,000 Br.—Live Oak Stud (Fla) Tr.—Ritvo Kathy — 117 — 6 0 0 1 $1,400
22Nov91- 4Hia fst 6f :221 :462 1:13 ⒻMd 15000 6 8 76½ 44½ 35 37 Velez J A Jr b 119 6.40 70-16 FightingTune1196½UnrealRose115½MedievalFlyer1193½ Rallied 12
5Nov91- 3Crc gd 6f :22 :461 1:134 ⒻMd 20000 2 9 97¾ 89½ 55¾ 54 Lee M A b 119 19.10 77-13 RditionLdy1151½ClssyPistol119½TrsFinss1191 Lck rally, 5-wde 12
4Oct91- 7Crc fst 6f :221 :464 1:143 ⒻMd 25000 12 4 2hd 3nk 119¾ 119½ Hernandez R b 118 16.30 60-18 OhMySallyBarnes1181Mybellette1112CgedHert118hd Faltered 12
20Sep91- 6Crc fst 6f :222 :463 1:133 ⒻMd 30000 3 4 53½ 68 811 910½ Ramos W S b 117 13.40 71-18 TuneInToTheCat1153SpecialTale117nkHelpOnHigh1131 Faded 12
8Sep91- 1Crc sly 6f :22 :461 1:134 ⒻMd 35000 4 7 84¾ 55 55½ 44¾ Valles E S b 117 43.90 76-12 GoldnBimmr1171½FirstCourtship1172½SistrNin117½ Late rally 12
7Aug91- 6Crc fst 6f :221 :462 1:134 ⒻMd 35000 6 5 21 21 58 68¾ Lee M A b 116 5.40 73-16 ShowNoFer116½StrSpngledGirl1162Concord'sSolo1121 Faded 8
Speed Index: Last Race: -14.0 3-Race Avg.: -12.6 6-Race Avg.: -12.0 Overall Avg.: -12.0
LATEST WORKOUTS Oct 31 Crc 4f fst :512 B Oct 13 Crc 3f fst :372 B

Medieval Flyer certainly appeared as the dominating factor in the race, to be sure. However, for the horse to qualify as a Monster, the Pole Speed of its best race AND second-best race must be higher than the Pole Speeds of the best and second-best efforts of any other competitor. Medieval Flyer seemed to favor the role as a closer despite the fact that his good early speed figures indicated that he could a pacesetter if he had to be.

This is how Medieval Flyer appeared on the *Pace Analyst*:

```
Race:   2    HIA      6 f
                               Morn.  Pole
PP  Horse                      Line   Speed

 2  TicTocker        85/77      8:1     85
 1  InAFlurry        84/76      2:1     82
 4  PhoenixSquare    81/71     12:1     81
 5  SilentWizard     81/78     10:1     81

12 >MedievalFlyer    86/77      3:1     84
 2  TicTocker        85/77      8:1     84
11  ImperialLure     81/77     12:1     81
 5  SilentWizard     81/78     10:1     81

11  ImperialLure     81/77     12:1     80
12 >MedievalFlyer    86/77      3:1     79
 9  P.M.'sHope       79/71     20:1     79
 1  InAFlurry        84/76      2:1     77
```

```
* PACE ANALYST *
Expected Pole Speed.... 86 - 0:46.4
Pure Speed Estimate.... 79 - 1:14.0
Required Last Quarter..174   L/S  737

CAPABLE AT THIS PACE:                L/S
~~~~~~~~~~~~~~~~~~~~~ Best        ~~~
12->MedievalFlyer 86/77   80/185   752
 4-PhoenixSquare  81/71   81/181   744
 1-InAFlurry      84/76   82/180   744
 9-P.M.'sHope     79/71   74/184   740
 6-SpinninCannon  78/77   76/182   740
                        2nd
12->MedievalFlyer 86/77   84/180   745
 1-InAFlurry      84/76   79/182   743
 4-PhoenixSquare  81/71   56/195   738
11-ImperialLure   81/77   81/177   738
                        3rd
12->MedievalFlyer 86/77   79/180   740
 1-InAFlurry      84/76   77/180   737
11-ImperialLure   81/77   80/179   737
00-                       00/000  0000

         RACE FILE: 11-29-91.hia
         Pacesetters: # 12  #   2
```

It can be seen that Medieval Flyer's second-best Late Speed (745) is better than the BEST Late Speed of every other horse in the race and that he was identified, along with Tic Tocker, to be one of the two pacesetters in the contest. Medieval Flyer's second-best race was notable because he ran an 84 Pole Speed (47 1/5 seconds), two-fifths faster than any other horse when we compare only the two or three best races of each contender.

The way the race would be unfolding was also clearly illustrated by the *Graphics* Module:

```
Race:  2     HIA    6 f
                          WINNING AT THE TRACK - Graphics                    BEST RACE

PP | Horse          Notes      Pole Speed          Last Quarter               Pole/LS

 1 | InAFlurry      84/76   ==============)))))))))))))))))))))))))))))))))))   82 / 744
 2 | TicTocker      85/77   ==================)))))))))))))))))))))))           85 p 726
 3 | LarksCasting   80/64   ============)))))))))))))))))))))))))                78 / 726
 4 | PhoenixSquare  81/71   =============)))))))))))))))))))))))))))))))))))     81 / 744
 5 | SilentWizard   81/78   ============)))))))))))))))))))))))))))))))          81 / 737
 6 | SpinninCannon  78/77   =======)))))))))))))))))))))))))))))))))))))         76 / 740
 8 | Smart&Pretty   79/64   =========)))))))))))))))))))))))))))))))             79 / 729
 9 | P.M.'sHope     79/71   =====)))))))))))))))))))))))))))))))))))))           74 / 740
11 | ImperialLure   81/77   ========)))))))))))))))))))))))))))))))))))          77 / 739
12 | >MedievalFlyer 86/77   =========)))))))))))))))))))))))))))))))))))))))))))  80 p 752


    Pole Speed:    82    0     0:00.0  Out: 0    TV:17   Min. L/S:   0         n/a
```

In A Flurry was obviously in a tough spot being assigned to the inside post position. Tic Tocker, a horse with good early speed, would be in front of him early and Phoenix Square or Silent Wizard would be there also. This meant In A Flurry would be boxed in behind two tiring horses. He would be forced to work hard to get into the contest. In effect, there would be less competition for Medieval Flyer, already the logical choice.

Here is the result chart of the race:

SECOND — $6500; 6 fur.; fil 2-YOs; clg $16,000-15,000; winner $3900; time 22 3/5, 46 3/5, 1:13 3/5; winner ch f 1989 by Medieval Man—Peace Movement; trainer, Kathy Ritvo; owner, Mekamy Oaks Inc.

PP-Horse, Weight	St	½	Str	Fin	Eqv
12-Mdval Flyr,117	1	6-1½	5-1½	1½	2.80
5-DH-Slt Wzrd,115	4	2-2½	1-1½	2	17.80
11-DH-Imp Lure,115	10	5-hd	4-hd	2½	25.50
1-In a Flurry,119	7	7-1	3-hd	4-1¾	2.60
8-Smrt & Prtty,115	11	9½	6-1½	5-2	21.40
6-Spinnin Cnon,115	3	8-1½	8-1	6½	11.70
10-Distly Blue,119	2	1-2	2-1	7-1	5.60
3-Larks Castng,115	8	4-1	7-hd	8-hd	57.30
4-Phoenix Sq,110	12	11-1	9-1	9-1	9.00
9-PM's Hope,115	9	12	10-2	10-2	46.50
7-Sun Vlly Spt,115	5	10-1	11-5	11-9	15.70
2-Tic Tocker,115	6	3-hd	12	12	7.10
12-Medieval Flyer (Cst)			7.60	4.00	3.80
DH-5-Silent Wizard (Valles)				7.20	9.20
DH-11-Imperial Lure (Vernzla)				7.60	8.60

PERFECTA (12-5) paid $69.00
QUINELLA (5-12) paid $37.00
TRIFECTA (12-5-11) paid $742.60
DAILY DOUBLE (2-12) paid $37.00
PERFECTA (12-11) paid $76.40
QUINELLA (11-12) paid $38.40
TRIFECTA (12-11-5) paid $758.80

This section explains only one of many methods to identify the Monster. Most experienced handicappers have personal formulas that have proven successful over the years. There are probably many. To recap our approach:

- Rank the best and second-best past races for each horse.
- Rank the best and second-best Pole Speeds of those races.

The "Monster" will appear at the top of all four lists.

The Magic Triangle

If a trainer abides by the rules of "The Magic Triangle," you could be looking at a winning effort ... and quite often at a very respectable price!

The Magic Triangle is simply a pattern that appears in the newspaper that indicates a horse's improving form. When this pattern is combined with the trainer's ability to place the horse competitively in today's race, it indicates a potential key horse.

The pattern in the newspaper appears in the form of a right triangle indicating consecutively improving running positions (of non-winning contests), as shown by the following diagram example:

	Second Call	Stretch Call	Finish Position
Most recent race ...			3
Next most recent race ...		5	6
Third most recent race ...	8	7	9

Note the improving running positions 8-5-3 and 9-6-3. These consecutively improved figures constitute the right angle pattern and the indicator we call "The Magic Triangle." If the trainer enters the horse in a contest today (within 30 days of its last race) at a class no higher than that of its third most recent race, you have a key horse candidate.

When The Magic Triangle is coupled with one or more of the other key horse patterns that we've outlined in this book, you have probably identified a very serious contender in today's race!

Actually, our triangle pattern isn't especially new or earthshattering. In fact, it is nothing more than a variation of an improving horse pattern that writers have illustrated for many, many years; most notably, Danny Holmes in his recent book, *Ten Steps to Winning*. Nevertheless, our version, The Magic Triangle, is worth adding to your arsenal of handicapping tools.

EXAMPLE: REGALISUN DANSUR

Cam Gambolati, one of South Florida's better trainers, signaled a winning effort on November 7 when he entered Regalisun Dansur (*nine days* after his last race) in a Md15000, below the Md18000 of October 4.

Regalisun Dansur — B. g. 2(Apr), by Sunny North—Limerick Lace, by Coastal — $15,000 — Br.—Big C Farm (Fla) — Tr.—Gambolati Cam — 117 — Lifetime 6 1 0 1 $4,940 — 1991 6 1 0 1 $4,940
Own.—Peregrine Stable Inc

3Dec91- 4Hia	fst	7f	:222	:453	1:253	Clm 20000	12	11	127	115¾	119½	99¾	Thibeau R J Jr	b	119	38.20	65-22	MyLuckRunsNorth1172Srwl113hdIrshToothch1132¾	No factor	12
21Nov91- 5Hia	fst	7f	:22	:443	1:242	Clm 16000	2	9	98¾	817	811	313¾	DeCarlo C P	b	118	33.00	67-18	LognofthMst122¾UnrlMt12213RglsnDnsr118nk	Bumped inside	10
7Nov91- 1Crc	fst	6f	:223	:472	1:144	Md 15000	4	8	73½	53½	84¾	1hd	DeCarlo C P	b	119	12.80	76-17	Regalisun Dansur119hd Tragna1151 Once Regal1151	Stead trn	12
29Oct91- 4Crc	fst	6f	:221	:462	1:131	Md 15000	9	2	64¾	45½	57½	411	DeCarlo C P	b	118	7.40	73-13	Turpial1186 Darn Proud1111½ Dr. R. F.1143½	Lacked rally	10
17Oct91- 6Crc	fst	6f	:221	:463	1:131	Md 16000	7	10	86½	75½	56½	57½	DeCarlo C P	b	114	145.30	76-15	MyLckRnsNorth1144LgnfthMst1181½FrtntEdtn1141	Stead trn	12
4Oct91- 4Crc	fst	6f	:213	:454	1:134	Md 18000	8	8	911	1017	1014	1017¾	Velez J A Jr		118	29.90	63-18	Commdor'sDr1142Twomchsntngh113½FlghtSrgn118nk	Outrun	10

Speed Index: Last Race: -13.0 3-Race Avg.: -11.6 6-Race Avg.: -12.8 Overall Avg.: -12.8

The Magic Triangle (10-5-4 and 10-5-4) clearly illustrated the horse's improving form and trainer Cambolati provided yet one more indication when he brought his runner back almost immediately.

Regalisun Dansur won the maiden contest by a head and paid a handsome $27.60 return for each $2 bet.

EXAMPLE: SHINE ON SARAH

In this example, trainer Hicks returned this green baby in the Spring after waiting for the track to thaw. Assuming that the horse's position was 6th at the second call point in the fog, the filly displayed an improving form with The Magic Triangle (6-4-2 and 6-3-2).

Shine On Sarah B. f. 3(Mar), by Secreto—Hytania, by Buckpasser
Own.—Manfuso R
Br.—Calumet Farm & Leet L G (Ky)
Tr.—Hicks John W III
112
Lifetime 9 1 4 3 $29,030
1991 5 1 2 2 $20,950
1990 4 M 2 1 $8,080
Turf 1 1 0 0 $9,900

16Jly91- 4Lrl	fst	1 1/16	491	1:142	1:444	3↑ⒻAlw 18500	7	6	75 1/2	68	46	36 1/2	Wilson R	L	110	2.50	82-12	Nuniyjissive108 4 1/2 TwoEyesFerYou1102ShinOnSrh110no	Rallied	7
5Jly91- 6Lrl	fst	1 1/16	471	1:131	1:452	3↑ⒻAlw 18500	5	5	55 1/2	32	12	21 1/2	Wilson R	L	112	3.40	84-13	Goldi'sPpoos1171 1/2 ShinOnSrh1121 1/2 DownthOcn1082	Weakened	7
31May91-10Pim	fm	1 1/16 Ⓣ	:472	1:122	1:443	3↑ⒻMd Sp Wt	2	7	78	75 1/2	33	1nk	Prado E S	L	112	3.00	82-17	Shine OnSarah112nkEmpornette114hdTundraBird114 3/4	Driving	9
4May91- 4Pim	fst	6f	:232	:464	1:114	3↑ⒻMd 50000	1	1	32	42 1/2	41 1/2	21	Prado E S		112	3.30	85-13	Maid of Glory112 ShineOnSarah112noShortHunt1143	Bumped	7
23Apr91- 1Pim	fst	6f	:223	:454	1:11	3↑ⒻMd 50000	5	7	79	57 1/2	45 1/2	35 1/2	Prado E S		112	5.10	84-14	CafeWest114noShortHunt1145 1/2 ShineOnSarh1125	Tried lug in	7
29Dec90- 6Lrl	my	7f	:231	:463	1:252	ⒻMd Sp Wt	6	—	—	—	—	622 1/2	Rowland M F		119	*1.50e	57-17	SocialLaunch119 8 1/2 HppilyEverAfter119 4 1/2 MissAlethi1143 1/2	Fog	8
22Nov90- 5Lrl	fst	6f	:222	:462	1:12	ⒻMd Sp Wt	10	1	87	98 1/2	66 1/2	22 3/4	Desilva A J		119	9.80	82-14	LovelyLily1142 3/4 ShineOnSarh119noHppilyEverAfter1191 3/4	Wide	12
13Oct90- 7Lrl	my	6 1/2f	:223	:464	1:191	ⒻMd Sp Wt	3	7	55 1/2	45	33 1/2	34 3/4	Desilva A J		119	14.00	78-17	Minnu1193 Fittingly Proud1191 3/4 Shine On Sarah1192 3/4	Rallied	11
23Sep90- 5Lrl	fst	6f	:222	:472	1:122	ⒻMd 25000	5	13	106 1/2	107 1/2	48	212	Hutton G W		119	24.40	71-18	SilverTango11912ShineOnSrh1191 1/2 Serch'sEmmy1191 1/2	Rallied	14

Speed Index: Last Race: -1.0 1-Race Avg.: -1.0 1-Race Avg.: -1.0 Overall Avg.: -6.6
LATEST WORKOUTS Jun 19 Lrl 3f gd :364 H

23 Apr- As expected, Shine On Sarah improved against the older competition following her layoff of almost four months.

4 May- Shine On Sarah continued to improve, finishing second, despite being bumped.

31 May- Placed on the turf, stretching out, and being given Lasix for the first time was enough to produce the necessary win. One could argue that this MSW race represents a higher class than that of 29 Dec. If so, it would not qualify according to our earlier rule. It's a fine line, to be sure, but this is still a worthwhile example. Shine On Sarah won the contest by a neck paying $8.00.

EXAMPLE: GALLANT HITTER

When Owner/trainer Garren entered his colt in a route *eight days* after finishing second in a 6f sprint, some questioned the horse's ability. After all, in a similar route a month earlier, the horse finished a tired ten lengths behind the victor.

Gallant Hitter Dk. b. or br. c. 4, by Star Gallant—Ruthless Lady, by Annihilate 'em
Own.—Garren M M
Br.—Old Westbury Farms South Inc (NY)
Tr.—Garren Murray M
117
Lifetime 36 2 11 6 $103,485
1991 18 1 9 2 $67,620
1990 11 1 2 2 $29,908
Turf 1 0 0 0

25Jly91- 1Sar	fst	1 1/4	:503	1:404	2:061	3↑Clm 25000	6	4	41 1/2	31	21 1/2	2hd	Velazquez J R	b	117	3.30	73-23	Syret115hdGllntHitter1172 3/4 SpceAbove117nk	Sted'd repeatd'y	6
15Jly91- 2Bel	fst	1 1/16	:461	1:104	1:431	Clm 25000	8	9	75	3 1/2	1 1/2	2no	Vasquez M O5	b	112	5.40	86-08	Fake Out115noGallantHitter112nkRomanCat117nk	Just missed	11
10Jly91- 4Bel	fm	1 1/16 Ⓣ	:472	1:112	1:413	Clm 45000	3	5	77 1/2	95 1/2	99	910	Vasquez M O5	b	108	19.00	80-10	SfetyCtch1152Comeindownthlin1131 1/2 Cllonzo113hd	Done early	10
1Jly91- 8Bel	fst	1 1/16	:46	1:10	1:413	3↑Alw 31000	1	5	56	54	34 1/2	36 1/2	Vasquez M O5	b	114	15.20	87-06	Vermont1132 1/2 Majesterian1114 Gallant Hitter114nk	Mild gain	5
22Jun91- 9Bel	fst	1 1/16	:462	1:103	1:413	Clm 25000	3	6	54	3nk	2 1/2	2 3/4	Vasquez M O5	b	114	6.70	93-11	Johnny Ross117 3/4 Gallant Hitter1147 Willy Day1175	2nd best	7
10Jun91- 9Bel	fst	1 1/16	:473	1:123	1:444	3↑ⓈAlw 29000	8	6	41	1hd	13 1/2	1 1/2	Velazquez J R	b	117	7.10	78-22	GallntHitter117 1/2 SoundInvestment117nkLedingStr1090	Driving	14
2Jun91- 9Bel	fst	6f	:221	:451	1:101	Clm 22500	2	5	72 3/4	61 1/2	3nk	2 3/4	Velazquez J R	b	115	9.00	88-12	CrftyMn115 3/4 GllntHitter115hdSlem'sRvng1172 1/2	Svd grd rallied	10
18May91-10Bel	fst	7f	:223	:461	1:252	3↑ⓈAlw 27000	7	6	63 1/2	2 1/2	2 1/2	2 1/2	Velazquez J R	b	119	8.10	76-19	MichaelMunyk113 1/2 GllntHitter119noCochFreddy1191 1/2	Gamely	10
12May91- 7Bel	fst	1 1/16	:481	1:134	1:46	3↑ⓈAlw 29000	3	5	31 1/2	51 1/2	54	69 1/2	Cordero A Jr	b	119	3.60	62-30	Quite An Eiffel1191 Wild Chris115 1/2 Nora's Prayin'1122 1/2	Tired	12
2May91- 4Aqu	fst	6f	:221	:46	1:121	3↑Clm 25000	5	8	77 1/2	55	42	31 1/2	Velasquez J	b	119	5.20	78-23	Talc's Bid112 3/4 Scorecard Harry1191 Gallant Hitter119 3/4		8

2May91-Broke slow,steadied bumped 3/16 pole
Speed Index: Last Race: -4.0 3-Race Avg.: -5.6 6-Race Avg.: -3.5 Overall Avg.: -3.5
LATEST WORKOUTS Jun 19 Bel tr.t 3f fst :381 B

Actually, for those of us who saw it, the trainer was telling us loud and clear that his horse had a solid chance to win. Gallant Hitter's Magic Triangle (5-2-2 and 6-2-2) was easy to spot which pointed to an improving form. The horse won driving and paid the lucky ticketholders a healthy $16.20.

EXAMPLE: SCREAMIN EMMA

Screamin Emma is another example of a young, improving filly stretching out and dropping down with its Magic Triangle pattern (12-4-2 and 8-4-2) there for all to see.

Screamin Emma — Dk. b. or br. f. 3(Apr), by Wild Again—Miss Royal Kret, by Royal Nore
Br.—Agnew Dan J (Ky)
Own.—Schwartz Barry K — Tr.—Alexander Frank A — 115
Lifetime 7 1 2 0 $14,300 — 1991 7 1 2 0 $14,300 — 1990 0 M 0 0

6Dec91- 6Aqu	fst	1 1/16	⊡:48	1:13^2	1:46^3	3↑ⒻAlw 29000	1	5	6^3	5$^{1\frac{3}{4}}$	6$^{2\frac{1}{4}}$	6^6	Santos J A	115	16.20	69-22 Oriane115^{no} Cozzinia115^{no} Tuned Way Up115$^{4\frac{1}{2}}$	No factor	6
17Nov91- 4Aqu	fst	1 1/8	:49	1:15^3	1:55^1	3↑ⒻMd 30000	6	5	4$^{4\frac{1}{2}}$	1^1	1^9	1$^{17\frac{1}{2}}$	Antley C W	116	*.90	60-32 ScrmnEmm116$^{17\frac{1}{2}}$Prsd116^{1}MuscInstrmnt116$^{2\frac{1}{2}}$	Kept to drive	8
1Nov91- 2Aqu	fst	6f	:21^3	:47^3	1:13	3↑ⒻMd 30000	6	4	6$^{8\frac{1}{2}}$	6^6	3^3	2$^{\frac{1}{2}}$	Antley C W	116	2.10	75-17 FondRomnc116$^{\frac{1}{2}}$ScrmnEmm116^{2}CircusAct120$^{2\frac{1}{2}}$	Rallied wide	9
7Oct91- 3Bel	fst	1 1/16	:48^1	1:13^4	1:46^1	3↑ⒻMd 35000	2	7	7^6	6$^{2\frac{1}{2}}$	4$^{2\frac{1}{2}}$	4$^{3\frac{3}{4}}$	Antley C W	119	*1.50	67-25 DreddCrdit115^{2}CountryMous118$^{1\frac{1}{2}}$SwtAbility110^{no}	Impr. pos.	9
15Aug91- 5Sar	fst	6½f	:21^4	:44^3	1:16^3	ⒻClm 35000	4	12	12$^{2\frac{1}{2}}$	12$^{9\frac{1}{2}}$	11^{11}	8$^{6\frac{1}{2}}$	Antley C W	116	9.70f	85-10 No Cost116^{no} Quick To Blame111$^{1\frac{1}{2}}$Inciting116^{no}	Never close	12
19Jly91- 1Bel	fst	7f	:22^3	:45^4	1:23^2	3↑ⒻMd Sp Wt	6	2	3^1	4^4	6^{14}	6$^{26\frac{1}{2}}$	Antley C W	116	5.70	60-15 LovBird116$^{11\frac{1}{2}}$DoublsMtch116$^{5\frac{1}{2}}$WingdTruth116^5	Lacked rally	8
1Jly91- 2Bel	fst	6f	:22^4	:46^3	1:12^1	3↑ⒻMd 50000	4	6	6$^{8\frac{1}{2}}$	6$^{4\frac{1}{2}}$	5$^{4\frac{1}{2}}$	2$^{1\frac{1}{2}}$	Antley C W	116	8.50	77-15 LdyBliss112$^{1\frac{1}{2}}$ScrmnEmm116^{hd}MyHwiiTrip116$^{2\frac{1}{2}}$	Rallied wide	8

Speed Index: Last Race: -9.0 3-Race Avg.: -8.3 3-Race Avg.: -8.3 Overall Avg.: -10.1
LATEST WORKOUTS Nov 29 Bel tr.t 5f fst 1:03^4 B Oct 19 Bel 5f gd 1:03 B

Unfortunately, almost everyone did see it. Screamin Emma went to the post as the favorite and didn't disappoint the chalk players by romping in nearly 18 lengths ahead of the rest of the field!

EXAMPLE: KING ATHLETE

Here is an example where the colt appears to be moving up in class (ie., a higher claiming price), but not necessarily into a more difficult field of competition. The betting public saw it that way too.

King Athlete — Ch. c. 3(Feb), by Entropy—Beyond Illusion, by Visible
$5,500 Br.—Farnsworth Farm & Salner J (Fla)
Own.—Rey-Wan Racing — Tr.—Estevez Manuel A — 110^7
Lifetime 27 3 0 2 $13,519 — 1991 23 2 0 2 $10,042 — 1990 4 1 0 0 $3,477

29Nov91- 4Hia	sly	6f	:22^1	:46^1	1:11^4	Clm 7000	8	6	6$^{4\frac{1}{2}}$	9^5	10$^{5\frac{1}{2}}$	11$^{16\frac{1}{2}}$	Santos C M^5	Lb	110	16.70	76-17 This TimeTony113$^{\frac{1}{2}}$Bugmover113$^{\frac{1}{2}}$SunnyWalk119$^{1\frac{1}{2}}$	Thru early	12
21Nov91-10Hia	fst	6f	:22	:45^3	1:12	Clm 7000	4	3	1^1	1^2	1^2	1$^{\frac{1}{2}}$	Santos C M^7	Lb	106	4.50	82-18 King Athlete106$^{\frac{1}{2}}$ Bugmover113$^{\frac{1}{2}}$ T. J.'s Joy107^1	Driving	9
3Nov91- 2Crc	fst	7f	:22^4	:46^1	1:26	3↑Clm 5250	7	2	3^3	3^2	3$^{5\frac{1}{2}}$	5$^{4\frac{1}{2}}$	Sweeney K H	Lb	113	23.80	80-14 Unreal Currency115^{1}HotCandy111$^{2\frac{1}{2}}$RightStar114^1	Weakened	9
26Oct91- 4Crc	sly	1 1/16	:48	1:14	1:49	3↑Clm 5250	5	1	1^2	2$^{2\frac{1}{2}}$	7$^{7\frac{1}{2}}$	7^{11}	Rodriguez P A	Lb	111	19.50	66-21 Papa Gino118^{no} Mr. Blackhawk113^2 Robins Hope116^1	Faded	8
11Oct91-10Crc	fst	7f	:22^2	:46^2	1:25^1	3↑Clm 5250	3	8	8$^{6\frac{1}{2}}$	8$^{5\frac{1}{2}}$	10^{12}	10$^{14\frac{1}{2}}$	Sweeney K H	Lb	116	14.20	74-14 Lord Raja114^4 Tyrant Boss116^{hd} SunApolo-Ar114^{hd}	No speed	11
29Sep91- 1Crc	fst	7f	:22^4	:46	1:25^1	3↑Clm 5250	2	3	3^2	4$^{1\frac{1}{2}}$	3$^{3\frac{1}{2}}$	7$^{6\frac{1}{2}}$	Sweeney K H	Lb	115	8.90	83-11 ProudStepper116$^{3\frac{1}{2}}$ExubrntJohnP.116$^{\frac{1}{2}}$SilvrKris113^{nk}	Faltered	12
19Sep91- 2Crc	fst	7f	:22^3	:46	1:26^1	3↑Clm 5250	3	5	3^2	3^2	2^{hd}	1$^{1\frac{1}{2}}$	Sweeney K H	Lb	111	7.40	84-15 King Athlete111$^{1\frac{1}{2}}$ Master Duece116^1 Nutty Bird113^1	Driving	9
2Sep91- 1Crc	fst	6f	:22^1	:45^4	1:12^3	3↑Clm 5000	7	6	8$^{3\frac{3}{4}}$	9$^{6\frac{3}{4}}$	6$^{4\frac{1}{2}}$	4$^{4\frac{1}{2}}$	Rodriguez P A	Lb	109^4	7.40	82-12 Pipers Bold114^1 Nutty Bird113$^{1\frac{1}{2}}$ TruerandBluer114^2	Mild bid	9

2Sep91-Dead heat

Speed Index: Last Race: -7.0 3-Race Avg.: -4.3 8-Race Avg.: -5.6 Overall Avg.: -6.4
LATEST WORKOUTS Nov 13 Hia 5f fst 1:05^3 B

King Athlete's Magic Triangle (8-7-5 and 10-7-5) pointed to an improvement in today's contest as he and other South Florida horses returned to the speedy Hialeah course.

King Athlete went gate to wire and paid a respectable $11.00.

EXAMPLE: LOTSA SPRINKLES

If you keep dropping the horse's price tag, eventually something good might happen. Trainer Schwartz reduced the price of Lotsa Sprinkles from $30,000 to $22,500 to $20,000 from October 27 to November 16.

Lotsa Sprinkles — **B. f. 4, by Thunder Puddles—Jimmy's Girl, by Proudest Roman**
Own.—Schwartz Arlene — **$22,500** Br.—Schwartz Arlene (NY) Tr.—Schwartz Scott M — **115**
Lifetime 19 4 3 3 $80,800 — 1991 13 2 2 3 $40,120 — 1990 6 2 1 0 $40,680 — Turf 1 0 0 0

2Dec91- 7Aqu	gd	1	:463	1:12	1:382	3+ⒻAlw 31000	10	9	87	75¾	86½	711¾	Maple E	b	117	15.00	58-33	ⓓMonstnGm1052EmprssOfRm1172¾FlyngCrss1151½	No factor	10
21Nov91- 6Aqu	fst	1	:474	1:124	1:374	3+ⒻClm 17500	6	2	21	23	12	17	Smith M E	b	117	2.30	73-30	Lotsa Sprinkles1177 Lois L.1171½ Blessings1172½	Mild drive	8
16Nov91- 1Aqu	fst	1⅛	:474	1:14	1:53	3+ⒻClm 20000	2	2	3½	41½	53½	35	Ortiz F L5	b	108	6.10	66-23	PcdllyLlly1171½FtlRomnc1173½LotsSprnkls1082	Bumped early	7
5Nov91- 4Aqu	fst	1	:474	1:132	1:392	3+ⒻClm 22500	5	8	75½	74½	45½	45¾	Mojica R Jr	b	115	13.40	59-35	SophistictdSm1171½PcdllyLlly1171¾Bllyno1172½	Saved ground	11
27Oct91- 4Aqu	fst	1	:454	1:10	1:352	3+ⒻClm 30000	5	5	54½	77	611	615½	Mojica R Jr	b	113	35.80	69-16	EmprssOfRm1154AmPssbl1172¾EnglshChrm1172½	Done early	10
29Sep91- 2Bel	fst	1 1/16	:464	1:114	1:444	3+ⒻClm 20000	4	5	43	42½	2½	1½	Mojica R Jr5	b	108	6.60	78-18	LotsSprinkls108½PcdllyLlly1172F:lRomnc1171½	Stedied 1/8 pl.	8
18Sep91- 5Bel	fm	1 1/16	Ⓣ:461	1:10	1:414	3+ⒻClm 35000	9	3	41½	87	1212	1216½	Velazquez J R	b	117	31.20	71-12	MmorBy1191½LifeOntheFrm1121½Hrvrd'sBst117hd	Done early	12
7Sep91- 3Bel	fst	1 1/16	:473	1:12	1:433	ⒻClm 30000	7	6	74	31	32½	35¾	Krone J A	b	113	9.40	78-12	SpdMnstr1174¾CoCoBmbn1131LtsSprnkls1133½	Flattened out	7
23Aug91- 2Sar	fst	1⅛	:48	1:123	1:512	3+ⒻClm 22500	9	1	2hd	2hd	1hd	21½	Mojica R Jr5	b	110	5.60	78-14	FlyingCross1121½LotsSprinkles110¾MoonDron1172	Held place	9
11Aug91- 4Sar	fst	1⅛	:472	1:12	1:512	3+ⒻClm 35000	4	5	65½	86	73½	47	Mojica R Jr5	b	112	5.30	73-23	French Quill1175 FairPropina1122MeanScreen117no	No threat	8

11Aug91-Originally scheduled on turf

Speed Index: Last Race: -9.0 3-Race Avg.: -5.6 9-Race Avg.: -7.1 Overall Avg.: -8.1

With this drop in value, the horse managed to improve its record and produce a Magic Triangle (7-4-3 and 6-4-3) that signaled a potential winning effort. Trainer Schwartz saw the improvement and waited only *five days* to make his move, entering the family's filly in a $17,500 claimer. The horse responded by finishing the race with seven lengths of daylight, paying her patient backers a generous $6.60.

EXAMPLE: PAIGE MARTY'S DR.

In South Florida, veteran trainer Harold Rose is well known for his long shot surprises. Paige Marty's Dr. proved to be no exception to those who are not aware of The Magic Triangle.

Paige Marty's Dr. B. c. 2(Apr), by Rexson's Hope—My Lady Doctor, by Family Doctor

$16,000 Br.—Harold Rose (Fla) Tr.—Rose Harold J **119**

Lifetime 12 2 1 0 $10,440 1991 12 2 1 0 $10,440

Own.—Elsie A Rose Stable Inc

6Dec91- 6Hia	fst	6f	:22	:46	1:12	Clm 16000	7	10	$6^{3\frac34}$	$3^{1\frac12}$	$2^{3\frac12}$	$1^{\frac34}$	Nunez E O	117	33.40	82-20	PigeMrty'sDr.$117^{\frac34}$PlesureRolo114^{2}ARelMircl117^{4}	Drvg 6 wide 12
7Nov91- 8Crc	fst	6f	:22	:46	1:13	Clm 16000	6	1	$4^{\frac34}$	$3^{4\frac12}$	5^{9}	$4^{8\frac12}$	Nunez E O	114	41.00	76-17	BlazingCt$114^{\frac12}$UnrelConnection$114^{4\frac12}$Rockfine$114^{3\frac12}$	Weakened 7
23Oct91- 3Crc	sly	6f	:22	$:45^{3}$	$1:12^{2}$	Clm 15000	7	2	4^{3}	$6^{6\frac12}$	$6^{9\frac34}$	$6^{12\frac34}$	Sipus E J Jr	114	56.10	75-17	Oslan$114^{6\frac12}$ It's One Rhythm$118^{\frac12}$ Stetson Led112^{hd}	Faltered 8
10Oct91- 5Crc	gd	6f	$:22^{3}$	$:46^{2}$	$1:13^{1}$	Clm 16000	6	8	$7^{5\frac12}$	8^{11}	8^{15}	$8^{13\frac12}$	Green B	114	49.70	70-19	CristalandBrie114^{nk}BlzingCt114^{2}AmericnFethers113^{nk}	Outrun 8
20Sep91- 2Crc	fst	6f	:22	$:45^{4}$	$1:13^{2}$	Clm 16000	8	1	$1^{\frac12}$	$3^{3\frac12}$	$4^{8\frac12}$	$5^{7\frac34}$	Green B	116	34.60	75-18	UnrealConnection$114^{4\frac12}$RealScore$116^{1\frac12}$Wiscsset$114^{\frac12}$	Faltered 8
30Aug91- 5Crc	fst	6f	:22	$:46^{1}$	1:14	Clm 22500	9	1	$3^{\frac12}$	6^{5}	10^{14}	$10^{11\frac14}$	Green B	116	56.10	69-18	Licencido114^{no}[D]SweetBbyGlen114^{2}TrndyGuy$108^{1\frac12}$	Gave way 10
21Aug91- 5Crc	fst	6f	$:22^{2}$	$:46^{4}$	$1:14^{3}$	Clm 25000	7	1	$2^{\frac12}$	$5^{4\frac34}$	$7^{9\frac12}$	$7^{10\frac12}$	Green B	116	9.20	66-18	Watula116^{2} A Native Decor$116^{1\frac12}$ Buck 'n Tuck116^{1}	Stopped 7
7Aug91- 1Crc	fst	6f	$:22^{1}$	$:46^{2}$	$1:14^{2}$	Md 16000	2	2	$1^{2\frac12}$	1^{3}	1^{4}	1^{2}	Green B	114	5.20	78-16	PigeMrty'sDr.114^{2}TrendyGuy112^{nk}ActDeturmnd$113^{1\frac12}$	Driving 10
31Jly91- 2Crc	gd	$5\frac12$f	$:22^{4}$	$:47^{4}$	$1:08^{3}$	Md 16000	4	1	1^{4}	1^{5}	1^{3}	$2^{2\frac14}$	Green B	116	9.40	81-15	JohnnyBush$116^{2\frac12}$PigeMrty'sDr.$116^{1\frac34}$ColdNovel$116^{1\frac12}$	Faltered 10

Speed Index: Last Race: +2.0 3–Race Avg.: –4.3 9–Race Avg.: –7.7 Overall Avg.: –7.7

LATEST WORKOUTS ●Dec 1 Crc tr.t 3f sly :38 B

Trainer Rose had family money on the line with this 2-year-old colt. The Magic Triangle (8-6-4 and 8-6-4) signaled a winning effort. Entering the horse, after 29 days, at the same $16,000 level as 10 Oct gave us the green light. Our winning ticket paid an astounding $68.80!

The *Also Eligible* Contender

Racegoers are forever trying to measure "trainer intentions." Of all the trainer moves that can be considered reliable, this simple indicator has to rank as one of the best!

When a horse makes it into the race from the "Also Eligible List," it is almost always an indication that the trainer is serious about the contest. We can, therefore, expect the new entry to make a meaningful effort most of the time. If the trainer is intent on using today's race as a "conditioner" for another, more important contest at a later date, it can usually be detected. On the other hand, if today's race appears to be nothing more than another mountain to climb, don't be surprised if the horse does just that! And, best of all, an also-eligible entry is oftentimes an overlay, having received no more than a cursory glance by the "late night" handicappers.

Our rule in this case is very straight-forward: When a horse is coming into the race from the A/E List and appears to be a viable contender without any apparent major negative, consider this newcomer a key horse candidate.

Before continuing with examples, there are other signals that can measure the seriousness of this trainer's intentions:

First, is this race an allowance race or a claiming race? And is the horse over its head at this level? An answer to these questions helps us determine whether the trainer is entering the animal for conditioning to get it ready for another day. A competitive A/E entry into a claiming race indicates that the trainer *wants* to be in this race and is willing to risk selling it to go for the gold. It could also be true with an allowance race, but it's a little less certain.

Second, is the horse an owner/trainer entry? This condition isn't mandatory by any means. But if it's an O/T horse, it's nice to know that whatever the trainer might be planning is being done with personal funds at stake!

Third but no less important, is the horse in form or coming into form?

EXAMPLE: CUTANDTHRUST

Here is an Also Eligible entry into a 6 1/2 furlong $20,000 claiming race at Calder for fillies and mares. Cutandthrust help set the early pace in both races immediately following her layoff of four months. In an earlier section we described how "improving newcomers" can return to form after a layoff of 45 days or more. In this case, trainer Julian had to be disappointed by Cutandthrust's September 12 effort. Today, October 6, it's "let's try that one again" time.

12 Sep- As in the 31 Aug race, Cutandthrust showed some early speed which is probably what trainer Julian wanted to see. As before, the horse failed to deliver. She's coming back into form and, if so, she should be ready next time out.

If Cutandthrust makes it into today's race, she figures to be one of the two pacesetters. A morning scratch allowed her to get in. When the gate opened, she went to the front as expected and was clocked at the half in 45 1/5 -- much the same as before. This time, she didn't stop. Cutandthrust won by two, paying a generous $16.80 and topped a $93.80 perfecta with one of the two favorites in the contest.

In this example, the horse was rounding into form and appeared competitive at this level. The trainer wanted her in the race because he thought she could win the purse.

EXAMPLE: CHEZVOUS

It's now November 12 at Hialeah Park. Trainer and part-owner Jerry Paradise is hoping that Chezvous can get into a $14,000 allowance route. A morning scratch gave the horse an opportunity to be included in the turf contest.

14 Sep- At Calder, following a 60-day layoff Chezvous was placed on Lasix for the first time and showed marked improvement from his mid-summer effort. Clearly, this is a closer that prefers the grass.

29 Sep- Returning to the turf, moving up in class, and going a little longer, the horse is definitely coming into form. He rallied, as before, but still managed to come up short. So, trainer Paradise decides to drop him back to a more competitive level.

In South Florida, as it is with most parts of the country, the difference between the Calder and Hialeah turf surfaces is much less significant as a handicapping variable than it can be with dirt surfaces. As we all know, regardless of the track, a move from dirt to turf, or vice versa, is *always* significant.

Today, taking no chances, the trainer drops his regular rider and asks one of the top jockeys on the circuit, Pedro Rodriguez, to do the honors. Bingo! Chezvous is less than a length off the lead at the top of the stretch and wins by four paying $14.80.   Chezvous was also the first half of a $71.80 perfecta.

EXAMPLE: TICKERTAPEPARADE

On November 24, a $20,000 claiming race for 2-year old fillies at Hialeah had a full field of twelve before two scratches. One of the two A/E entries in this 6f contest was a shipper from Canterbury Downs, finishing 34 lengths out in her last appearance on 5 Oct. The other, Tickertapeparade, had run ten days earlier at Hialeah and was dropping further down the ladder.

This example points to one of the major complaints that many serious handicappers have with "full disclosure" rules to the racing public. The owner of Tickertapeparade is "JFT Stable." The racing public is entitled to know whether the trainer has a financial interest in this horse's ownership. If so, his name should also be listed as an owner. Anyway, we'll assume that trainer Vivian doesn't own a part of Tickertapeparade.

Aside from the fact that Tickertapeparade is being offered for sale at a tag 60% below the claiming price at Calder only a month earlier, we can only guess that the horse is ready to win today's contest.

6 Nov-   Tickertapeparade flashed a little early speed on the slower
            Calder surface at the $35,000 level.

14 Nov-   Eight days later, at the $25,000 level, she showed little, although
            rider Rodriguez noticed that she made a "mild bid" in the later
            stages of the race.

Today, ten days later, trainer Vivian wants her in this race and apparently believes that she'll be more competitive at this lower level.

Sure enough. Tickertapeparade stalked a 46 2/5 pace and finished driving to win by one length. She paid $17.60 and was part of a $182.80 quinella.

EXAMPLE: SILENT WIZARD

On December 22, the computer pointed to a "lock" in a 6 furlong maiden claiming contest at Hialeah for 2-year-old fillies. That is to say, Silent Wizard appeared to be the one to beat IF she managed to get into the race from the A/E List. The figures suggested that she could beat this field by at least three lengths -- excluding, of course, the three first-time starters.

Owner/trainer Julie King must have thought her horse was ready after two gamely Hialeah efforts at the same price tag. After a morning scratch allowed Silent Wizard in, few were surprised when the public made her the favorite at just under 2 to 1. The record was there for everyone to see:

Also Eligible (Not in Post Position Order):

Silent Wizard — Ro. f. 2(Jun), by Westheimer—Reel Sterling, by Silent Screen — Lifetime 4 0 1 2 $2,285 — 1991 4 M 1 2 $2,285
Own.—King Julie A — $14,000 Br.—Wisniewski Mary F (Mo) — Tr.—King Julie A — 115

8Dec91- 2Hia	fst	6f	:22⁴	:47	1:12⁴	ⒻMd 14000	8	6	31½	3nk	2½	35	Vasquez J	115	4.70	73-19	PurplProspct1191SpinninCnnon1154SlntWzrd1151½	Weakened 12
29Nov91- 2Hia	sly	6f	:22³	:46³	1:13³	ⒻMd 14000	5	4	3nk	22	11½	2½	Valles E S	115⁴	17.80	73-17	MedievlFlyer117½DHSilentWizrd115DHImperilLur115½	Gamely 12
29Nov91-Dead heat																		
5Nov91- 3Crc	gd	6f	:22	:46¹	1:13⁴	ⒻMd 18000	12	2	87½	77¾	911	911½	Rodriquez H Q	115	10.60	69-13	RditionLdy1151½CissyPistol119¾TresFiness1191	Showed little 12
24Oct91- 1Crc	fst	6f	:22²	:46⁴	1:14¹	ⒻMd 16000	3	8	62¾	75¼	57	36½	Rodriquez H Q	114	15.70	72-14	Priceless Rosemary1183Delson1093½SilentWizard114no	Rallied 12

Speed Index: Last Race: -8.0 3-Race Avg.: -12.0 4-Race Avg.: -12.5 Overall Avg.: -12.5

LATEST WORKOUTS Nov 23 Hia 3f fst :35³ H Nov 15 Hia 4f fst :49³ B Oct 22 Crc 3f gd :36³ Hg

The race was passed due to the odds, which proved fortunate since the winner was one of the first-timers, beating Silent Wizard by a length. Silent Wizard finished six lengths ahead of the rest of the field and paid $3.20 to place. She was also part of a $29.80 quinella.

EXAMPLE: FORO

Trainer and part-owner Pedro Sobarzo apparently believes that his Also Eligible entry has a solid chance to win today's $7500 claiming race at Gulfstream. It's January 11, only nine days since his last race, a sprint in the slop. Now Foro is returning to his normal distance and at a price tag below his most recent victory. A morning scratch lets him in.

22 Dec-   Foro is competitive in this Hialeah $10500 route and finishes a respectable third at long odds. The horse clearly indicates that he's in form and ready to run.

2 Jan-   Aside from the flash of early speed in the prior race, it isn't clear why trainer Sobarzo enters Foro in this sprint -- other than to keep him fit.

The horse breezes a slow 6f workout on January 8. Again, it appears that the trainer is trying to keep him sharp.

Today, Foro stalks the pacesetters by less than two lengths behind a slow time and closes in the final strides to catch the leader by a nose. The winning ticket pays $9.80 and the perfecta is a modest $46.80.

It can be seen by these and countless other examples that the Also Eligible List is often a gold mine of opportunity. ALWAYS give the A/E entry a second look. When a horse is entered into the race from this list, most of the time the trainer has serious intentions. Many profitable key horses are found in this way.

Appendix

The Purse Value Index

For years, the *Daily Racing Form* has published a Purse Value Index for North American Tracks showing the value of Allowance Race purses. This has been a way for handicappers to relate one race track to the next when horses ship in from another location.

We have modified this approach to include a figure that relates all tracks to Churchill Downs, the "home" of the Kentucky Derby, and to its Index, equal to 100. For example, when our table indicates that another track has a Purse Index of 93, it has an average purse $7,000 less than the average purse at Churchill Downs. A race track with a Purse Index of 104 has an average purse $4,000 higher than Churchill Downs. These are our estimates, not those of the *Daily Racing Form*.

Here is a list that includes most of the North American race tracks in the *Winning at the Track* computer program:

Agua Caliente, Mexico (AC)	85	Bay Meadows, Cal. (BM)	95
Ak-Sar-Ben, Neb. (Aks)	88	Belmont Park, N.Y. (Bel)	122
Albuquerque, N.Mex. (Alb)	85	Beulah Park, Ohio (Beu)	84
Aqueduct, N.Y.(AQU)	108	Birmingham Race Course, Ala (Bir)	83
Arlington Park, Ill. (AP)	97	Blue Ribbon Downs, Okla. (BRD)	82
Assiniboia Downs, Canada (AsD)	84	Boise, Id. (Boi)	82
Atlantic City, N.J. (Atl)	88	Calder Race Course, Fla. (Crc)	92
Atokad Park, Neb. (Ato)	81	Canterbury Downs, Minn. (Cby)	87
Balmoral Park, Ill. (Bml)	88	Charles Town, W.Va. (CT)	83
Bandera Dowons, Tex. (BnD)	82	Churchill Downs, Ky. (CD)	100
Bay Meadows Fair, Cal. (Bmf)	90	Columbus, Neb. (Cls)	82

Del Mar, Cal. (Dmr)	115	Northlands Park, Canada (NP)	86
Delaware Park, Del. (Del)	85	Oaklawn Park, Ark. (OP)	97
Delta Downs, La. (DeD)	83	Penn National, Pa. (Pen)	84
Detroit Race Course, Mich. (Det)	86	Philadelphia Park, Pa. (Pha)	89
Ellis Park, Ky. (ElP)	89	Pimlico, Md. (Pim)	97
Erie Downs, Pa. (ErD)	84	Playfair, Wash. (Pla)	82
Evangeline Downs, La. (EvD)	84	Pleasanton, Cal. (Pln)	91
Exhibition Park, Canada (EP)	88	Portland Meadows, Ore. (PM)	82
Fair Grounds, La. (FG)	89	Prairie Meadows, Iowa (PrM)	82
Fair Meadows Okla. (FMT)	83	Prescott Downs, Ariz. (Pre)	81
Fairmount Park, Ill. (FP)	84	Puerto Rico (PR)	90
Fairplex Park, Cal. (Fpx)	104	Remington Park, Okla. (RP)	89
Ferndale, Cal. (Fer)	82	Rillito, Ariz. (Ril)	81
Finger Lakes, N.Y. (FL)	86	River Downs, Ohio (RD)	85
Fonner Park, Neb. (Fon)	85	Rockingham Park, N.H. (Rkm)	86
Fort Erie, Canada (FE)	85	Ruidoso, N.Mex. (Rui)	84
Fresno, Cal. (Fno)	87	Sacramento, Cal. (Sac)	86
Garden State Park, NJ (GS)	90	Santa Anita Park, Cal. (SA)	118
Golden Gate Fields, Cal. (GG)	96	Santa Fe, N.Mex. (SFe)	83
Grants Pass, Ore. (GrP)	81	Santa Rosa, Cal. (SR)	91
Greenwood, Canada (Grd)	96	Saratoga, N.Y. (Sar)	120
Gulfstream Park, Fla. (GP)	99	Solano, Cal. (Sol)	89
Hawthorne, Ill. (Haw)	93	Sportman's Park, Ill. (Spt)	95
Hialeah Park, Fla. (Hia)	90	Stampede Park, Canada (StP)	85
Hollywood Park, Cal. (Hol)	114	Stockton, Cal. (Stk)	86
Jefferson Downs, La. (JnD)	84	Suffolk Downs, Mass. (Suf)	86
Keeneland, Ky. (Kee)	110	Sun Downs, Wash. (SuD)	81
La Mesa Park, N. Mex. (LaM)	81	Sunland Park, N.Mex. (Sun)	83
Laurel Race Course, Md. (Lrl)	96	Tampa Bay Downs, Fla. (Tam)	84
Lincoln State Fair, Neb. (LnN)	83	Thistledown, Ohio (Tdn)	87
Longacres, Wash. (Lga)	88	Timonium, Md. (Tim)	85
Los Alamitos, Cal. (LA)	92	Trinity Meadows, Tex. (TRM)	86
Louisiana Downs, La. (LaD)	92	Turf Paradise, Ariz. (TuP)	84
Marquis Downs, Canada (MD)	82	Turfway Park, Ky. (TP)	91
Meadowlands, N.J. (Med)	95	Woodbine, Canada (WO)	103
Monmouth Park, N.J. (Mth)	97	Woodlands, Kansas (Wds)	85
Mountaineer Park, W.Va. (Mtn)	82	Yakima Meadows, Wash. (YM)	83
Northampton, Mass. (Nmp)	83		

Index

Liberty Publishing Company is a leading supplier of handicapping products to the serious racing fan. Included are books, special reports, software and videos. LPC's books are available from better bookstores everywhere, or you may contact the publisher directly.

Winning at the Track - David L. Christopher $9.95 160 pgs. (book only)

Winning at the Track Software package for IBM PCs/Compatibles (book included) 5 1/4" or 3 1/2" disc $59.95

Modules for Winning at the Track Software:

- **The Pace Analyst** $39.95

- **The Graphics Software** $39.95

- **The Database Software** $149.95

Special Report I - Computer Handicapping $30.00 35 pgs.

Special Report II - The Performance Cycle $25.00 21 pgs.

Special Report III - Pace Handicapping For Profit $30.00 35 pgs.

Quarter Horse Handicapping - Fred M. Faour $9.95 160 pgs.

The Mathematics of Horse Racing - David B. Fogel $9.95 144 pgs.

Fast & Fit Horses - Bob Heyburn $9.95 172 pgs.

Ten Steps to Winning - Danny Holmes $9.95 144 pgs.

Horse Racing Logic - Glen Jones $9.95 144 pgs.

Horses Talk: It Pays to Listen - Trillis Parker $19.95 160 pgs.

Complete Guide to Racetrack Betting - David Rosenthal $9.95 168 pgs.

How Will Your Horse Run Today? - William L. Scott $9.95 216 pgs.

Total Victory at the Track - William L. Scott $12.95 288 pgs.

Handicapping Trainers - John Whitaker $12.95 168 pgs.

Liberty Publishing Company, Inc.
440 South Federal Highway, Suite 202
Deerfield Beach, Florida 33441

Okay, now you have the Key Horse...

Winning at the Track Software will run on any IBM PC or IBM-compatible using MS-DOS (including Tandy model 1000, Compaq, Hewlett Packard, etc.) with a minimum memory of 256k.

The software, written in pascal, automatically corrects to more than 140 track surfaces, dirt or turf, and features a parallel speed table to adjust 14 different distances.

The package includes a 5 1/4" or 3 1/2" disk and a copy of the 160-page best-seller book, **Winning at the Track**. The complete package is $59.95 plus $3.00 for shipping. If you would like it sent more quickly (2nd Day Air), please include $5.00 rather than $3.00. The package does not include the modules (**The Pace Analyst, The Graphics Software**, or **The Database Software**) which are sold separately.

(305) 360-9000

SOFTWARE ORDER FORM

To: **Liberty Publishing Company, Inc.**
      440 South Federal Highway
      Deerfield Beach, Florida 33441

Gentlemen:

Please rush my **Winning at the Track** software program. I expect the package to be shipped to me UPS. The price below includes shipping costs. Please indicate format.

_____ Enclosed is $62.95.   _____ 5 1/4" _____ 3 1/2"

_____ Yes, I would like to learn more about **The Pace Analyst, The Graphics** and **The Database** Modules.

Ship to: _____
                             (Name)

           _____
                             (Street)

           _____
                       (City, State and Zip)